"Very few thinkers in the world today understand as clearly as Vishal Mangalwadi does the impact of the Bible on Western civilization. He brings a unique perspective. Born and educated in India, he sees the West as others see us, which breaks the myopic view that so many politically sensitive Westerners have today. This is refreshing, invigorating, and very valuable reading. A tour de force from someone who sees us from the outside as well as the inside."

CHUCK COLSON
Founder, Prison Fellowship Ministries
Author of *How Now Shall We Live?* and *The Faith*

"There is urgency about Vishal's excellent argument. He is right on with respect to the moral and spiritual dynamics of Western civilization. As an outsider, he is in a strong position to address Western minds because of his knowledge of history and facts, and because of the level of concreteness with which he lays out his case. His logic is impeccable and forceful. Of course, our sophisticates will be dismissive of him, but multitudes of 'ordinary people' will see the point and perhaps will do something about it."

DALLAS WILLARD
Professor of philosophy, University of Southern California
Author of *The Divine Conspiracy*

"The current worldwide economic crisis shows what happens when distrust rules nations. Vishal Mangalwadi illuminates the path to restoring trust by embracing truth."

MARVIN OLASKY
Editor-in-chief, *WORLD*; provost, The King's College, New York City
Author of *The Tragedy of American Compassion*

"Vishal is authentic. From jail for civil disobedience to church planting, from debate with great gurus and national newsmen to grassroots community development, from video studies to sweltering jungles, Vishal has shaped a truly original vision. This is no ivory tower writer."

MIRIAM ADENEY
Associate professor of global and urban ministry, Seattle Pacific University
Teaching fellow, Regent College; author of *Daughters of Islam*

"From his own life experience Vishal has gained a profound understanding of those things found at the very core of our cultures. In *Truth and Transformation* he diagnoses where the West has been losing its way. He unveils how Jesus-centered truth has transformed each area of life, from morality to justice and the economy, from education to technology, from family to society, and more. He succinctly reveals how regaining a Christ-centered view can make a lasting change in any culture. Vishal's voice is one worth listening to for truth and change."

LOREN CUNNINGHAM
Founder, Youth With A Mission; president, University of the Nations

"The Ten Commandments carted out of courthouses, school children cannot pledge allegiance to one nation under God, Christian pastors cannot pray in the name of Jesus at public events—all of this would have been a nightmare for our Founding Fathers, but is all too real in America today. As a civilization, we are cutting ourselves off from the source of our liberty and our culture. Into this scene, Vishal Mangalwadi gives us a highly accessible work with a profound message for our times. I pray that we respond to its call."

GORDON ROBERTSON
CEO, The Christian Broadcasting Network

"It is a rare and weighty combination when in one person you get someone intimately familiar with the development of Western civilization and also a total outsider with no personal ties to warp his understanding. This book will be widely read."

RALPH D. WINTER
Chancellor, William Carey International University
Founder, U.S. Center for World Mission

"If you are concerned with the health and development of your nation, then *Truth and Transformation* is a must read. The world has it wrong—money, technique, and technology are not the keys to a nation's healing and prosperity. Truth is the root from which vigorous and wholesome societies flourish. No one says it better than Mangalwadi."

DARROW L. MILLER
Cofounder, Disciple Nations Alliance; author of *Discipling Nations*

"Unlike most upwardly mobile, young Indians, Vishal Mangalwadi turned down three job offers in the West and another three in Indian cities to return unsponsored to a backward village to work for a better life for someone else. He has faced assassination attempts, had his farm burnt to the ground by those in whose interests it is to abuse the poor, and has contested national elections on behalf of the powerless, knowing that he didn't stand a chance. *Truth and Transformation* was born out of such experiences and is one of the best books on how truth transforms."

JENNY TAYLOR
Founding director of Lapido Media, London

"The church as a 'threat'? The church as 'dangerous'? The implications of *Truth and Transformation* for the church of this generation are not comfortable, but they are precisely on target. The 'truth' Vishal unpacks here needs to first challenge our churches before it can be used of God in the transformation of our societies."

BOB MOFFITT
President, Harvest Foundation; cofounder, Disciple Nations Alliance

"The voice of Vishal Mangalwadi from the nation of India comes through with clarity, conviction, and truth as he makes the case for pursuing truth in troubled times."

LUIS BUSH
International facilitator, Transform World Connections

"Of all his books, this is Mangalwadi's most prophetic—and timely. Although this book began in prison some thirty years ago, it has the capacity that it had when first penned—to jolt and provoke us to thoroughgoing discipleship."

BOB OSBURN
Executive director, Wilberforce Academy

"*Truth and Transformation* is a succinct diagnosis of current trends. Its keen observations should be studied by anyone interested in global missions, discipleship, and church planting."

THOMAS WANG
President emeritus, Great Commission Center International

"This timely book invites us to appreciate the beauty, profundity, and current application of timeless truth through a prism of multi-culture and multi-class perspective. Many ideologies have been constructed and deconstructed, but the simplicity of God's Word stands forever. Vishal's 'lived-truths' are forceful because they are grounded in history and reason and distilled from his life among the poor."

KEITH KISUNG PARK
Senior pastor, Church of Southland, Santa Fe Springs, California

"In *Truth and Transformation* Vishal Mangalwadi excellently reveals the important lesson he learned from the West, that the Bible is the foundation for the great liberty and prosperity of Western civilization. Having largely forgotten this truth, the nations of the West must learn from this man from the East the biblical art of nation-building if they hope to solve their current national problems."

STEPHEN MCDOWELL
President, Providence Foundation Biblical Worldview University

"When I read the earlier version of this book, I told myself, 'This is what I have been looking for—a Christian worldview that makes Christianity relevant in public space.' I was struggling with real issues in Indonesia, but my theological roots were in Western evangelicalism, which had reduced Christianity to being only about me. Vishal's convincing book helped me integrate a Christian worldview with issues in my nation. This expanded version of the book could change how Indonesian Christians study the Word of God and help them become agents of change in their culture and their host nations."

KIE-ENG GO
Founder, Fellowship of Indonesian Christians in America
Indonesia country coordinator, Jubilee Campaign

TRUTH
AND
TRANSFORMATION

Other Books by Vishal Mangalwadi

Burnt Alive (with Babu Verghese, Vijay Martis, and others)

Corruption Vs. True Spirituality (with Francis Schaeffer)

Dear Rajan: Letters to a New Believer

India: The Grand Experiment

The Legacy of William Carey: A Model for the Transformation of a Culture (with Ruth Mangalwadi)

Missionary Conspiracy: Letters to a Postmodern Hindu

Obama, the Presidency and the Bible

The Quest for Freedom and Dignity: Caste, Conversion, and Social Transformation

Spirituality of Hate

What Liberates a Woman? The Story of Pandita Ramabai (with Neil McNeil)

When the New Age Gets Old: Looking for a Greater Spirituality

Why Must You Convert?

The World of Gurus

VISHAL MANGALWADI

TRUTH
AND
TRANSFORMATION

A MANIFESTO FOR AILING NATIONS

YWAM PUBLISHING
P.O. Box 55787 Seattle, WA 98155

YWAM Publishing is the publishing ministry of Youth With A Mission. Youth With A Mission (YWAM) is an international missionary organization of Christians from many denominations dedicated to presenting Jesus Christ to this generation. To this end, YWAM has focused its efforts in three main areas: (1) training and equipping believers for their part in fulfilling the Great Commission (Matthew 28:19), (2) personal evangelism, and (3) mercy ministry (medical and relief work).

For a free catalog of books and materials, call (425) 771-1153 or (800) 922-2143. Visit us online at www.ywampublishing.com.

Truth and Transformation
Copyright © 2009 by Vishal Mangalwadi
www.VishalMangalwadi.com

Published by YWAM Publishing
P.O. Box 55787, Seattle, WA 98155

13 12 11 10 09   1 2 3 4 5

ISBN: 978-1-57658-512-2

Library of Congress Cataloging-in-Publication Data has been applied for.

This book incorporates an earlier book by Vishal Mangalwadi titled *Truth and Social Reform* (New Delhi: Nivedit Good Books, 1985, 1996; London: Hodder and Stoughton Religious, 1989). Chapters 1–4 summarize the thesis of an eleven-part lecture series, "Must the Sun Set on the West? An Indian Explores the Soul of Western Civilization." Appendix I, "Corruption Vs. the Culture of the Cross," is adapted from Francis A. Schaeffer and Vishal Mangalwadi, *Corruption Vs. True Spirituality* (New Delhi: Nivedit Good Books, 1998). Used by permission.

Unless otherwise noted, Scripture quotations in this book are taken from the HOLY BIBLE, NEW INTERNATIONAL VERSION®. Copyright © 1973, 1978, 1984 International Bible Society. Used by permission of Zondervan. All rights reserved.

Printed in the United States of America

Dedicated
with deep gratitude to
Dr. David and Amber McDonald

Contents

Foreword

Many have spoken and written on the crises of our times—economic, religious, moral, and political. Some have said that the culture wars are over and secularism has won. Others have maintained that we have a window of ten to twenty years in which we can still work for spiritual renewal and transformation. If there is still the opportunity for radical (root) change, and I believe there is, we need a way forward, an agenda that will set forth the principles we need to follow—a manifesto for our times.

We have this set before us in Vishal Mangalwadi's *Truth and Transformation*. Vishal has been dubbed by some as "India's Francis Schaeffer." He studied with Schaeffer in his earlier days and spent extensive time at Cambridge University researching the content of this book. However, Vishal is not merely an academic writing from an ivory tower. Many stories throughout this book demonstrate his extensive work with the poorest of the poor in India. In fact, this book began when Vishal was thrown into jail for (guess what?) serving victims of a hailstorm. Because of his extensive study and work in an Indian context, he can be of great help to us in the West (and throughout the world) as we face formidable cultural challenges.

Why, you might ask, can an Indian philosopher/activist help us? Because, as C. S. Lewis once argued, every culture has its own blind spots, its own outlook. It is good at "seeing certain truths and especially liable to make certain mistakes."[1] As a corrective, Lewis recommended that we read old books. Lewis's rule was to read one old book for every new one, or if that is too much, one old one for every three new ones. Thus, we can let the "clean sea breeze of the centuries" blow through our minds and get a clearer perspective on our times.

I have often said that another way to get this increased clarity on our times is by living for an extended time in another culture or among people of another culture who also know the USA (or the West). C. S. Lewis placed great value on seeing through other people's eyes. He said, "My own eyes are not enough for me, I will see through those of others."[2] Unless we see the world through others' eyes, we inhabit a tiny universe, one in which we will suf-focate. Vishal gives us such an illuminating perspective on our times; not only is his scholarship and analysis profound, but his Indian perspective allows us to see the United States and Western culture with a stark, new clarity.

In the first four chapters Vishal vividly makes the case that the foundations of what has made the West great are crumbling. The rug is being pulled out from under morality, human dignity, rationality, technology, and character. These foundational ideas that have shaped our culture are rooted in the Bible. As these and other principles are replaced by lies, we need to transform our culture by returning to the truth.

As Vishal points out, this will not be an easy task. There are powerful vested interests in the West (and elsewhere) bent on perpetuating falsehood. There is also the need to put on the whole armor of God, because our battle is not merely against flesh and blood but against principalities and powers in high places

1. C. S. Lewis, "On the Reading of Old Books," in *First and Second Things: Essays on Theology and Ethics*, ed. Walter Hooper (Glasgow: Collins, 1985), 207–208.

2. C. S. Lewis, *An Experiment in Criticism* (Cambridge: Cambridge University Press, 1961), 140.

(spiritual warfare). Resisting falsehood with truth involves conflict; that conflict may lead to retaliation and persecution as it has in countries around the world. In order to sustain our strength and not be overwhelmed, we need power that comes from the Holy Spirit and prayer. In this context we desperately need community, the church, so that we are stimulated to love and good deeds. The church, as Paul said to Timothy, was intended to be "the pillar and foundation of the truth" that transforms. We can hope for victory not because of our own strength but because the battle is the Lord's. We can trust in the character and purposes of our Lord. We need to intervene in the conflict, but we also need to maintain our strength through intercession. Even if we lose personally, our God wins in the end. That is our sure and certain hope.

The power of Vishal's presentation lies not only in its stories and illustrations but in its expression of truths often neglected in the evangelical church—sin, the cross, the church, judgment, social justice, the law, and repentance. Vishal's work also, by contrast, demonstrates the falsity of the belief that all religions are the same and that beliefs and doctrines don't matter. In fact, truth (or lies) has profound consequences in personal as well as public life.

If we continue to follow the falsehoods of our culture, we will lose that truth, goodness, and beauty that made the West a beacon of light for so many throughout the world. Vishal calls us to uphold truth like a torch, act upon it (intervene), and sustain our action until the goal is realized. You will find many of the observations he makes and the stories he tells unforgettable.

DR. ART LINDSLEY
C. S. Lewis Institute
March 2009

Preface

These are not the best of times. Even secular Americans are looking for a messiah. Therefore, during his presidential campaign Senator Obama had to remind his supporters, "Contrary to the rumors that you may have heard, I was not born in a manger."

People are desperate for good news as America's biggest automakers—who just received $25 billion for emergency bailout—lay off more workers, ask for another $100 billion, and/or file for bankruptcy, which could send an economic tsunami throughout the industrial world. No wonder, soon after President Bush signed an emergency bill authorizing $700 billion to bail out America's financial institutions, President Obama had to sign a new "Stimulus Package" worth $787 billion to try to revive the economy; announce a $275 billion mortgage rescue plan to prevent families from losing their homes; and promote an effort likely to cost $2 trillion to rescue failing banks, which serve as the backbone of the world's economic superpower. And yet . . .

The Dow Jones Industrial Average dived down to its lowest level in twelve years and the shares of Bank of America and Citi Bank to their lowest point in history.

Why would a promise of massive infusion of capital in banks make investors so jittery? Because, at its root, the problem is not economic! Facing accusation that the government was bailing out the corrupt, the US Treasury secretary announced a "stress test" for the banks being bailed out. He said that the Administration will examine the banks' books. Those who *know* no longer trust certified auditors. Investors know that a genuine investigation will reveal to the world that some of America's biggest banks are even more insolvent than poor home owners who cannot pay their monthly mortgages. No doubt confidence will return to the financial market.

But do you know *why*?

A super-wealthy, super-confident, super-informed "Mafia don" in Arizona said to a friend of mine, "Don't worry! This is the time to buy shares in (XYZ) bank. The government cannot possibly allow this bank to fail because it has been participating in the corruption of the banks for a long time. It will force helpless citizens to bail out the corrupt banks."

The don may be exaggerating, but many wonder if this culture of corruption is spreading through other sectors of the economy. The FBI is investigating over three hundred fifty cases of fraud in corporate America. The US government has sued Switzerland's largest bank, UBS AG, to try to force disclosure of the identities of as many as fifty-two thousand wealthy Americans who were allegedly hiding at least $14.8 billion from US tax authorities in secret Swiss accounts. John DiCicco, acting assistant attorney general in the Justice Department's tax division, said in a statement: "At a time when millions of Americans are losing their jobs, their homes, and their health care, it is appalling that more than 50,000 of the wealthiest among us have actively sought to evade their civic and legal duty to pay taxes." Few expect this case to go anywhere; nevertheless, a government that is taking from honest tax payers on "Main Street" to save the corrupt on Wall Street has to appear to be holding Wall Street accountable.

Examples can be multiplied, but the critical question is, Will this culture of corruption filter down to what used to be America's Moral Majority, or will America experience a grassroots awakening that brings about an all-around transformation? President Obama has three options:

- Force honest taxpayers to bailout the corrupt. But for how long?
- Punish the corrupt. But can anyone throw 10 percent of America's most powerful one million people in jail?
- Lead the nation in repentance.

President Obama is right—those who look to him as the savior will be deeply disappointed. It is time for the *church* to recover and unleash the power of the Good News to transform the brokenness of our times.

Some cultures believe that evils—whether corporate corruption or an innocent child dying of preventable malaria, hunger, adulterated medicine, or terrorism—are God's will. Others think it is karma. But from beginning to end the Bible reveals a God who grieves over evil (Gen. 6:6), who judges evil (Isa. 11:3–4), and who is committed to making all things new (Rev. 21:5).

Jesus wept over our world full of sin, corruption, oppression, poverty, disease, demons, and death. He neither bowed his knee before the devil nor sought escape from suffering in contemplation, meditation, or inner ecstasy. He brought God's kingdom of forgiveness, healing, and liberty into a world ruled by sin and Satan.

Satan deceived Adam and Eve to corrupt the creation. Jesus began transforming their children to become the light of the world. "If you abide in my word," he told them, "you are truly my disciples, and you will know the truth, and the truth will set you free" (John 8:31–32 ESV).

I began writing *Truth and Social Reform* in 1980, when I was jailed for serving the victims of a hailstorm. That explains why the first chapter in the original version[1] was entitled "Jesus the Troublemaker." I was looking at "the Establishment" from the perspective of the disciples of John the Baptist and the Lord Jesus, who saw their rulers as wicked and brutal. That chapter

---

1. *Truth and Social Reform* (New Delhi: Nivedit Good Books, 1985 and 1996; London: Hodder & Stoughton, 1989).

was presented at a conference at Wheaton, Illinois, in 1983. The portrayal of the Messiah as a reformer cost me many friends, but it intrigued Dr. Miriam Adeney enough that she went on to read the entire manuscript, edit it without being asked, and encourage me to publish the book.

The second chapter portrayed the apostle Paul also as a troublemaker who turned a corrupt world upside down. That perspective on Paul's evangelism upset even more friends. But Hodder and Stoughton decided to publish a British edition—again, without being asked. They, at least, signed a contract. A Korean doctor living in the shadow of Communist China and North Korea found a copy of the book at the British L'Abri and started translating it without even asking for permission!

I wanted to revise a book that had been written in jails and jungles, but as demand for the book kept coming and the plans for revisions kept getting postponed, our older daughter, Nivedit, decided to publish the third edition without major revisions. This fourth and much enlarged edition was inspired by a request for a few hundred copies by Dr. Robert Osburn at the University of Minnesota. Dr. Luis Bush played an equally important role by initiating a global movement that is redefining mission as transformation. The title of the book has been "transformed" also, because I have added seven new chapters to the third edition of *Truth and Social Reform*. Earlier the book was focused on India; the new chapters seek to make the book relevant also to the West.

Acknowledgments

Although the core insights of this book were born in rural India, I have been able to apply them to the wider world because, between 1997 and 2009, at least thirty families and institutions have provided short- and long-term housing for me and my wife, Ruth; and many more individuals, families, churches, and foundations have financially supported us and our projects.

Ruth and I continue to be humbled by the faithful "Little People" who love us, pray for us, and send us $20, $50, or $100 every month. Each gift fills us with gratitude to God. However, it would be dishonest not to admit that we could not have accomplished much without those who have trusted us with major grants. The audio series "Must the Sun Set on the West?" was the first fruit of that support. The videos—the second—are being edited now. *Truth and Transformation* is the third result. Several other products should follow from this ongoing study, including a curriculum and a new kind of college hinted at in Appendix 3.

I would also like to acknowledge the following:

- Dr. James Hwang sponsored the retreat of Transform World USA leaders who encouraged me to undertake this project.

- Dr. David & Amber McDonald made it possible for Dr. Mark Harris, Samraj Gandhi, Laura Dixon, and Emily Lewis to provide the practical support to prepare this edition.
- William Carey International University, where I served as an adjunct professor, provided the context for preparing this edition.
- Scott Allen sent the manuscript to the publishers and encouraged them to publish the book. He also put together the Disciple Nations Alliance (DNA) team that prepared the Study Guide in less than two weeks.
- Bobby and Jean Norment have hosted us at the wonderful facilities of Bethany Fellowship in Bloomington, MN, for the month that I have spent in getting the book ready for press. Along with their son, Davis, and his wife, Michelle, they are pioneering Rivendell Sanctuary—a new kind of college, a sanctuary of higher education, based on Jesus' model of apprenticeship. I am participating in this adventure to transform America.
- Ryan Davis has been a superb and enthusiastic editor.
- YWAM Publishing has made a daring attempt to publish this book in six weeks, in time for the Transform World Houston conference.

Encouragement, counsel, and prayers of Bob Osburn, Art Lindsley, Tom Victor, Luis Bush, and Rich & Sue Gregg were important for this project. I remain perennially dependent on Prabhu Guptara for wisdom and on the unconditional support of my family—Ruth, Nivedit & Edwin, and Anandit & Albert—for at least every good thing I do.

PART I

Do We Need Transformation?

ONE

Morality

The Floundering Secret of the West's Success

A Secret of the West's Success

Six months after our marriage, Ruth and I left urban India to live with poor peasants in one of the most backward districts in central India. We lived on less than ten dollars per month, trying to understand chronic poverty and developing practical projects to help our neighbors get out of its grip. As word of our work began to spread, I started getting invitations to speak in different countries. In 1980 I was invited to England to speak at a conference on simple lifestyle and economic development.

My plane took off from Delhi at about two in the morning. I was sleepy, but when Mr. Singh, who was sitting next to me, found out that I was living in a mud house near an obscure village in an unheard-of district, he concluded that, more than sleep, I needed counseling. He made it his mission to persuade me to change my vocation, relocate to England, and become a businessman. He went on and on, describing how easy it was to establish a successful business in England. By 3:30 in the morning it was getting difficult to pretend I was listening, but just when I was ready to tell him I needed to sleep, something intrigued me: while my English was poor, his was worse. I began to wonder how someone who couldn't speak English well could succeed as a businessman in England.

So I asked him, "Mr. Singh, why is it so easy to do business in England?"

He replied without pausing, "Because everyone trusts you over there."

Because I wasn't a businessman, I didn't understand what *trust* had to do with the economic success of an individual or a nation. Had Mr. Singh defended capitalism or socialism or communism, I might have become interested in listening; but his answer didn't square with any of the pundits—neither with the Left nor with the Right. So I pushed my seat back and fell asleep.

A few months later Ruth and I were in Holland to speak at the annual conference of one of Holland's largest charities. One afternoon our host, Dr. Jan van Barneveld, said to me, "Come, let's go get some milk." The two of us walked to the dairy farm through the beautiful Dutch countryside with gorgeous moss-covered trees. I had never seen such a dairy! It had a hundred cows, there were no staff on site, and it seemed amazingly clean and orderly. In India we had a small dairy of our own, but our dairy had two workers and it was filthy and smelly.

The contrast captured my attention because in the region where I served, at least 75 percent of the women spent an hour or two every day collecting cow dung with their bare hands. They carried it in baskets on their heads to their backyards and turned it into cow-dung cakes for cooking fuel.[1]

The Dutch dairy surprised me because no one was there to milk the cows. I had never heard of machines milking cows and

---

1. Poorer families cooked the food in the same room where they slept. The poisonous fumes burned their lungs so that by the time the women turned fifty, they looked like ninety-year-old European women.

pumping the milk into a huge tank. We walked into the milk room, and no one was there to sell the milk. I expected Jan to ring a bell, but instead he just opened the tap, put his jug under it, and filled the jug. Then he reached up to a windowsill, took down a bowl full of cash, took out his wallet, put twenty guilders into the bowl, took some change, put the change in his pocket, put the bowl back, picked up his jug, and started walking. I was stunned.

"Man," I said to him, "if you were an Indian, you would take the milk and the money." Jan laughed.

A few years ago I told this story in Indonesia, and an Egyptian gentleman laughed the loudest. As all eyes turned to him, he explained, "We are cleverer than Indians. We would take the milk, the money, and the cows."

Back in Holland, in that moment of laughter, I understood what Mr. Singh had been trying to explain to me on the plane to London. If I walked away with the milk and the money, the dairy owner would have to hire a salesgirl. Who would pay for her? Me, the consumer!

However, if the consumers are dishonest, why should the supplier be honest? He would add water to the milk to increase the volume. Being an activist, I would protest that the milk was adulterated; the government must appoint milk inspectors. But who would pay for the inspectors? Me, the taxpayer!

If the consumer and the suppliers are dishonest, why would the inspectors be honest? They would extract bribes from the suppliers. If they didn't get the bribes, they would use one law or another to make sure that the sale is delayed enough to make the nonrefrigerated milk curdle. Who would pay for the bribes? Initially the supplier, but eventually the consumer.

By the time I had paid for the milk, the salesgirl, the water, the inspector, and the bribe, I wouldn't have enough money to buy chocolate syrup to add to the milk. Without the syrup, my children don't like milk. Consequently, they are not as strong as the Dutch children.

Having paid for all of these things, chances are I wouldn't have surplus money to take my children for an ice cream treat on Saturday night. The person who makes and sells ice cream adds value to the milk, whereas the sales girl, the water, the inspectors, and the bribe add nothing. In paying for them I simply pay for my sin: my propensity to covet and steal my neighbor's milk and money. The high price of sin makes it difficult for me to buy ice cream; that is to say, the price of sin prevents me from patronizing genuine economic activity. My culture of distrust and dishonesty robs me of money that could be used to provide a better life for my children and productive employment for my neighbors.

My visit to the dairy farm helped me understand why a small country such as the Netherlands is able to donate money to a much larger nation such as India. It also helped me get what my fellow passenger, a semiliterate businessman, was explaining to me. He could say what economic experts avoid discussing: that moral integrity is a huge factor behind the unique socioeconomic/sociopolitical success of the West.

Where did this morality come from? Why isn't my society equally trustworthy?

Education was a key force that transformed Western Europe. Religious reformers such as Martin Luther, John Knox, and John Amos Comenius universalized education precisely to civilize generations that could create a new Europe. The pioneers of modern education made character formation a primary function of education because they accepted the Judeo-Christian ideas that

- God is holy;
- he has given us moral laws, such as the Ten Commandments;
- obedience to God's Word is the precondition of *shalom* (peace) and the source of good life;
- disobedience to God's moral law is sin that does not go unpunished;
- sinners can repent and receive forgiveness and new life.

This good news became the intellectual foundation of the modern West, the force that produced moral integrity, economic prosperity, and political freedom.[2]

Why Are Moral Foundations Floundering?

If moral integrity is foundational to prosperity, why don't secular experts talk about it? The reason is that the universities no longer know whether moral laws are true universal principles or mere social conventions made up to restrict our freedoms.

And why don't they know?

Economists have lost the secret of the West's success because philosophers have lost the very idea of truth.

Why?

The truth was lost because of an intellectual arrogance that rejected divine revelation and tried to discover truth with the human mind alone. Scottish philosopher David Hume (1711–1776) demonstrated that unaided logic and experience could not prove God, human self, or some of the basic assumptions of science, such as that every effect has to have a cause or that the laws of physics have to be the same everywhere and at every time in the universe.

Hume's recognition of the limits of logic should have humbled the Enlightenment's arrogance. However, instead of admitting that our logic had its limits, many assumed that if logic could not prove God, then God could not exist. Hume tried to build a case for morality without God, but German philosopher Immanuel Kant (1724–1804) recognized that without divine revelation the human mind was incapable of knowing whether the universe was moral. In this life we see the righteous suffer

2. Early eighteenth-century England was as corrupt as my country; it was transformed by a religious revival led by John Wesley, the founder of the Methodist Church. For that story, see chapter 7 of my book *Missionary Conspiracy: Letters to a Postmodern Hindu* (New Delhi, India: Nivedit Good Books, 1996).

and the wicked prosper, but without revelation we cannot know if there will be a final judgment after death.

Kant tried to save morality, but Friedrich Nietzsche (1844–1900), the nineteenth century German philosopher, concluded that if logic could not know morality, morality had to be a mere social construct. Since Judeo-Christian morality favors the weak, it must have been made up by the slaves to restrain the freedom of the powerful—the Aryans.

Existentialist philosophers that followed Nietzsche decided that since the universe had no God-given meaning and moral norms, the quest for freedom required us to create our own values and purpose. For example, the German existentialist Martin Heidegger (1889–1976) began his intellectual carrier as a champion of the Nazi thought. Nazism was defeated militarily, but logic's inability to know God or morality has produced postmodern universities that no longer know if anything is right or wrong. Having rejected God and his revelation, educational institutions have become incapable of teaching goodness, beauty, and truth. I encountered this aspect of the West two years after my trip to the dairy farm in Holland.

Corruption in the West

In 1985 Ruth and I were back in Holland—this time with our two daughters. One day, when Ruth was lecturing, I took the girls on a sightseeing tour of Amsterdam. I tried to use a machine to buy a day pass for buses and trams. Since the instructions were in Dutch, I asked two young women, "How do I get tickets from this machine?" They turned out to be Americans.

"Why do you want to get tickets?" they responded. "We've been riding around for a week. No one has ever come to check any tickets."

Their shamelessness shocked me more than their immorality. They represented the new generation, liberated from "arbitrary" and "oppressive" religious ideas of right and wrong. University education had freed them from commandments such as "You shall not steal."

"It is wonderful," I said to them, "that there are enough commuters who pay so that the system can carry some who don't. Once your schools succeed in producing enough clever commuters, your country will catch up with mine. You will have to have ticket inspectors on every bus and have super-inspectors to spy on the inspectors. Everyone will then have to pay more. But corruption won't remain confined to the consumers; it is a cancer that will infect politicians, bureaucrats, managers, operators, and the maintenance staff. They will take kickbacks, commissions, and bribes to use substandard parts and services. Soon your public transport will resemble ours: frequent breakdowns will slow down not only the transport system but also your roads, efficiency, and economy."

Corruption and Poverty

Every year in August, Transparency International (TI), a nongovernmental agency in Germany, publishes what it calls the *Corruption Perceptions Index*, which lists countries from the least corrupt to the most corrupt. No country is totally free from corruption, but some countries are so corrupt that TI is not able to survey them. These countries are ruled by mafias, gangs, and warlords. Their chronic poverty proves what Adam Smith, a father of capitalism, knew: real-world economics are the result of the kind of morality you have, which in turn is a fruit of the kind of philosophy you have. For example, why have health care costs become so obscene in America that they are destroying the very culture of compassion? Insurance and pharmaceutical companies that sustain health care are blamed only because the intellectual elite can no longer calculate the economic costs of academic godlessness that separates economics from moral truth.

Transparency International, a secular agency, knows that corruption is costly. Its official Web site tells stories such as these:

Around the globe, corruption impacts people's lives in a multitude of ways. In the worst cases, corruption costs lives. In countless other cases, it costs their freedom, health, or money. . . . In May 2000, 950 people were injured and 22 killed, when a fireworks factory in Enschede, the Netherlands, burst into flames. The explosion reached such catastrophic levels because government regulators turned a blind eye to grave security breaches with regard to storing explosives on the factory premises. In return for remaining silent, the officials are said to have received free fireworks for years. Even an illegal enlargement of the factory was legalized by the authorities a *posteriori*. The local government official in charge of monitoring fireworks factories in the area admitted to not knowing the specific regulations on the storage of explosives. Though considered an expert, he hadn't read the relevant literature, nor had he taken part in any training seminars. He only followed the instructions of his superiors, one of whom was arrested on corruption charges two years ago.[3]

The Source of Moral Transformation

What created the trustworthy England that Mr. Singh saw? Modern England's moral transformation began with John Wesley, the founder of Methodism. Wesley would have agreed with Transparency International that sin is a serious matter. Sin's initial economic costs are trivial compared to its ultimate cost—death. John Wesley learned from the Bible that sin does not lead to physical death alone; its ultimate result is spiritual death, or separation from God. Initially the separation is temporal and reversible, but if we choose not to repent and get right with God, we risk eternal separation from him. Wesley taught English masses that the God who loves us takes sin so seriously that he incarnated to take our

3. Transparency International, Frequently Asked Questions About Corruption, http://www.transparency.org/news_room/faq/corruption_faq#faqcorr7 (accessed March 18, 2009).

sin and its consequence—death—upon himself. He died on the cross of Calvary so that we might find forgiveness and eternal life. This was the good news—the gospel—according to the Bible and John Wesley. This gospel, rooted in the moral absolutes of God's law, created the culture of trustworthiness that facilitated Europe's economic progress.

Why don't simple Dutch peasants steal the milk and money? Why, instead, are they able to give money for India's development?

Following the sixteenth century Reformation, the Heidelberg Catechism played a huge role in shaping the Dutch religious culture. The Catechism was drafted in Germany in 1563 and translated into Dutch in 1566. The Catechism was approved by four synods from 1568 to 1586 and finally by the Synod of Dort (1618–1619), which officially adopted it as the second of the Three Forms of Unity and made its weekly exposition by the ministers obligatory. As a result, Dutch churches began to teach it every Sunday. The Catechism expounds the command "You shall not steal" in two questions:

Question 110: What does God forbid in the eighth commandment?
Answer: God forbids not only those thefts and robberies that are punishable by the courts; but he includes under the name of "stealing" all deceitful tricks and devices, whereby we design to appropriate to ourselves anything belonging to our neighbor—whether it be by force or under the appearance of right, as by unjust weights, inaccurate measurements, false reckoning of time spent in service, fraudulent merchandise, false coins, exorbitant interest, or by any other means forbidden by God. God is forbidding covetousness as well as all abuse as waste of a person's gifts.

Question 111: But what does God require in this commandment?
Answer: That I seek the advantage of my neighbor rather than my own every instance I can and deal with my neighbor as I desire to be dealt with by others. Further, that I faithfully

labor and generously give, so that I may be able to care for the
hurting and relive the needy.

Why was the Catechism reading all these extra things into a
simple commandment against stealing? The Catechism was not
injecting anything into the Ten Commandments which the Bible
did not. It was God who said that his people who did not tithe
were robbing him (Mal. 3:8). People in the Netherlands had
money to give because generation after generation was taught to
work hard and give tithes and offerings to God. The Dutch made
money to give to the poor in India because the Bible taught, "He
who has been stealing must steal no longer, but must work, doing
something useful with his own hands, that he may have something to share with those in need" (Eph. 4:28).

In terms of Gross Domestic Product (GDP), China is the
fourth largest economy, India is twelfth, and Saudi Arabia, with
a much smaller population, is twenty-fifth. But these budding
economies are not top "donor nations."[4]

Economists know that corruption causes poverty, but they
lack intellectual framework and spiritual resources to help corrupt nations ask tough cultural questions: Why are the Dutch or
the English able to trust each other in a way that the Indians or
the Egyptians cannot? What makes some cultures more honest,
less corrupt, more trustworthy, and therefore more prosperous?
And why is the postmodern West discarding the moral secret of
its success?

---

4. Top ten richest countries in the world in terms of GDP per capita
in US$: (1) Luxembourg 80,800; (2) Qatar 75,900; (3) Bermuda 69,900;
(4) Norway 55,600; (5) Kuwait 55,300; (6) United Arab Emirates 55,200;
(7) Singapore 48,900; (8) USA 46,000; (9) Ireland 45,600; (10) Equatorial
Guinea 44,100.

Top ten donor countries of foreign aid in billions $ (in 2003–04): (1) USA
12.9; (2) Japan 9.2; (3) Germany 5.4; (4) France 5.2; (5) United Kingdom
4.8; (6) Netherlands 3.4; (7) Italy 2.3; (8) Canada 2.0; (9) Sweden 1.8; (10)
Norway 1.8.

Corruption and Philosophy

For me the ironic fact is that while my culture teaches that each one of us is God, the Netherlands and England were built on the biblical idea that human beings are sinners and accountable to God. India's religious philosophy taught that since the human soul was divine, it could not sin. In fact, our most rigorous religious philosophy teaches that everything is God.[5] God is the only reality that exists, and therefore there is no ultimate distinction between good and evil, right and wrong.

Swami Sivananda of the Divine Life Society summarized classic Hinduism in this way: "The world is neither good nor bad. The mind creates good and evil. Thinking makes it so. The evil is not in the world, it is in the mind. . . . If you become perfect [God] the world will appear good [perfect]."[6]

Acharya-turned-Bhagwan-turned-Osho Rajneesh, who gave widespread publicity to the tantric idea of salvation through sex, summarized the Indian as well as the postmodern Western worldview in similar terms: "We have divided the world into the good and the evil. The world is not so divided. The good and the evil are our valuations [not God's commandments]. . . . There is no good, there is no bad. These are two aspects of one reality."[7]

The data collected by Transparency International shows that the least corrupt countries are overwhelmingly those whose soul was nurtured by the Bible (not the "church"). However, many intellectuals have been forced to conclude that if God has not given any moral commandments to human beings, and if he will not judge us, then morality is an artificial cultural construct. There are no moral norms that are binding on everyone; morality

5. This philosophy is called pantheism (*pan* = all; *theos* = God; i.e., all is God) or monism (all is one).

6. Swami Sivananda, *Bliss Divine* (Sivanandanagar, India: Divine Life Society, 1964), 459.

7. Acharya Rajneesh, *Beyond and Beyond* (Bombay: Jeevan Jagruti Kendra, 1970), 12–13.

is flexible or relative; different norms apply to different individuals or communities.

Moral Relativism and Poverty

These experts plan "economic development," but they do not understand the first lesson Ruth and I learned when we began living with the poor. Remember, we were living on a farm outside a village. No one did that. It was an invitation to robbers called *dacoits*. It took us no time to learn that one factor behind our people's poverty was that they were not able to make use of the land they had. If you don't live on your land, you can't protect vegetables, fruit, or livestock. You don't grow fruits or vegetables, or keep chickens or rabbits, because they will be stolen. A mango from India sells for as much as three dollars in America. Growing mangoes or guavas alone could lift whole families out of poverty. But if hardworking peasants grew good mangoes and guavas, the higher castes would come and take them. If the peasants tried to protect their fruit, they would be beaten and their wives raped.

Why?

Because there is no God who has said, "You shall not covet your neighbor's [mangoes]" or "You shall not steal or commit adultery."

Is it really wrong to covet, steal, or rape?

Postmodern relativism, like my traditional culture, says, "Yes, it is wrong for *you* to do so, but it is not wrong for *us*, because *we* make the rules and have the power to enforce them. Morality is merely a function of cultural power. Moral rules are relative. You have no power to enforce *your* rules on us; therefore, they do not apply to us." This Nietzschean/Nazi/Aryan "truth" is now being propagated by many universities.

Our "upper castes" practice moral relativism (different moral norms for different castes) not because they are more wicked than other human beings. They do so because our pantheism dismisses morality and our polytheism worships corrupt gods. Now corruption rules our public life in India, because the West's intellectual and cultural elite also teach us moral relativism. The West is becoming corrupt like us because it is developing a "new spirituality" without morality. This new spirituality is no different than our old spirituality.

The Dutch dairy gave me a glimpse into the moral soul of the West, but it did not explain why their dairies were cleaned mechanically while our women had to collect cow dung with their bare hands and carry it on their heads.

TWO

Rationality

The Forgotten Force Behind Western Technology

Why Do They Haul Water on Their Heads?

Several years after my visits to England and the Netherlands, I was invited to teach a course on community development in a university in Uganda. I had assumed that Uganda was poor because it was a resource-deprived desert. En route from Entebbe airport to Jinja, I saw hundreds of women and children carrying water on their heads. The sight made me feel at home because that is what women did in our villages and towns. It reinforced my assumptions about Africa's poverty, even though all I could see was lush greenery. The next day my assumptions collapsed into confusion.

I discovered that I was staying on the banks of Lake Victoria, one of the largest bodies of fresh water in the world. The mighty river Nile originated just a few miles from my guest room. The river starts with such force that in 1954 the British began generating hydroelectricity. Uganda produces more power than it consumes. Some of it is sold to Kenya. The question was, with so much water and so much power, why were human beings carry-ing water on their heads?

The image of women carrying pots of water on their heads powerfully symbolized the contrast between Western civilization and my culture (non-Western civilization). Why are women in my country forced to carry water, cow dung, and bricks on their heads, when women in the West are not? I asked this question to some Western visitors who came to India as spiritual seekers.

What Made the West a Thinking Civilization?

Some of these visitors came to me because they had heard of my book *The World of Gurus*, which had been published by Asia's larg-est publisher. They wanted to talk about Yoga, Tantra, meditation, reincarnation, or vegetarianism. They were surprised that I wanted to learn from them how to deliver my neighbors from the degrad-ing toil that stunted their minds and destroyed their bodies.

These Western pilgrims in India had taken the technological and economic progress of their societies for granted. Some were critical of it. They mentioned books such as *The Tao of Physics* by Fritjof Capra and *The Aquarian Conspiracy* by Marilyn Ferguson. These books condemned the Bible for inflicting science and tech-nology upon the world. This confused me, because until then I had generally heard the accusation that Christianity was opposed to science and technology. These books criticized the Bible for birthing science and technology.

Western critics of technological progress saw women haul-ing water on their heads as something romantic. For me, that sight was not cute; it was a challenge. I needed no research to know that this method of carrying water meant limited water in homes. People could not wash their hands, dishes, fruit, and salad adequately. Waterborne diseases would give them stomach dis-eases that sap energy and require otherwise avoidable treatment. I wanted to know: why do some cultures do with their minds what the rest of us do with our muscles?

When you use the mind, water brings itself to you: water produces electricity, and electricity pumps water into your home. A handful of workers using the mind can pump more water into every home and factory than can millions of women carrying it morning and evening, 365 days a year. Why do Indians and Africans waste billions of man-hours hauling water or collecting cow dung, when women could be reading or teaching or planting or playing?

Could it be that the West uses the mind because the white race is more intelligent? I already knew that people living on the banks of the Nile were not dumb. They built pyramids thousands of years before the West learned how to make palaces. The problem is that the cultures that made pyramids and Taj Mahals did not make wheelbarrows for their slaves. Why?

The answer came from historian Lynn White Jr.'s study *Medieval Religion and Technology.* His pioneering research into the history of technology led him to conclude that it was the Bible that made the medieval West the first civilization in history that did not rest on the backs of sweating slaves.

The first chapter of the Bible presents a God who is a worker, not a meditator. God worked for six days—so must we! To work is godly. The third chapter of the Bible teaches that toil came as a curse upon Adam's sin. Humans became the only species that had to eat of the sweat of their brow. Since toil is a result of sin, salvation includes deliverance from sin as well as toil—from mindless, repetitive labor that requires no choice.

So, why don't Western women haul water or dung on their heads? It is because, while the elite in other cultures used technology for power and pleasure, prestige and torture, Christian monasteries began developing technologies that liberated powerless individuals from dehumanizing slavery. Toil is dehumanizing because it forces a human being to do what can be done by an ox, a horse, wind, water, or wheels.

Why Christian Monks Developed Technology

Having studied Hinduism I already knew that Hindu and Buddhist monks were no less intelligent than Christian monks. The philosophies they constructed, the caves that they sculpted, and the temples that they built testify that they were second to none in imagination, ingenuity, architecture, engineering, discipline, and organization.

Christian monks shared a common problem with the Buddhist monks: neither of them had wives to haul water, grind wheat, or find fuel for cooking bread. One difference was that the Buddha required his monks to beg for food while the New Testament said that whoever does not work should not eat. Christian monks invented machines because they had to bring their own water, clean their own dairies, grind their own wheat, and bake their own bread. Christian monasteries developed technologies because their religious requirement to work was coupled with

- a spiritual quest for salvation from sin and its consequences, including toil;
- a theological commitment to the dignity of every human being—male or female, high or low; and
- a religious obligation to cultivate the human mind.

As religious institutions, Christian monasteries were unique; some of them evolved into universities because they were created to cultivate the mind as much as character. They made a distinction between myth and truth, and believed that the human mind could know the truth. Therefore, they required monks to study logic, philosophy, rhetoric, languages, literature, law, mathematics, music, agriculture, and metallurgy in addition to the Bible. These religious institutions became the nursery of rational disciplines such as medicine and music, law and technology, astronomy and botany, capitalism and morality.

European monasteries cultivated the mind because they were founded upon St. Augustine's exposition of the Bible, which taught that the human mind was different from the animal brain; it was made in God's image. They did not think that the mind was a product of blind chance or primeval ignorance (*Avidya*). They believed that the human mind can know God, goodness, and beauty; that human words can communicate truth because God made our minds in his image; and that God gave us the gift of language so that he might communicate with us, his children.

These schools of piety created a uniquely *rational* religious man who became capable of developing complex theories. These theories created capitalistic economy and institutions that produced civil societies where power was subject to agreed-upon principles.

Why Buddhist Monks Did Not Develop Technology

Given our early start, India and China should have been eons ahead of the West in developing technology and economy. Why did we fall behind? The answer is that our cultures were shaped by worldviews that taught us that intellect was our problem and salvation depended on deliverance from intellect, not from sin.

In 1974 I spent some time in Rishikesh at the ashram of the late Maharishi Mahesh Yogi, the founder of Transcendental Meditation (TM). The Beatles helped him build this beautiful ashram on the banks of the river Ganges, where it comes down to the plains from the Himalayas. I was interested in Mahesh Yogi partly because he is a graduate of Allahabad University, my alma mater. I had read several of his books, including his commentary on the Bhagavad Gita, a sacred Hindu scripture. The president of the Indian branch of his movement initiated me into TM in Maharishi's own living room. He gave me a mantra: the name of a minor Hindu demigod. He asked me to recite this sound silently for twenty minutes, twice a day. In advanced stages, he said, I would need to fast and recite that mantra for several hours at a time.

I asked the initiator what my mantra meant, but he told me not to bother with meaning. The principle of Transcendental

Meditation is not to know truth but to empty one's mind of all rational thought—to "transcend" thinking. To think is to remain in ignorance, in bondage to rational thought. Meditation, he explained, is a means of escaping thinking by focusing attention on a sacred though meaningless sound like *Om*. His explanation helped me understand why our monks did not develop technology, universities, and science.

Did the Printing Press Make the West a Rational Civilization?

At the turn of the millennium, secular scholars were telling us that the printing press made the West a rational civilization because it made books easily and cheaply available. The problem is that the same scholars were also telling us that China had invented printing five hundred years before Guttenberg and that Koreans had invented moveable metal fonts centuries before the West did. But that did not turn these nations into rational societies that replace the use of muscles with machines.

By AD 823 Chinese monasteries had so many books that they had invented rotating bookcases. By 836 at least one monastery at Xuzhou in eastern China even designed a brake to stop the rotation. What did these bookcases do?

In the middle of the twelfth century, when Christian monasteries in Oxford and Cambridge were growing into universities, a Buddhist monk named Yeh Meng-te (d. 1148) traveled through many temples and monasteries in China and reported that "in six or seven out of ten temples, one can hear the sound of the wheels of the revolving cases turning"[1] day and night.

Were the monks turning the bookcases in order to find and read books? Had that been the case, their scholarship would have been far ahead of Oxford and Cambridge. Many of these temples belonged primarily to the Ch'an sect, which minimized

---

1. L. C. Goodrich, "Revolving Book Case in China," *Harvard Journal of Asiatic Studies* VII (1942): 154.

the importance of the written word. Professor Lynn White Jr. explains that the sound of the rotating bookcases was "not a result of scholarly activity."[2] The monks were using the sound of the rotating wheels of these bookcases as a mantra. A word (Greek, *logos*) is a sound with sense; a mantra is a sound separated from sense. The monks sought "salvation by rotation of sacred writings." They considered the rational act of reading and thinking about the meaning of the words and text a hindrance to mystical enlightenment. Their idea of meditation was the opposite of the Western or biblical idea of meditation: they believed that salvation comes from emptying our minds of all thoughts and words.

My meditation on the banks of the river Ganges helped me understand why our monks did not harness her energy to liberate our women from dehumanizing drudgery and toil. Our monks were not using their minds to replace muscles; they were trying hard *not* to think—and they had succeeded.

Why Is the West Replacing Reason with Mysticism?

We have already noted that once European philosophers separated reason from revelation, their confidence in the mind's ability to know the truth began to decline. Eventually, philosophy's failure to answer life's fundamental questions forced thinkers to ask even more probing questions: What is language? What is logic? Why do we assume that logic can lead us to truth or that truth can be communicated in words?

During the second half of the twentieth century, Western philosophers such as Michel Foucault (1926–1984) and Jacques Derrida (1930–2004) began deconstructing the foundational assumptions of the West. Universities found that having given up revelation they had no reason to trust reason. They assumed that since there is no Creator, the mind could not be anything but

2. Lynn White Jr., *Medieval Religion and Technology* (Berkeley: University of California Press, 1978), 47.

an accidental by-product of blind chance. It must have evolved merely to aid our fierce struggle for survival. Therefore, the mind had to be an instrument of manipulating the environment; it could not possibly be a means of knowing truth.

How, then, can we know truth?

Once it was assumed that the mind could not know truth, many gave up the quest for truth, while others started searching for truth with the help of drugs, meditation, or yogic or sexual techniques of altering rational consciousness.

In California I have met university graduates, even doctoral candidates, who spend ten days at a time practicing Vipassana. During this time they read nothing, ask no philosophical questions, and listen to no discourses. They sit and sit and sit, inhaling and exhaling, observing their breathing. Their breathing becomes the mantra, like the sound of rotating bookcases. These educated Americans follow Indian and Chinese monks in seeking enlightenment by emptying their minds. This is the opposite of what Jesus said to his audience, who were like sheep without a shepherd, harassed and helpless, weary and oppressed: "If you abide in my word...you will *know the truth*, and the truth will set you free" (John 8:31–32 ESV).[3] Since this book asserts that it is *truth* that transforms, we will revisit this issue in later chapters.

For now the question is: If the DNA of Western character, rationality, technology, and universities developed in monasteries, then why were these monasteries rejected? And how did these ideas spread beyond monasteries to emancipate ordinary housewives from their drudgery and toil?

3. Italics added here and in all other biblical quotations with italics throughout this book.

THREE

Family

The Failing School of Western Character

Some people think that it was the right to vote that empowered Western women; others give credit to education or job opportunities. As early as the 1870s—fifty years before American women started voting—Indian reformers such as Keshab Chandra Sen had realized that the social institution that liberated Western women was *monogamy*: marriage being a permanent and exclusive union of one man and one woman. This definition of marriage gave Western women unique power over their husbands and children. Physically, intellectually, socially, and morally strong women nurtured strong children, strong men, strong communities, and strong nations.

Because of this realization, Sen asked British colonial rulers to make monogamy the law for all Indians. But polygamy (both polygyny and polyandry) were such integral parts of our religious culture that monogamy would not be made a law for Hindus for another eighty years, in 1956. However, even in the late 1990s we had a member of parliament who had thirty-nine wives, and he did not know all of their names. Polygamy devalued our women and weakened our children.

Few sociologists will dispute the fact that the West became stronger than other civilizations because something liberated and empowered Western women. This was an important conclusion reached by the celebrated French magistrate Alexis de Tocqueville, who visited America in 1831–32 and wrote the classic account *Democracy in America*. Tocqueville concluded that America was becoming stronger than Europe mainly because the American women had become stronger than European women: "If anyone asks me what I think [is] the chief cause of the extraordinary prosperity and growing power of this nation, I should answer that it is due to the superiority of their women [and family life]." And again: "Certainly of all countries in the world America is the one in which the marriage tie is most respected and where the highest and truest conception of conjugal happiness has been conceived."[1] Indeed, until recently, America was the only country in the world where a presidential candidate would have to withdraw if he was found to be involved in an extramarital affair.

The question is: why did the West define marriage as a permanent *and* exclusive union of one man and one woman?

Sex and Social Reform

One man who transformed the Western view of marriage and took the seeds of Western civilization from monasteries into the wider culture was the sixteenth century German reformer Martin Luther. Once an Augustinian monk, Luther denounced monasteries and promoted marriage and family as the divinely ordained school of character.

Luther knew firsthand that despite their success in developing rationality, monasteries and nunneries were not cultivating

1. Alexis de Tocqueville, *Democracy in America* (New York: Harper Perennial, 1988), 603 and 291.

the character that they were meant to create. In 1522 Luther was hiding in the Castle of Wartburg, studying the Bible and translating the New Testament into German. A fresh reading of the Bible taught him that the monastic movement was built on a wrong belief: that holiness required perpetual virginity and that sex and marriage were "carnal." In fact, Luther discovered that the Bible teaches that God created male and female to love one another, to become one flesh, and have children. God instituted marriage before sin entered the world. Sex was a part of God's good and perfect creation. The Creator commanded Adam and Eve to have children, to fill the earth, and to establish their culture over nature (Gen. 1:27–28).

Luther's writings began to change his society. At the risk of their lives, nuns escaped nunneries to get married. Katharina von Bora was one of ten nuns who hid in empty beer barrels to flee their nunnery. Nine of them found husbands, but Katie didn't. So she decided she would marry Dr. Luther.

Luther's senior colleagues advised him to live by his beliefs and marry Katie. He agreed to marriage to please his father and despise the devil. Predictably, his marriage became a weapon in the hands of his opponents; they used it to hit at the entire movement for reform. The Reformation, they said, was nothing but rationalization of Luther's sinful desire to give up his quest for personal holiness and fulfill his carnal lust for sex.

Luther responded that the monks who condemned him for giving up the pursuit of holiness had no idea of what they were talking about. Rather, "one year of marriage was more sanctifying than ten years in a monastery." Marriage brings out the worst in us. But it also refines us, provided we *stay* in that school; seek grace to change our values and behavior; and honor, love, and serve our spouses whose views, values, and habits irritate us.

The statement ascribed to Luther may be apocryphal, but he did propagate the radically new idea that *marriage*, not *monastery*, was the school of character. Sex, not celibacy, builds a strong culture. However, Luther knew that not every form of marriage empowers women. When harnessed properly, sexual drive builds individuals, families, and communities; but when it is unleashed without the restraints of morality and wisdom, it destroys.

In advocating marriage Luther was promoting the morally demanding idea of an exclusive and lifelong love relationship between one man and one woman. Such a relationship implies that sex inside of loving marriage is sacred and honorable, but sex outside of marriage is sin. This understanding of marriage spread around the world from Luther's home in Wittenberg.

Before Luther, European priests did not marry, which made Luther's home the first Christian vicarage in Europe. The house used to be a monastery; but the monks had left it because of Luther's teachings, and Fredrick the Wise gave it to Luther as his home. Katie turned the place into a guest house and invited university students to live with them as paying guests. Some of these students started recording their after-dinner discussions with Dr. Luther. These *Table Talks* shaped the Western definition of marriage for five hundred years, until the sexual revolution of the 1960s. Luther's biblical idea of marriage so empowered the West that monogamy began to spread around the world.

Although my culture accepted polygamy, in practice most men had only one wife. Nevertheless, one result of polygamy was that our traditional culture did not and could not require men to love their wives. To hold your wife's hand and to walk beside her is still a revolutionary idea for a majority of Indian men. Wives must walk behind their husbands. Yet our people did not consider it morally wrong for a man to love a mistress instead of his wife. In fact, our temples offered our leaders the services of religious prostitutes (called *devadasis*) for companionship, pleasure, and enlightenment. One of our most popular gods is said to have sixteen thousand wives, but none of his wives is worshiped— his consort is. Mahatma Gandhi did not sleep with his wife for decades, but we know the names of at least ten women he did sleep with. Polygamy makes marriage a nonexclusive relationship; therefore our people have no moral problem voting for a mistress to become the chief minister of a state, even if her political opponent is the wife of the deceased politician.

In cultures that permit polygamy, monogamy may be a social fact, but it is not a moral restraint to an exclusive sexual relationship with one person only. The Beatles turned against their guru Mahesh Yogi, calling his celibacy a lie (John Lennon), because they did not understand that in Hinduism "celibacy" does not mean absolute abstinence from sex; it means abstinence from marriage and harnessing of sexual energy for becoming divine (Brahma). The Hindu word for celibacy is *brahmacharya*, which involves an effort to become Brahma. The Hindu deity named Brahma himself has a consort named Saraswati.

What difference does it make whether one reserves sexual energy for a single spouse or spends it in many affairs? Some Indian reformers advocated monogamy because they understood that permissive sex is like a river that flows in an unregulated manner; its waters make little direct contribution to culture. A river becomes useful for irrigation, water mills, or electricity when it is dammed and controlled, when its flow is limited and regulated. The greater the control, the greater the river's usefulness.

So why don't American women haul water and cow dung on their heads? Our women do so because they cannot say to their husbands, "You bring water today, because you are sitting and playing cards. I want to put my feet up and read *Good Cowkeeping*." Polygamy and temple prostitution made our women weak. If a wife asked her husband to stop playing cards or smoking pot in order to haul water or organize the community and get the village council to vote for a twenty-four-hour water supply, then the husband would simply love the second wife or go worship the temple goddess.

The amazing irony is that some women reject monogamy because they think that to be tied exclusively to one person is slavery. In reality monogamy makes a husband a virtual slave to his wife. When told he has to stop playing cards and get water, the poor fellow cannot protest and take a second wife who would be less demanding. He cannot go to the temple and love a goddess or sleep in his mistress's home. He cannot divorce his bossy wife. In fact, he is not even allowed to hate her. He has to bring not just water but also a bouquet of flowers, preferably with a love note that says, "Honey, why don't you rest for a change! I will make dinner tonight."

Does this make the husband weak or henpecked? It makes him meek and also creative. He has to make not only dinner but also a wheelbarrow to haul water, or better still, organize his community to get water pumped into his home, dairy, or factory.

A Lost Definition of Marriage

As a school that transforms character, monogamy is tough. That is why no culture in history ever made it mandatory. It is a peculiarly New Testament idea rooted in the Jewish Scriptures that God made only one Eve for Adam and intended for the two of them to be permanently one. Monogamy is tough because it cannot be sustained without a spirituality that mandates love above lust, submission as the secret of greatness, meekness as the source of glory, and service as the path to power. The question is: Are these biblical, Western ideas of sex, love, marriage, and family true? Do they matter? Or should the law in India, America, or Africa welcome multiple definitions of marriage and family as equally true, good, and valuable? Obviously, these are not mere academic issues. If the West is still reaping the positive results of monogamy, many more countries in Africa are already paying a massive socioeconomic price for sexual permissiveness of one or both partners in terms of slavery of women, weak children and men, orphans, HIV/AIDS and other sexually transmitted diseases, and the loss of their working generation.

In Europe, the impact of unstable marriages has frightened millions of people from having and nurturing children. This will enable Islam to take over Europe through reproduction alone, without firing a gun or winning a debate. Even before Islam takes over Europe, democracy and the Muslim vote are forcing Europe to legalize polygamy. It is legal in the Netherlands and permitted in Norway, Britain, and also Canada for Muslims to have multiple wives.

The West was able to sustain monogamy only as long as it believed that love was a gift of grace, a fruit of the Spirit. Now people are taught that *spirit* does not exist and that love is only chemistry; once chemistry has changed, you cannot love the same person; chemistry is selfish, and no spirit can overrule chemistry in favor of self-sacrificing character. As a result of this thinking, divorce has become commonplace. One does not need to ask for divorce three times, as in Islam. Once is enough. Easy divorce has already turned monogamy—the school of Western character—into serial polygamy.

The new West no longer looks at Martin Luther's vicarage as the source of its definition of marriage. Many now look to Hugh Hefner's harem as offering a more interesting definition of sexuality. The tragedy is that Europe will soon graduate from Hefner's harem to Muhammad's harem, further devaluing its women.

For Luther sex was for pleasure, procreation, and bonding a family into permanent unity. The sexual revolution of the 1960s separated the pleasures of sex from the bonding role it plays in building stable and secure relationships. The separation of the pleasures of sex from its role as bonding glue is turning men into boys—playboys—who take little or no responsibility for the women they love or the children they produce. It is also turning the West's strong women into single mothers and "Desperate Housewives."[2]

The problem with polygamy, permissiveness, and divorce is that they undermine the most potent idea behind Western civilization—the dignity of women, men, and children. To that subject, therefore, we must now turn.

---

2. Between 1999 and 2004 the suicide rate in America is said to have increased 19.4 percent among men and 31 percent among women ages 45–54.

FOUR

Humanity

The Forsaken Soul of Western Civilization

My visit to Africa recounted in chapter 2 led me to ask: Why is it that cultures that built pyramids and Taj Mahals could not make wheelbarrows for their women and children, slaves and laborers? I discovered that it was a particular belief that enabled the West to abolish slavery and grant to their women greater liberty than even matriarchal cultures. The belief was that all human beings, whether high or low, educated or illiterate, rich or poor, healthy or sick, male or female, or black or white, were equal. And what made the strong and the weak equal? It was not that everyone evolved equally but the *fact* that every human being was made in God's image and therefore was endowed with dignity.

This peculiar doctrine of the dignity of man was the force that made the West different from the rest of the world, but now it is no longer a part of Ivy League universities. At the dawn of the modern era, Michelangelo painted this idea on the ceiling of the Sistine Chapel. He depicted God reaching out his arm to create Adam in his own image, while Eve is in the other arm of

God, looking at the marvel that is Adam and awaiting her own creation, which will be a marvel for Adam. The contemporary West mocks Michelangelo's worldview and devalues human life to the level of mere animals. Let me illustrate the transforming power of this truth by sharing a true, though tragic, story.

When Ruth and I moved out of the city to serve poor peasants, I was writing my first book *The World of Gurus*, which became recommended reading in universities such as Cambridge. We had no tables or chairs. I sat on a stool and handwrote the book on a small wooden plank that came out of the wall on one side of our bed. Ruth sat on the other side of the bed, editing my manuscript and typing it on a typewriter. When I didn't have enough work for Ruth, she would cycle to the village and go door-to-door to learn about our neighbors. She wanted to know how many children were studying and what we could do to help those who were not going to school. Ruth ran into a ten-year-old girl and asked her, "How many brothers and sisters do you have?"

"Three, maybe four," the girl replied.

"Do you have three or do you have four?" Ruth asked, seeking clarification.

"Three," she said. "The fourth is almost dead."

"Can I come and see this child?" Ruth asked.

Ruth had to bend down to go through a little door into a mud hut without a window or lighting. In the middle of the room was a bare string cot, and on this was an eighteen-month-old skeleton of a girl's body with pus oozing from sores all over, including from her head. Flies covered her face because she couldn't raise her hand to chase them away.

The girl was so weak that she couldn't cry. When she tried to cry, she only sighed. Her thighs were as thick as an adult's thumb. As Ruth looked at this dying child—Sheela—she started to cry.

"What's wrong with her?" Ruth asked the mother.

The mother smirked and said, "Oh, she doesn't eat anything. Whatever we give her she vomits."

"Have you taken her to the doctor?"

"What's the use? What can the doctors do if she will not eat anything?"

"How do we know what doctors can or cannot do? Shouldn't we give her the medical attention that is available?"

The mother got a little irritated. "How can we afford to go to the doctor?"

Ruth was sorry that they were too poor to go even to a free clinic in the city, so she said, "I will give you the money to take this child to the hospital."

The mother said, "I am afraid of the city. I can't go there."

"Well, take your husband."

"How can he go? Who will look after the fields and the cattle?"

"What if I gave him money to hire a laborer for a day to look after his field? Would he then come with you? I will come with you and help you navigate your way around."

"I will speak to my husband." With that the mother ended the conversation.

Ruth bicycled back to our house and got after me. "You have to talk to the husband." Though I wasn't playing cards or watching TV, I had to submit. I went, even though the couple wasn't expecting me.

They had made up their minds that they were not going to the hospital.

"Why?" I asked.

"We don't have the money."

"But my wife told you that we will give you the money."

"We don't want to get into debt."

"I will give it to you in writing that this is a gift, not a loan. We are never going to ask you for this money back."

"But we don't have the time."

"My wife told you that we will pay for a laborer so that you can create time to come."

That really got them irritated.

"Why are you bothered? She is *our* daughter."

I didn't know how to answer that. *Why am I bothered?* The only way I could interpret that question was that they wanted Sheela to die. Although I didn't believe that any parent could do that, there was no other way to interpret their behavior. So I decided to raise my voice and at least pretend to be angry.

"Are you killing this child? If you are killing her, why are you being so cruel? Why don't you pick up a knife and stab her, instead of letting her go through this pain and suffering?"

They were stunned, but I continued. "Look, if you don't take this child to the hospital, tomorrow I am going to bring the police here and lodge a complaint that you are killing this child."

By this time there was a crowd around us, and I tried to put the pressure of public opinion upon the parents. I looked around for moral support, but everybody looked at me as though I was a fool. It took me months to realize that I was, in fact, utterly ignorant. The parents were doing what was customary in the village. They already had one girl; why did they need the second girl? The first one can cook and clean and look after the siblings. Why should they take on additional trouble to bring up another girl who will need a dowry to qualify for marriage?

One elderly gentleman told the parents, "Look, this fellow is crazy. He might actually bring the police. If the police take your daughter to the hospital, you will have to pay the bill. Since he is offering to pay, why don't you go?"

The next day Ruth took Sheela and her mother to a hospital that was not free but was of better quality. Sheela was so anemic that the hospital staff couldn't give her any medication or feed her fluid through her nose. She had to be put on intravenous. In a week she gained enough strength so that they could start treating her and feeding her with a tube. After another week the doctor said, "The bill is getting too high. Why don't you take Sheela to your home and feed her? I will come once a week to look at her."

Sheela stayed in our home for a month. India did not have disposable diapers, and we had no washing machine. Dirty diapers had to be washed by hand. It was a new experience for the men in our household—especially because Indian men did not change, let alone *wash*, their children's diapers. Once we made the decision to do whatever it took, we really fell in love with Sheela, and she began to respond to that love. For the first time we could see her smiling. Her smile was worth all the trouble. Few experiences have been more satisfying for us as a family. But a month or so later the mother came and started fighting.

"Everyone in the village is saying that our daughter is eating your food and this is polluting our caste. We will be excommunicated. We want our daughter back."

Ruth said, "We have no intention of taking Sheela away from you. We want you to take your daughter and look after her. I will pay for the milk, but I will give it directly to the milkman. You take care of Sheela, and we will come and visit her."

Ruth started paying the milkman, but within a few weeks Sheela was back to square one. The milk was being fed not to Sheela but to her brothers. The whole process had to be repeated. Ruth had to fight with the mother, I had to fight with the father, and then Ruth had to take Sheela and her mother to the hospital. Sheela was again put on intravenous, then fed by tubes, and eventually brought to our home. And the mother came back and fought again. We assumed that she had learned her lesson, so we gave her another lecture on parental responsibility and gave Sheela to her along with some clothes, hoping that this time things would be better.

Within days, dear Sheela was dead.

I was convinced that her parents had killed her. Ruth didn't believe that any parent could possibly do that. After we had three more experiences of that kind, Ruth began to realize that infanticide was a common practice in our area and decided, therefore, that we should never take this risk. If parents do not want a child, we should take the baby and find a home for her (or him). We made that our practice: no questions, no arguments—if you don't want the child, we will find a home for her.

This is no place to go into those stories. The point is that what we experienced with Sheela's parents was a clash of two worldviews, both of which cannot be true. We saw this child very differently than the parents saw their own daughter. For us she was a precious individual. For them a second daughter was a liability: you feed her for ten to twelve years, treat her, educate her, and then you have to go into debt to get her married. That is not the end either. The in-laws may torture the girl to extract a larger dowry from her parents. Her whole life is suffering. Why not end this suffering quickly and smoothly and avoid hassles to yourself and the child? What is the truth—was Sheela a liability, or was she as valuable as her brothers and any other person in the world?

If an American were to argue with Sheela's parents, the parents might respond: "Look, if we had facilities for ultrasound, if we knew that this was going to be a second daughter, we would have aborted her. Since we didn't know that she would be a girl—an unwanted baby—we made the hard decision to end her life after she was born, after we knew she was a girl. We didn't do anything different than what you do when you know you won't be able to give a good life to your babies. You kill them too. You just don't see what you are doing because you pay the doctors to dispose of your babies for you. You soothe your conscience by giving it a different name. The fact that we took eighteen long months to make that painful decision only shows how difficult that decision was—how much we loved her."

"Why is it wrong to kill unwanted babies?" her parents may go on to question you. "We believe that cows are sacred, but you kill them. Your ancestors in Greece and Rome practiced infanticide as we do, but now you think that human life is sacred. Why should we be bound by your values? After all, according to your universities, a cow is one kind of animal and a human being is simply another kind of animal. Whatever value a society ascribes to either cows or humans is an arbitrary social convention. If your universities are right, if there is no God who has said, "You shall not kill," then why is murder wrong? Where does a person get a fundamental right to his or her life, property, or conscience, if not from society? Why can't a society take away the right to life, which it gives—or at least make exceptions to the normal rules? Our society allows us to kill unwanted babies. Who gave *you* the right to impose your moral values on us?"

Sheela's parents had no philosophical basis for affirming the positive value of Sheela's life. In fact, they did not realize their own human dignity. They did not know that poverty and misery are not inevitable and inescapable. They were Hindus, but like most Hindus they accepted the Buddha's first Noble Truth that life is suffering. They didn't know that life does not need to be suffering. Suffering is not written in our stars, karma, fate, or destiny.

Sheela's mother, grandmother, and great-grandmother may have experienced life as miserable. But could Sheela's parents give to her a different and better future? Could a poor family bring up a daughter in a way that she could become a source of a better future for the whole family? Could a girl lift an entire village out of poverty? Sheela's parents were poor, but their poverty was more than material. They knew we were willing to give a new life to Sheela, but they lacked faith. A second daughter was not valuable enough for them to resist the pressure of a culture that preferred she die rather than eat our food.

Compare this story with the story of Helen Keller. When she was nineteen months old, Helen became deaf and blind. Because she had not started speaking by then, she also became mute. Although physically she was capable of speaking, psychologically she couldn't. She was shut up in her own self, unable to communicate with anyone in the world, frustrated, angry, and irrational.

From the secular viewpoint of our age, Helen's life had little value. She was a girl—deaf, dumb, and blind. Today in the Netherlands she could be euthanized legally. Along with legally accepting polygamy, the Netherlands has become the first Western nation to legalize infanticide under certain circumstances. America will follow the Netherlands, China, and India as more and more people decide that a human being is nothing more than an animal: she has no intrinsic, God-given value; the only value she has is relative, arbitrarily assigned to her by other human beings.

Fortunately for Helen Keller, she was born in a different era, when the West still believed—on the Bible's authority—that a deaf and blind girl is still a human being, the image-bearer of God.

Anne Sullivan, Helen's nurse, teacher, and maid, loved and served Helen. One day she took Helen to a well where there was some fragrant honeysuckle. Someone was drawing water at the well, and Ann put Helen's hand in the water stream. As Helen was shocked by the sensation of water falling on her one hand, Ann started spelling *water* on Helen's other hand—first slowly, then quickly. Helen was mesmerized. All of a sudden she understood that what was being drawn on one hand was the name of this cool something falling on her other hand. Helen's world changed— the magic of language began to make sense. Excited, Helen went back home and started learning language. Although she was still mute, with writing she learned on the very first day words such as *father*, *mother*, *teacher*, *brother*, and *sister*. In a few weeks Helen began to speak. Then she learned to type on a special Braille typewriter and went on to become a mighty spokeswoman for handicapped children all over the world.

What made the difference for Helen? Was it her parent's wealth or their belief that a deaf, dumb, and blind girl was valuable? There are aristocratic families in Western India that boast that they have not had a single girl born in their clan in fourteen generations! They won't tell you that their female babies are aborted. (Earlier girls died mysteriously at birth.) Helen was helped to flourish because her culture believed that a deaf and blind girl was not a useless child without value. Helen was so important that God himself had come to earth to give her eternal life; therefore, people had to do all they could to help her find abundant life.

The belief in the unique dignity of human beings was the force that created Western civilization, where citizens do not exist for the state but the state exists for individuals. Even kings, presidents, prime ministers, and army generals cannot be allowed to trample upon an individual and his or her rights. The idea of human dignity liberated children from the dark, satanic mills of the Industrial Revolution in Britain. It led to the American Revolution, which ended colonialism, and to the American Civil War, which ended slavery. It continues to inspire all sorts of movements for justice and equity.

The West was never perfect, but it was a mighty achievement to create a civilization where the king of England or the president of America had all the power to do right but no power to do wrong by taking away the life of a deaf and blind girl. The West valued human beings because the Bible says:

> What is man that you [God] are mindful of him,
>   the son of man that you care for him?
>   [Even though a human being is but a speck]
> You made him a little lower than the heavenly beings
>   and crowned him with glory [*dignitas*] and honor.
> You have made him ruler over the works of your hands;
>   you put everything under his feet. (Ps. 8:4–6)

The contemporary West, especially Europe, is now busy amputating its soul. It is rejecting the source of its greatness, that is, the truth revealed by God's Word that defines the value of every individual and redefines the purpose and the function of the state. The West is discarding the source of its morality, rationality, family, and humanity: the intellectual foundation of human rights, justice, compassion, care, and education. In this depressing environment one comforting fact for me as an Indian is that Bollywood movies such as *Taare Zameen Par* (*Stars on Earth*) are trying to change India by injecting into our culture the biblical idea of the dignity of every child.

Serving a weak, unwanted girl may be a more attractive idea than killing her, but why should Sheela's parents pay the price to follow an idea simply because it sounded attractive? Why not choose an easier, more convenient, and cheaper course of action— killing her? Helen Keller's parents chose the emotionally and monetarily costly course because they *believed* that as a human being endowed with a soul, Helen was infinitely valuable. It is truth that transforms.

But is transformation possible in our world? As Old Testament prophets such as Isaiah realized, a commitment to truth can be costly in a society that has sold its soul. Reflecting on the cost of ultimate healing and transformation, Isaiah wrote, "The punishment that brought us peace was upon him, and by his wounds we are healed" (53:5). It is by his wounds that the Messiah brings healing to a nation.

PART II

Can Nations
Be Healed?

FIVE

His Wounds

For the Healing of the Nations

"Americans Can Do Anything"

On February 24, 2009, President Barack Obama gave his first address to the joint session of Congress, repeatedly using the word *crisis* to describe the fact that many Americans are spending "sleepless nights" with their dreams "hanging by a thread." He reminded the world's sole economic superpower of "a trillion-dollar deficit, a financial crisis, and a costly recession." The president acknowledged that the economy is in trouble because some of America's biggest financial institutions have been so mismanaged that they have become incapable of sustaining American capitalism. Before a skeptical nation, President Obama defended his plan simultaneously to give trillions more of taxpayers' money to these same institutions and to cut the national deficit in half. On what did he base such an "audacious hope"?

The president asserted that "the weight of this crisis will not determine the destiny of this nation. The answers to our problems don't lie beyond our reach. They exist in our laboratories

and universities; in our fields and our factories; in the imagina-
tions of our entrepreneurs and the pride of the hardest-working
people on Earth."

A few minutes after the president's speech, Bobby Jindal,
America's first Indo-American governor, from Louisiana, gave the
Republican Party's response to the president. While strongly dis-
agreeing with Obama's philosophy of big government, the governor went beyond the president in affirming his own father's naive
faith that "Americans can do anything."

Really?

Can Americans sustain their liberty?

On Christmas Day 2002, my wife Ruth and I were flying
from Florida to Minnesota. When our airline's crew joined us in
the airport shuttle, I wished them "Merry Christmas." While the
shuttle driver responded warmly with "Same to you," the crew
merely nodded politely. I wondered if they were unhappy that
they were working on Christmas Day while the rest of us were
enjoying a holiday. I understood better in the plane when a flight
attendant greeted us with "Happy Holidays."

I asked her, "Are you not allowed to say, 'Merry Christmas'?"

"No," she replied. "We have to say, 'Happy Holidays.'"

"This is amazing," I said to her. "I thought America was tol-
erant—the land of the free and the home of the brave. The world
respects your forefathers for saying, 'Give me liberty or give
me death.' And here you are—you cannot even wish us 'Merry
Christmas'!"

At that time most Americans were still excited about the war
against terror and Islamic militancy. So I pressed my point harder:
"If you surrender your heritage of freedom, how can you ask the
people in Afghanistan or Iraq to stand up for their liberty?"

She responded politely, "Religious terms such as 'Christmas'
offend liberals."

"If so," I inquired, "should you surrender your freedom or
teach them tolerance?"

Is American character still as strong as President Obama and Governor Jindal assume it is?

Can American scientists express sincere convictions?

As I began watching Ben Stein's movie *Expelled: No Intelligence Allowed*, I felt that he was overstating the case that America, the land of the free, is turning into a Nazi-like authoritarian regime that persecutes scientists who pursue truth and express their convictions that their scientific investigations reveal intelligent design in creation. At one point I got so upset at the film's portrayal of the loss of intellectual integrity in America that I wanted to walk out of the theater. By the end, however, I was convinced not merely that Ben Stein is right but that his courage is heroic. His movie shows that the American academy has become adamant about "suppressing the truth with unrighteousness." In Romans 1:18–32, the apostle Paul describes what follows such actions.

Can Hollywood make honest movies?

"Americans can do anything"—but who in Hollywood has the courage to tell the story of a final-year medical student that I met in the Hollywood district of Los Angeles?

"How did your day go?" I inquired of him.

Very sadly, he responded, "It was an easy day until the end."

"What happened?"

"A handsome young man came into the clinic at the end of the day with some minor symptoms. I examined him and recommended prescriptions, but he kept sitting, hesitating to leave. I asked him, 'Is there something else we need to talk about?'

"'Can I get tested for HIV?' he requested sheepishly. When we found that he was positive, he burst out crying. He confided, 'My partner just died of AIDS.' I held his hand, talked to him, and prayed with him."

More funds are available to fight HIV/AIDS than any other epidemic. And yet, thanks to Hollywood's brazen promotion of homosexual and bisexual behavior, after a period of decline HIV/ AIDS has bounced back in America and has become the number-one killing epidemic in China.

Can Americans donate according to their conscience?

"Americans can do anything"—fearlessly. A few weeks after that Christmas Day flight in 2002, I saw media reports of a sixteen-year-old high school girl performing a sexual act on her classmate in a school bus as their friends cheered them on. Another story reported a similar incident that occurred in a middle school classroom while the teacher was present in the class, showing a film to other students. Now, because of widespread Internet pornography, readers are no longer shocked by such stories, and, therefore, such stories have no place in the media. In early 2009 the media is reporting that Californians can do anything—except fearlessly say that adultery, fornication, and divorce are destructive evils, or donate to Proposition 8 to preserve marriage as a covenant between one man and one woman. Voters who donated to Proposition 8 have been blacklisted on the Internet and have had their personal information released. As a result, gay rights activists can intimidate them fearlessly, making it hard for them to live, speak, donate, and vote according to their conscience.

Truth transforms. But if you work for an airline, truth can cost you your job. If you work in Hollywood, it will cost you a nomination for an Oscar. If you exercise your democratic duty in California, you will be blacklisted on the Internet. For testifying to the truth, the Messiah had to bear the cross.

The Cost of Hope

The Bible climaxes with an awe-inspiring vision of hope, in which John sees a river flowing from the throne of God, down the central street of a heavenly Jerusalem. "On each side of the river stood the tree of life, bearing twelve crops of fruit, yielding its fruit every month. And the leaves of the tree are for the healing of the nations" (Rev. 22:2).

What is the price of this hope? Isaiah 53:4–5 says:

Surely he took up our infirmities
    and carried our sorrows,
yet we considered him stricken by God,
    smitten by him, and afflicted.
But he was pierced for our transgressions,
    he was crushed for our iniquities;
the punishment that brought us peace was upon him,
    and by his wounds we are healed.

Who was the prophet talking about when he said, "By his wounds *we* are healed?" Who is the "we"?

Hope for the Nations

American individualism has so permeated the church that most Christians automatically assume that "we" means "she, you, and I as individuals." That is, a collection of individuals makes a "we." But if you look at the book of Isaiah, you will find a very different description of "we."

Who is sick and needs healing? Isaiah answers that question beginning in verse four of his first chapter:

Ah, sinful nation,
    a people loaded with guilt,
a brood of evildoers,
    children given to corruption!
They have forsaken the LORD;
    they have spurned the Holy One of Israel
    and turned their backs on him.
Why should you be beaten anymore?
    Why do you persist in rebellion?
Your whole head is injured,
    your whole heart is afflicted. [You have a heart disease.]
From the sole of your foot to the top of your head

> there is no soundness—
> only wounds and welts
>   and open sores,
> not cleansed or bandaged
>   or soothed with oil.
> Your country is desolate,
>   your cities burned with fire.

Who is sick and needs healing? Isaiah could be describing American financial institutions responsible for the present financial crisis when he goes on to say in verse 21–23:

> See how the faithful city
>   has become a harlot!
> She once was full of justice;
>   righteousness used to dwell in her—
>   but now murderers!
> Your silver has become dross,
>   your choice wine is diluted with water.
> Your rulers are rebels,
>   companions of thieves;
> they all love bribes
>   and chase after gifts.
> They do not defend the cause of the fatherless;
>   the widow's case does not come before them.

It is the nation of Israel that is sick, and the prophet is proclaiming the good news that there is healing for the nation in the wounds of the Messiah. In chapter six, Isaiah uses the word *healing* again. Isaiah saw the Lord and heard the call, "Whom shall I send? And who will go for us?"

Isaiah responded, "Here am I. Send me!"

And the Holy One said, "Go."

And do what? God answers in Isaiah 6:9–10:

"Go and tell this people:
'Be ever hearing, but never understanding;
　be ever seeing, but never perceiving.'
Make the heart of this people calloused;
　make their ears dull
　and close their eyes.
Otherwise they might see with their eyes,
　hear with their ears,
　understand with their hearts,
and turn and be healed."

If you look at words such as *heal* and *healing* in the book of Isaiah, you will find that Isaiah is not talking about individuals. He consistently uses these words for *nations*. God called Abraham, Isaac, and Jacob so that through their descendants he might bless all the nations.

"But you, O Israel, my servant,
　Jacob, whom I have chosen,
　you descendants of Abraham my friend,
I took you from the ends of the earth,
　from its farthest corners I called you.
I said, 'You are my servant';
　I have chosen you and have not rejected you.
(Isa. 41:8–9)

"I have seen his ways, but I will *heal* him;
　I will guide him and restore comfort to him,
　creating praise on the lips of the mourners in Israel.
Peace, peace, to those far and near,"
　says the LORD. "And I will *heal* them." (Isa. 57:18–19)

In Isaiah 58:7–8 the Lord explains through Isaiah that the spirituality that brings *national* healing is more than a matter of observing rituals. What is true fasting?

"Is it not to share your food with the hungry
    and to provide the poor wanderer with shelter—
when you see the naked, to clothe him,
    and not to turn away from your own flesh and blood?
Then your light will break forth like the dawn,
    and your *healing* will quickly appear."

Because God chose Israel in order to heal and bless all the nations of the earth, Isaiah had to correct the narrow nationalism of his countrymen:

> So the LORD will make himself known to the Egyptians. . . . The LORD will strike Egypt with a plague; he will strike them and *heal* them. They will turn to the LORD, and he will respond to their pleas and *heal* them.
>   In that day there will be a highway from Egypt to Assyria. . . . The Egyptians and Assyrians will worship together. In that day Israel will be the third, along with Egypt and Assyria, a blessing on the earth. The LORD Almighty will bless them, saying, "Blessed be Egypt my people, Assyria my handiwork, and Israel my inheritance." (Isa. 19:21–25)

The idea that the wounds of the Messiah are for the healing of the nations raises a theological problem for Christian individualism: For whom or for what did Jesus die?

If Isaiah meant that the Messiah would suffer for the healing of Israel, is that consistent with the Gospels? Did Jesus die only to take our souls to heaven, or did he die also for the healing of our nations?

For Whom Did Jesus Die?

Let us turn to the Gospels and face the question head-on. To discover truth that can transform your nation, you have to be like the Bereans, who were noble because they searched the Scriptures to judge whether Paul's teaching was heresy or truth (Acts 17:11). I invite you to do the same.

The implication of Isaiah is radical: could the individualistic gospel usually heard be a caricature of the biblical gospel?

The cross is the original source of Western individualism. It inspired individual reformers such as John Wycliffe, Jan Hus, Martin Luther, and William Tyndale to stand against the entire tradition and teaching of their church and risk their lives. But the individualism of the cross was very different from its secularized counterfeit. The individualism of the cross says, "Not my will, but thine, be done." The cross involved Jesus surrendering himself to the Father in such a radical way that God could give his Son's life for the world. Secularized individualism is self-centered; it sees the passion of the Christ as something for "me."

This counterfeit individualism reads the Gospels with colored glasses and filters out anything that does not fit the presumption that Jesus died only to take our souls to heaven. This has resulted in a spirituality that Os Guinness says is "privately engaging but publicly irrelevant." It has become the source of the cultural ineffectiveness of the Western church. Therefore, let us take a fresh look at whom the Messiah was healing and whom he had compassion on.

SIX

His Compassion

Jesus the Troublemaker

Compassion for the suffering individual and concern for the glory of God were undoubtedly the prime motives of Christ's service. But if compassion had meant for Christ merely what it means for most Christians today, Jesus would never have been killed. He would have been a fit candidate for a Nobel Prize, not the cross.

Christ's compassion was prophetic. Instead of being a gut-level response to pictures of starving children, it grew out of a prophetic insight into the root causes of human misery. Jesus went to the source of suffering and dealt with it.

In an earlier age, when Protestants still believed in social protest, the following commentary would have been redundant. To many Christians today it will seem too radical, because for a few centuries now the world has heard the gospel as articulated by the Western church, which has enjoyed a position of privilege. In spite of the "wall of separation" between the church and the state, no John the Baptist was beheaded in America or England.

Faith-based initiatives received state patronage. Therefore, the West had little reason to examine biblical ideas such as compassion from the perspective of the oppressed. Now, however, the secular West is squeezing the truth. A pastor can go to jail for reading in public the biblical injunctions against homosexuality. Therefore, the radical perspective of this chapter is becoming relevant even for the West.

When I wrote this chapter, I was trying to understand Christ from inside a prison in central India. Before sending me to jail, the police superintendent told me that if I did not cancel a public prayer meeting for the victims of a hail storm, he would kill me. Thankfully, his threat turned out to be a bluff. I was jailed only for a week, but that was enough to help me understand the transforming power of Christ's compassion.

Service: A Stirring of a Stagnant Pool

In John 5 Jesus healed a man who had been sick for thirty-eight years. The lame man was lying near a pool of water. When the waters of the pool were stirred, therapeutic powers went into action, and the sick who entered the water were healed. This was not the man's own superstition but was something he had been witnessing for decades. No one, however dumb, would have stayed by the pool for all those years if he had not seen the healing powers of those waters. The man was sick, the treatment was free and within sight, yet he could not get it.

Why not? He explained to Jesus that he did not have anyone to help him into the water when it was stirred. No one cared for him.

Jesus told this man who had not stood for almost four decades to pick up his mat and walk. He did! But it was the Sabbath. In Jerusalem you could forget whether it was Tuesday or Thursday, but no one ever forgot it was the Sabbath. It was forbidden to carry your mat on the Sabbath. The Jewish society was so well organized that in no time the authorities found out that this unknown man had dared to break the sabbatical rule by picking up his bed and walking. An on-the-spot inquiry began. How efficient!

Why was a religious establishment which had not cared for a sick man for thirty-eight years so prompt in caring for its own inhuman rules? I find it hard to believe that they were so keen to enforce the Sabbath legislation because they wanted to please God. I am more inclined to think that one of their interests was to impose a fine and collect a little extra revenue! The sick man had complained to Jesus that his problem was that his society had no compassion. It hadn't even bothered to enforce a basic etiquette of civilized behavior: first come, first served. The resourceful came late but got healed first.

It was not by mistake that Jesus asked this powerless man to challenge an inhuman society by a deliberate act of defiance. God had provided the stirred-up pool of water for the healing of this man. It was the social pool of a stagnant, selfish society that needed to be stirred up for the man's healing. Stirring the pool is precisely what Jesus did.

Does the healing ministry of the church today lead to such retaliation from society? No, because our service does not touch the real issues. Many sick men, women, and children in the villages and slums of my country die daily, not because treatment is unavailable or too expensive, but simply because no one cares to take treatment to them.

Our governments can send satellites to the sky, but they cannot take simple sanitation to the dying and destitute people in our slums. The church says it cares, yet so often it does not dare to expose the selfishness of the ruling elite, which is the real cause of hundreds of basic diseases that could have been wiped out by now if only clean water, basic sanitation, adequate nutrition, health education, and immunizations were made available to the poor masses. The technology and financial resources are available in abundance to take these services to the poor, but the powerful have other priorities.

The World Health Organization estimates that India loses twenty thousand crores of rupees[1] annually because of sicknesses caused by contaminated water alone. Christ's mercy did not touch the individual alone. It sought to touch the heart of a society. It sought to awaken the sleeping conscience of society. It troubled the stagnant waters and brought about a torrent of retaliation from vested interests.

Service: Judgment of a Blind Society

After he opened the eyes of a beggar who was born blind, Jesus did not portray himself as a healer or a servant. He said, "For judgment I have come into this world, so that the blind will see and those who see will become blind" (John 9:39).

Before this, the disciples had asked Jesus, "Rabbi, who sinned, this man or his parents, that he was born blind?" (9:2).

Jesus did not think that the disciples had a profound philosophical interest in the problem of suffering which deserved an answer.[2] Their question seems to have hurt him because at best the disciples were blaming the innocent man or his parents for his blindness. At worst they were looking for a rationale to justify their indifference to the man's need: true, the man was born blind, but did he have to be a beggar?

In reality, both the blind man and his parents were sinners—but no more than the disciples. Why did the disciples exist? For the glory of God! Why did the blind man exist? Equally for the glory of God! Was Israel justified in ignoring the fact that the blind man was a human being made in the image of God, worthy of love and care?

The man was begging neither because he was blind nor because he was a sinner, but because Israel was blind to the fact

1. US$58,000,000,000.

2. For a detailed discussion of suffering, see the chapter "Making Sense of Suffering" in my book *Missionary Conspiracy: Letters to a Postmodern Hindu* (New Delhi: Nivedit Good Books, 1996).

that he was an image-bearer of God, the crown of God's creation. He was a beggar because Israel had sinned by not caring for him. The disciples, instead of seeing their own sinful indifference to their neighbor, judged the man and his parents for his blindness.

Jesus sought to open his disciples' eyes by a brilliant act of civil disobedience. The healing incident in John 5 was not an isolated happening; it was part of Christ's pattern. On that occasion Jesus had simply asked the sick man to break the Sabbath law by picking up his mat. On this occasion in John 9, Jesus breaks the Sabbath himself. In order to open the eyes of the blind man, Jesus did not need to spit on the ground and make mud with the spit. He knew this would be seen as work on the Sabbath and therefore a deliberate act of defiance of the Establishment's laws. Yet he did it. It was intentional provocation of the ruling religious elite, who saw the beggar as a sinner. Jesus also asked the blind man to break their law. "'Go,' he told him, 'wash in the Pool of Siloam'" (John 9:7).

Jesus did not need to challenge the socioreligious establishment in order to heal the blind man, but healing the man was not his only objective. Jesus' objectives included exposing the blindness of the self-righteous religious establishment and condemning it publicly. Had not God commanded Israel to have mercy on its poor? If Israel was righteous and obedient, why did this man beg on the streets in order to live?

Civil disobedience is a deliberate, courageous, and compassionate act of a reformer to expose and condemn the institutionalized evils of his day. That is what Jesus was doing. And the cultural elite were blind enough to be thus exposed. Instead of containing Christ's service by patronizing it, they condemned the healing of a blind man simply because it was done on the Sabbath. They excommunicated the man from the synagogue and thereby further exposed their own blindness. The world was able to see that a mighty prophet had arisen among them who could open the eyes of a man born blind, yet the rulers could see nothing more than the violation of their own petty rules. Their values, ideals, attitudes, and priorities all stood exposed and condemned. The world was able to see that the rulers did not care for their people, but Christ did. The sheep were able to perceive that Jesus was their true shepherd, who dared to stand against the wolves pretending to be their custodians.

The blind man had to pay a heavy price for his healing. He was put out of the synagogue because he chose to speak the truth. The authorities also made it known that Jesus was persona non grata. Anyone who said that Jesus was the Christ would be put out of the synagogue. It became harder to associate with Jesus; being seen around him could land someone in trouble.

Genuine compassion calls us to confront social structures and cultural practices that make people miserable. Atheism destroys compassion by making human beings accidental products of random chance in an impersonal universe. This deprives compassion of all moral significance. If nature does not care for a creature too weak and powerless to care for itself, why should we, especially if he or she is of no use to us? Human beings are special only if they are seen as created beings, special to their Creator. If humans are created as image-bearers of the Creator himself, then they are even more special. And if individuals are to relate to the Creator in an intimate, personal relationship and carry out the Creator's will in this world, then they are very special indeed. That is how Jesus saw this blind beggar. "Neither this man nor his parents sinned . . . but this happened that the work of God might be displayed in his life" (John 9:3).

Because an "unknown" blind beggar is special to God, we must have compassion for him individually. This compassion must be visible in specific acts of mercy, but our compassion for him must go deep enough to create a society that can see that a blind man is a special person. He should not have to live a hand-to-mouth, insecure existence until one day he falls sick, becomes too weak to beg, and rots by the roadside to be eaten by beasts, birds, and worms.

A society that cannot see the intrinsic value of a blind beggar is blind to truth. Its blindness needs to be exposed so that it can be transformed into a humane and compassionate community.

Service: A Power for Social Change

Religious authorities made the decision to kill Jesus after he raised Lazarus from the dead (John 11). Jesus loved Lazarus and his sisters Mary and Martha. These sisters sent word to Jesus that Lazarus, his beloved friend, was sick. Jesus could have healed Lazarus by a word from wherever he was, saving the sisters from much agony. But his healing ministry had purposes other than mere healing. He waited till Lazarus died. He waited till the Pharisees in Jerusalem heard of Lazarus's death and assembled in his village, Bethany, to comfort his sisters. Then, in front of a crowd, Jesus displayed his love for the dead man and his sisters by raising him from the dead. Jesus displayed his anger as well as sorrow at disease and death, for he knew that this suffering was not what God desired or designed.

Jesus' prayer in John 11:41–42 makes it abundantly clear that even though he could have healed Lazarus and raised him from the dead without exhibiting who he was, Jesus felt it necessary at that point to enable the world to see his heart, his being, and his power.

The miracle had the intended effect: many people believed in Jesus. Their acceptance of Jesus as the Messiah was a rejection of the religious establishment (John 12:9–11). The Jewish rulers were aligned to the exploitative Roman regime (John 19:15); they had power because they allowed and enabled Rome to continue its exploitation of the people. The chief priests could not allow Jesus to extend his influence over the people, for that would create a new center of mass power which would be in the interest of the common man, not the rulers. Because the empire would not tolerate a leadership that defended the interests of the people, it was inevitable that "the Romans will come and take away both our place and our nation" (John 11:48). If the nation was to be "saved," the high priest reasoned, the shepherd had to be eliminated (John 11:49–50). "Slavery is better than destruction" was the rationale behind eliminating the good shepherd.

The raising of dead Lazarus shows that the compassion of Jesus did not merely heal individuals; it also built up a mass following—just as Jesus' preaching not only educated but also drew wholehearted dedication to follow him. The separation of evangelism and church planting has created a mentality among Christians all over the world that leads to preaching and serving, but not to building up a faith-filled following. Because of this mentality, many people cannot even see in the Gospels the obvious fact that Jesus was building up a disciple-based movement through his teaching, preaching, and healing.

A fresh look at the Gospels, however, will convince the reader that Jesus carefully built a large following that was not another religious sect but an alternative center of power in Israel. It was a threat to the status quo, not only naturally, but also intentionally, because it was the very antithesis of all that the Establishment represented.

First, this alternative center of power was a moral force in contrast to the immoral national leadership. Jesus healed physically and called people to sin no more (John 5:14). He called his disciples to righteousness that "surpasses that of the Pharisees and the teachers of the law" (Matt. 5:20).

Second, it was a social force that stood up for the smallest of people, in contrast to a religious leadership that protected the interests of the powerful exploiters, such as the traders in the temple, whom Jesus called "robbers" (Mark 11:17). Jesus called his followers to serve "the least of these"—the hungry, the naked, the sick, the homeless, and the imprisoned (Matt. 25:34–46).

Third, this alternative power was both a compassionate and courageous force. It required a determination to stand for the protection of the harassed and helpless sheep to the point of the laying down of one's own life (John 10:11). This was a contrast to the established leadership, which was concerned primarily for its own safety and well-being and was prepared, in the face of Roman threat, to sacrifice the interests of the common man (John 11:45–48).

Jesus intentionally built up his following, his *ecclesia*, as a power structure to withstand the mighty forces of destruction and death. He said to Peter, "You are Peter, and on this rock I will build my church, and the gates of Hades will not overcome it" (Matt. 16:18). The destructive forces of death will fight against Christ's new society but will not prevail against it. The church was meant to stand against the forces of oppression and death because it was asked to "feed my lambs" and "take care of my sheep." In an unjust, oppressive society, when a group stands up for the smallest of lambs, it automatically stands up against the mighty vested interests that grow fat on their flesh (see Isa. 61:1–2). In America today, it is the corruption of the corporate giants that is giving sleepless nights to the honest workers.

Jesus and his new community were naturally and intentionally a threat to the kingdom of darkness. Jesus set his face to go to Jerusalem and precipitate a confrontation. He forced Israel to choose between the status quo and transformation.

Generally speaking, the "Sunday school Jesus" confines himself only to the changing of people's hearts, but the Jesus of the Gospels aimed to change both human hearts and human society. He prepared shepherds to replace wolves as the leadership of Israel. Jesus made his intentions explicit in the parable of the laborers in the vineyard (Matt. 21:33–46). He concluded the parable by telling the chief priests, "Therefore I tell you that the kingdom of God will be taken away from you and given to a people who will produce its fruit" (v. 43). This was an explicit statement of a radical transformation, of a transfer of power from the wolves to the shepherds. The leaders understood Jesus' message and tried to arrest him on the spot, "but they were afraid of the crowd because the people held that he was a prophet" (v. 46).

The wise men had announced Jesus' kingship at his birth, and John the Baptist had announced some of the changes that the Messiah was to bring about before Jesus began his public ministry. But Jesus announced to the corrupt leaders his intention of social change only after he had carefully built up mass support. Jesus asserted his royal authority over Zion through the dramatic event of his triumphal entry into Jerusalem after the raising of Lazarus, which had created excitement among the masses.

Power was not an accidental byproduct of compassion. Jesus consciously used his service to cultivate a mass following to transform his society. Look at his strategy following the raising of Lazarus in John's gospel.

First, Jesus brought a dead man back to life. He allowed the story of this fantastic miracle to spread to the point when it started ringing alarm bells in the ears of the established leadership (John 11:45–53). Then he withdrew to a desert town called Ephraim (11:54). It was near the time of the Passover festival when many Jews poured into Jerusalem, and naturally they gossiped about Jesus (11:55–56). After Jesus had become the hot topic of debate, he returned to Lazarus's home in Bethany, just two kilometers from Jerusalem. The word of Jesus' return to Bethany spread in Jerusalem, and crowds flocked to see not only him but also Lazarus (12:9–11). Then, when a large enough crowd had gathered about Jesus, he asked for a colt and allowed his disciples to organize a procession. Jesus marched into Jerusalem, with the crowd proclaiming him to be the king of Israel. The whole city was stirred up, and "the Pharisees said to one another, 'See, this is getting us nowhere. Look how the whole world has gone after him!'" (12:19).

As a result of Jesus' strategy, the cultural elite decided to kill both Jesus and Lazarus (12:9–11). Christ knew that this would be the consequence of what he was doing, but he had no choice. Israel's leadership had refused to repent. It had refused to believe the truth and had decided to continue in its evil ways. Either

Jesus had to give up his call for repentance and change or he had to precipitate a confrontation to give the rulers a last opportunity either to repent or to kill him. He was prepared to pay the price of such a confrontation.

Jesus did not heal the blind man or raise Lazarus from the dead merely to have them live comfortably. He was paying a price for the world, and his followers had to pay a price too.

Compassion that does not ask the beneficiaries to pay a price tends to become patronizing; it violates their dignity and fails to produce a following. When Jesus sent the twelve apostles to preach and heal in Israel, he prohibited them from taking money with them (Matt. 10:5–10). The beneficiaries of their healing ministry had to pay for the apostles' upkeep and thus become participants, if not the owners, of Jesus' movement.

Jesus accepted his death, the price that he paid as a "criminal," as his glory. He carefully chose the time and place of his confrontation with the establishment and his death so that his cause could receive the maximum benefit from his crucifixion. Within six weeks of his despised and lonely death in Jerusalem, over two thousand people had accepted him as their Messiah in that very city.

The purpose of Jesus' cultivating a mass following was not to gain a selfish crown. Satan had offered kingship to Jesus at the very beginning of his ministry (Matt. 4:8–10), but Jesus refused to have the kingdom for himself. He wanted the kingdom for the poor (Matt. 5:3; Luke 6:20), the sorrowful (Matt. 5:4), the meek (Matt. 5:5). The poorer masses saw him as their Messiah and began to follow him, which threatened the existing leadership. The Jewish authorities had perceived that the whole world was following him, and therefore he had to be eliminated. For Jesus, real glory was not international recognition, but crucifixion— laying down his life for the poor, the harassed, and the helpless lost sheep.

Compassion and Cultural Transformation

The shocking incident in Matthew 15 can help us understand how Christ's compassion freed his disciples from the deep-rooted racial prejudices of their culture. The chapter begins with a heated encounter between the Pharisees and Jesus. The Pharisees were upset because Jesus' disciples did not observe the traditions of the elders, specifically the ritual washing of hands before eating. Instead of rebuking his disciples, Jesus condemned the religious leaders for breaking the commands of God for the sake of their traditions.

The conflict became so intense that Jesus had to leave the Jewish area and go to the non-Jewish area of Tyre and Sidon. Although Jesus wanted to remain incognito, a Canaanite woman heard about him and came to him with a desperate prayer: "Lord, Son of David, have mercy on me! My daughter is suffering terribly from demon-possession" (Matt. 15:22).

Matthew records that "Jesus did not answer a word." That was unusual enough, but then Jesus did something worse. When the woman's persistence became a nuisance, the disciples urged him, not to cast out the demon, but to "send her away, for she keeps crying out after us." Jesus perplexed his disciples by a culturally "correct" response: "I was sent only to the lost sheep of Israel." Had Jesus been a Pharisee, his disciples would have believed him. But his statement made no sense, because he had just been driven to this area because of his opposition to the Pharisaic culture. The disciples had every right to wonder, *If you really want to please the Jews by not associating with this unclean, Gentile woman, why do you irritate them by breaking their Sabbath laws and established traditions, such as the ritual washing of hands?*

The Canaanite woman also had good reason for not taking Jesus' statement seriously. She kept pleading, "Lord, help me!"

Jesus responded to her plea for mercy with an astoundingly racist statement: "It is not right to take the children's bread and toss it to their dogs" (15:26).

The statement would have shocked the disciples. Is this the man who asked an unclean Samaritan woman for water? Is he the same man who touched the untouchable lepers? Didn't he choose to offend the Pharisees by eating with social outcasts like the tax collectors? Why is he trying to please the Pharisees now? Is he attempting to win back the Jews' favor by compromising with their racist notions of clean and unclean, pure and untouchable human beings?

This was not the first time Jesus had done or said something that his disciples did not understand. You can imagine them saying to themselves, "We can see ourselves calling this woman 'a dog.' In fact, we do consider them unclean dogs. But we never expected *him* to say this, certainly not in public! Racism is something we practice discreetly. No one displays it publicly like this. What is he doing?"

While the disciples were trying to figure out Jesus' powerful drama that exposed the racism of their culture, the "unclean" mother did something even more amazing. In total contrast to the self-righteousness of the Pharisees, she conceded publicly that she had no merit that qualified her to receive God's favor. She was asking for grace—unmerited favor. "'Yes, Lord,' she said, 'but even the dogs eat the crumbs that fall from their masters' table'" (15:27). Jesus commended the woman's "great faith" and healed her daughter.

Was Jesus flip-flopping, identifying with the racism of his society one moment and respecting the woman's faith the next? Or could it be that our individualistic perspective makes it hard for us to understand Jesus?

The precious Canaanite daughter was oppressed by a demon and needed deliverance. But wasn't there a second demon that oppressed both the mother and the daughter—the demon of racism? This second demon was in the culture that corrupted the disciples. This demon had to be exorcised if the disciples were to become true children of Abraham, willing to take the blessing of the gospel to all the nations, embracing uncircumcised Gentiles as their own blood brothers and sisters. Jesus was freeing them from the "yeast of the Pharisees and Sadducees" before verbalizing that in Matthew 16:6.

Jesus needed to deliver his disciples from racism because he was making them the light of the *world*, the salt of the *earth* for the healing of the *nations*. As the high priest predicted in John 11:52, Jesus died to make the scattered children of God *one*.

There is hope for the healing of the nations because Jesus confronted sins that separate people into people groups, such as caste, tribe, and race, that prohibit us from loving our neighbors across these divisions. With his wounds he paid the price for the healing of the nations, which includes reconciliation among hostile people groups. The West's failure to understand the Jesus of the Gospels has at times had tragic consequences, such as slavery and racism. A distressing truth is that even today American missionaries continue to advise Brahmin followers of Christ not to worship with believers from people groups other than their own. In the name of propagating the gospel, they export racist segregation from America to India, as though we did not have enough sins of our own. These American missionaries seek to become "upper-caste" Brahmins in order to win Brahmins, ignoring the fact that Jesus did not become a Pharisee in order to win the Pharisees.[3] Jesus' opposition to his religious culture led him to the cross.

When people commit themselves to following God even if it means conflict with their culture, God is able to use them to transform unjust social structures in favor of the enslaved, exploited, and oppressed. If they are willing to take up their cross, they will create ripples that never cease.

Let's postpone the discussion of whether Satan can oppress a whole culture until the next chapter. Let's acknowledge that the Jews and the Romans did not kill Jesus in order to make him a

---

3. Ironically, this unthinking forum calls itself Rethinking Forum.

sin offering; the historical cause of Jesus' death was that he was a serious troublemaker (from the Establishment's point of view). The charge against him was that he had claimed to be the legitimate king of the Jews, which meant that the leaders' rule was illegitimate. Does that mean that Jesus did not die for our sin?

Jesus Died for Our Sin

As Jesus hung upon the cross of Calvary, it was literally the sin of the world that was hanging there at that moment of history. The people who physically saw the crucifixion, whether or not they were Christ's followers, saw that it was not the justice but the injustice of man that was being carried out that day. In the arrest, trial, and crucifixion of Christ, man's sin was more than visible. Man's disobedience to God, his rejection of truth, his cruelty, his lies, his hate, his greed, his vested interest, his oppression, his exploitation, his abuse of power, his deliberate choice of evil—all were there on the cross for everyone to see, hear, and feel. That is why the biblical statement that Jesus became the sin of the world is not some theological mumbo jumbo. It is a statement describing historical fact. It was not Jesus who was judged and condemned on that cross; it was human sin.

The eyewitnesses, such as the dying thief, could see that man's evil was hanging on Jesus' cross.[4] This is why the Bible declares that God has now decreed that because Jesus loved sinners and became the sin of the world on the cross, man can find forgiveness for his sin through faith in the death of Christ, the final and complete sin offering. Conversely, if a man does not personally accept the death of Christ as a means to salvation from sin, then he cannot be saved and will himself have to bear the full consequence of sin before a perfectly holy God.

4. The act of proclaiming forgiveness for sin through Jesus' death on the cross is described in legal terms as "witnessing" because it is first a historical statement and only then a theological statement.

Many people find it hard to accept that Jesus' sacrifice on the cross is the only means of finding forgiveness for one's sin. But if I sin against you, there is only one way for me to get right with you: that is for you to forgive me. Because sin is against God, the only way to get right with God is to receive forgiveness from him. Jesus is the only way to forgiveness because no one else has ever become sin for the world. God declares, "There is no other name under heaven given to men by which we must be saved" (Acts 4:12).

The New Testament focuses on the theological meaning of the cross (Jesus as the Savior from sin) far more than it focuses on the socio-historical meaning of the cross (Jesus the troublemaker) because the socio-historical meaning of the cross would have been obvious to the immediate audience of the New Testament writers. The divine purpose behind the Messiah's passion, as predicted by the prophets, needed exposition, defense, and practical application. We ignore the theological meaning of the cross only at eternal cost to ourselves. However, the assumption that the socio-historical meaning of the cross is irrelevant is equally mistaken. Jesus not only carried his cross, but he also asked his disciples to carry their crosses (Luke 9:23). What does it mean to carry one's cross?

The capital punishment of crucifixion was the weapon used to perpetuate Rome's reign of terror. Those condemned to die had to carry their own crosses to a public place where they were crucified. Jesus asked his disciples to fight Rome with its own weapon instead of trying to fight it with the sword.

Mahatma Gandhi well understood and imitated Christ on this point. Some Indians wanted to fight British colonialism with guns and bombs, but Gandhi asked his followers to fill the British jails and accept the British stick-blows and bullets. When the British threw Gandhi in jail, it was not Gandhi who was judged and condemned but the British themselves. When they beat and killed the peaceful protesters, they in fact destroyed their own empire.

This is what Jesus invited his disciples to do. To take up your cross means to become a rebel, to fight a corrupt establishment with moral weapons, to be a troublemaker and bear the consequences of that.

Today, in countries of the world where evil, corruption, and tyranny reign, heaping untold miseries on the weak and the poor, Christ calls his disciples to have practical compassion for the sheep. He calls his followers to take up their crosses and follow him in the path of compassionate service, protest, confrontation, and sacrifice. This meaning of the cross may have had little practical relevance in America while its political, judicial, economic, academic, and social institutions were committed to truth and justice. But that era is fading before our eyes. Even the president knows that the challenge before him is whether he will side with Wall Street or reform it in favor of the common man on Main Street. What he does is up to him, but what is clear is that a good shepherd will have to have the grace to stand up to the wolves, many of whom now control not just political parties and financial institutions but also religious denominations, universities, courts, the media, and the entertainment industry.

A person whose perception of Christianity is conditioned by the contemporary image of the church is very likely to dismiss this interpretation of the historical meaning of the cross as a heresy. But Gamaliel, a respected Jewish rabbi who had watched Jesus and the healing ministry of his cross-bearing community, described the Christians as well-intentioned political rebels. He classified the apostles with Theudas and Judas the Galilean who *also* led revolts against Rome. The entire Jewish Sanhedrin, both critics and sympathizers of the apostles, agreed with Gamaliel's perception of the church as a band of compassionate rebels (see Acts 5:33–40).

Through his service Jesus deliberately became a champion of the masses, but this does not mean that he sought cheap popularity with the masses. He demanded costly discipleship. Only by creating disciples who are prepared to care for the sheep at the cost of their own lives can we hope to stand up against the forces of evil and death—be they Third World tyrants, Wall Street crooks, or media moguls.

Our service today lacks power because, in some cases, it is marked by self-love. In other cases it is driven by a compassion that does not understand the social roots of human misery and gives no answer to them. And more often than not it is oblivious to the fact that religious, social, and political leaders of this world have been and are able to oppose, arrest, and even crucify innocent public servants, such as Christ, because the natural realm is often controlled by supernatural evil.

SEVEN

His Kingdom

The Natural and the Supernatural

Pastor Rick Warren was invited to pray during the Presidential Inauguration of Barack Obama on January 20, 2009. As millions of people watched around the world, Pastor Warren concluded his invocation with, "Your kingdom come, your will be done on earth as it is in heaven." Someone unfamiliar with the Bible could have wondered, *This is the inauguration of Obama's kingdom. Why is he praying for God's kingdom to come?*

In the Sermon on the Mount (Matt. 5–7) the Lord Jesus asked his disciples to pray for God's kingdom to come. Why? Because the Bible says that very often the kingdoms of this world become the kingdom of Satan. Such was the case at the time of Christ. Both Matthew and Luke begin their narrative of Jesus' ministry by telling us that while Jesus spent forty days in prayer and fasting, Satan repeatedly came to tempt him. "The devil led him [Jesus] up to a high place and showed him in an instant all the kingdoms of the world. And he said to him, 'I will give you all their authority and splendor, for it has been given to me, and I can give it to anyone I want to. So if you worship me, it will all be yours'" (Luke 4:5–7).

The devil claimed that at that point in time the kingdoms of this world had been given over to him. Was he bluffing Jesus? No! The Lord Jesus acknowledged that Satan was the "prince of this world" (John 16:11). The apostle Paul called Satan the "ruler of the kingdom of the air, the spirit who is now at work in those who are disobedient" (Eph. 2:2). The apostle John saw the beastly nature of the kingdom of Rome as he saw his morally beautiful friends looted, crucified, beheaded, stoned, and burned alive. How could human rulers commit such evils? John says, "We know . . . that the whole world is under the control of the evil one" (1 John 5:19).

Our pseudo-intellectuals would no doubt mock the biblical teaching on Satan and demons. But a heart attack in 2003 helped me question the wisdom of our age. My chest pain started soon after we left Portland, Oregon, on a long drive for California. Because I was also burping, I assumed that my problem was acidity. So for several days I kept taking antacids while driving around greater Los Angeles. Finally, just before I was to speak to a group of international students, I decided to see a pharmacist at Loma Linda Medical University to get better antacids. I was diagnosed as suffering from a heart attack, and they put a stent in one of my arteries!

A few weeks later a medical doctor in Alabama, a friend, saw my medical reports. He said, "Yes, your blood sugar, blood pressure, and cholesterol were higher than normal, but none of these numbers explain the heart attack. Your heart is strong. There had to be another factor at work."

Loma Linda is one of the best hospitals in the world. I loved the warm, friendly atmosphere of the place. I have no doubt that my cardiologists were also wise enough to know that some factor other than heredity and observable ("natural") factors such as blood pressure had caused the heart attack. But not one doctor went beyond the natural, physical phenomenon. Why?

I know what caused my heart attack. I had been angry at my wife for several days. How does that work? My anger was an "emotion," as Charles Darwin or William James would have called it. But my anger had become sin. Let's analyze it.

An event happens; your wife says something or does something (or doesn't do something) that upsets you. You hurt. The good woman may not even know that you are hurt, if hurting you was never her intention. How do you deal with your hurt? You have two voices inside of you: One says, "Husbands, love your wives" and "Love is patient, love is kind. . . . It is not easily angered, it keeps no record of wrongs. . . . It always protects, always trusts, always hopes, always perseveres. Love never fails" (Eph. 5:25; 1 Cor. 13:4–8). The other voice says, "She has done it again; you have to teach her a lesson; you can't let this go; she must know that there are consequences; she can't have happiness unless she makes you happy."

The first voice is God's word. It is in your memory, and the Spirit is asking you to obey it. The second voice has been planted in you by your culture controlled by God's enemy.[1] You have to choose whether you will believe and obey God's truth or follow falsehood. What are the results of following the wisdom of the world? Unresolved anger and domestic unhappiness are only the starters. The real results could be anything from separation, divorce, and costly litigation to heart attack, paralysis, cancer, or death.

Surely a medical university knows that something more than "natural," physical factors (such as blood pressure or blood sugar) caused my heart attack. The critical question is: why didn't a single doctor help me consider the root cause—my sin—and help me deal with it? The answer: a doctor who discusses nonmaterial (supernatural) matters such as sin or soul would be fired

1. If you have been conditioned to think that chemistry and evolution can explain emotion, I invite you to listen to my lecture "From Michelangelo to Freud: The Devolution of Human Dignity" available at www.soughtaftermedia .com/musunsetonwe.html.

by a university that does not want a patient or the ACLU suing them. The implication: naturalism, or materialism, has become an intellectually totalitarian philosophy that intimidates Americans away from seeking truth about ourselves and our universe. Thankfully, my heart attack forced me to reconsider whether Sunday school teachers who talk about the devil speaking into one's heart may have more wisdom than doctors and researchers who have been bullied into silence by a kingdom of lies.

The New Testament's perspective on the grip of evil over our sociopolitical systems comes from the Old Testament prophet Daniel. Daniel was a young boy when the Babylonians destroyed his city of Jerusalem, brutally massacred his people, and carried the royalty into slavery in Babylon. Later they returned to destroy God's temple and placed God's sacred vessels in the temple of their god. This humiliating horror raised disturbing theological questions: Who really rules in the affairs of this world? Who is in control of history, at least at this moment? How can the kingdoms of this world become so cruel, brutal, exploitative, and oppressive at times?

As Daniel humbled himself, fasted, and prayed for understanding, he was given a glimpse into the supernatural realm: behind the sociopolitical evils of his time lay supernatural powers. In Daniel chapter 2, King Nebuchadnezzar saw in a dream a statue made of gold, silver, bronze, and iron, representing four successive empires: Babylonian (gold), Medo-Persian (silver), Greek (bronze), and Roman (iron). After that period a mere stone—the kingdom of God—brought to an end all the evil kingdoms of this world.

In chapter 7 we read that Daniel, a slave turned learned governor, humbled himself in fasting and prayer, seeking to understand where history was going and God's role in it. He was given the vision of the same four kingdoms that Nebuchadnezzar had seen earlier, except that Daniel saw them not as a dazzling statue of precious metals but as beasts that devour: the lion (Babylonian), the bear (Medo-Persian), the leopard (Greek), and the "fourth beast—terrifying and frightening and very powerful. It had large iron teeth; it crushed and devoured its victims and trampled underfoot whatever was left" (Dan. 7:7). This fourth beast was Daniel's vision of the Roman empire, which Satan told Jesus was his. In contrast to these beastly kingdoms, which came up from below, Daniel saw the humaneness of the coming kingdom of God as "a son of man, coming with the clouds" from above (Dan. 7:13).

As Daniel fasted and prayed to understand history further, it was revealed to him that the kingdoms of this world were beastly because behind them were evil, supernatural forces. The angel said to Daniel:

> Since the first day that you set your mind to gain understanding and to humble yourself before your God, your words were heard, and I have come in response to them. But the prince of the Persian kingdom resisted me twenty-one days. Then Michael, one of the chief princes, came to help me, because I was detained there with the king of Persia. . . . Soon I will return to fight against the prince of Persia, and when I go, the prince of Greece will come. (Dan. 10:12–13, 20)

This understanding of evil as something more than natural, human, or sociopolitical does not begin with Daniel. Israel's first king, Saul, became evil, despotic, and murderous, and the Bible explains that God's Spirit had left him and an evil spirit began to torment him (1 Sam. 16:14–23). Likewise, in the book of Judges (9:23), sociopolitical evils are seen as a direct result of spiritual evil.

Each of the above-mentioned biblical texts affirms that God remains sovereign in his creation, even when he gives authority to evil spirits or the devil. The apostle Paul explains in Romans 1:18–32 that God gives whole cultures over to evil when humans choose to suppress the truth in wickedness.

Are Demons Real?

Philosophically, if the supernatural realm does not exist, if the material universe is all there is, then words such as *good* and *evil* have no real meaning. At most they would describe our feelings. Phrases such as "this is evil" or "that is good" would really mean "I do not like this" or "my community approves of that." To have any real, objective meaning, the terms *good* and *evil* must refer to nonmaterial, supernatural, or moral realms.

I experienced supernatural evil in 1982 when an educated but mentally challenged, homeless young man from Bombay (now Mumbai) was sent to our rural community in central India. He was an intelligent and pleasant person who also had a personality disorder which even the best medical and psychiatric experts were unable to diagnose and treat. He lived with us for several months, and many of us got to know him. For a variety of reasons, some of us began to suspect that his problem might be demonic. So we began to pray for him.

One night as I was riding my motorcycle back from the town to our village, for no apparent reason I felt in my spirit that it was going to be a crucial night for this young man. Soon I found myself praying out loud and singing as I drove home. When I arrived at our gate, there he was, telling me that he was leaving us. I asked him to wait until the morning, as he would have to walk thirteen kilometers to reach the nearest lodge or bus station. He agreed to stay. I called the community together for prayer, and we prayed for the young man the whole night, apparently without any results. He disappeared the next day. We had a great sense of failure, and I felt that we had simply made fools of ourselves. (Months later we learned that the young man's personality disorder had begun when his uncle had sorcerers cast spells on him in order to take over his father's restaurant business.)

Meanwhile, three young people in our community decided to persevere. They prayed that God would bring before us a simple case of demon possession to initiate us into the realm of supernatural battle between good and evil. These three decided to fast and pray over a weekend. On their first night of prayer, a ten-year-old Hindu girl in our community had an attack of fits, which she had never had before. Because she was only a girl, her parents decided not to disturb any of us at night. By morning the girl was better, so no one took much notice of her illness.

Two days later she had another severe attack of fits. As I was walking back to my home after morning prayers, I saw the girl lying on her string cot. She was writhing in pain and had a high fever. In a rhythmic fashion she was lifting her head and banging it back on the cot in much agony.

One of the three young people who had been praying the previous weekend suggested the girl had an evil spirit and that we pray for her. Someone else insisted the girl simply had an attack of fits and should be taken to a doctor. I was indecisive, hesitant to say that my Christian friend was mistaken yet unwilling to make a fool of myself as before, when the whole night of prayer ended in failure. I thought it best to have my breakfast before deciding whether to take the girl to the hospital or to pray for her. Meanwhile, as I had breakfast, one of our Hindu friends rode his bicycle to the house of a snake charmer/exorcist and brought him to see the girl. This sorcerer abused the demon in filthy language, telling it to come out. To everyone's amazement, the girl instantly became normal.

I felt humiliated. I had to admit that even though I was a Christian, my secular education had really made me quite naturalistic. I had lived in Hindu ashrams and written about the *siddhis* (supernatural powers) of well-known gurus such as Sathya Sai Baba and Swami Muktananda, and yet deep down I was not really sure whether evil spirits affected human beings. Perhaps my illiterate, animist neighbors understood the supernatural character of the universe much better than my secular professors. That is why they were able to handle this situation more confidently. Our community had another prayer meeting to repent of our unbelief, praying for another opportunity to discover the power of God.

A week later a twenty-year-old man had a similar attack of fits, except that it was much worse. By the time we reached him, he was screaming out loud that he was about to die. He complained of a splitting headache and body ache. He, too, was lifting and banging his head on his bed in a rhythm. Because the symptoms were so similar, we believed this might be the same evil spirit that had troubled the girl. So we began to pray for the young man. We prayed for about an hour, but nothing happened. Gradually the prayer warriors began to leave the room. The young man's condition became worse, and a self-confessed agnostic in the community began to mock us and advised us to take the young man to the hospital instead of playing with his life.

Finally, only Kay Kudart (now Holler) from Wheaton, Illinois, and I were left praying. Doubts began to enter my mind. There was nothing much left to pray about, so I had to choose again: do we take him to the hospital or pray more? With my eyes open, looking at the agony of our friend, I made my decision out loud. "This time I refuse to be deceived. This is demonic, and the evil spirit must go." In an instant, the fever, pain, and fits vanished.

The young man got up as from a trance and walked with us to the next house, where many of the community members were having coffee. He announced, "I was dying, brother Vishal prayed for me, and the Lord Jesus has healed me." He didn't know that everyone there had been praying for him just half an hour ago.

Does Supernatural Evil Rule?

Today's intellectual climate makes us doubt that demonic forces seek to control intellectual, economic, religious, and sociopolitical institutions. However, most animists, traditional Hindus, Buddhists, and Muslims, as well as Bible-believing Christians, would acknowledge that just as computer viruses are created and sent by evil intelligences, so also some disease-causing viruses may be generated or spread by supernatural entities to inflict suffering upon innocent individuals.

Whatever your belief, it is unwise not to ask how a respectable investor on Wall Street could spend decades devising strategies to cheat his trusting friends of $50 billion.[2] Why shouldn't the same factors that compelled one individual propel the American Establishment into cheating trusting Americans out of trillions of dollars? (According to M. R. Venkatesh, one of India's highly respected journalists on economic affairs, whereas Americans are hiding approximately $15 billion in secret Swiss accounts, Indian political, administrative, and business leaders are hiding as much as $1500 billion.) Is it unwise to ask how university-educated Nazis could have killed six million Jews? Couldn't the chemical, intellectual, or supernatural factors that controlled Nazi Germany also lead to the killing of millions of Americans in the twenty-first century, simply because rulers of a new America don't like the faith or race of a particular group of people?

My nation's conscience was shaken on January 23, 1999, when a mob of militant Hindus burned alive an Australian missionary, Dr. Graham Staines, along with his two young sons, while they were asleep in their jeep.[3] Graham had devoted his life to serving the victims of leprosy in Orissa, on the east coast of India. His "crime" was that he followed a Healer who healed both the leprosy of the body and the leprosy of the soul—sin. The people who killed Graham worshiped many gods, including demons. They killed him in order to terrorize Christians and keep them from inviting people into the kingdom of Christ. For a few centuries now the West has not burned anyone for preaching righteousness; therefore, it is hard for modern Americans to understand why anyone would kill someone for preaching justice, grace, or liberty.

2. This was the case with Bernie Madoff, a former chairman of NASDAQ.

3. For the complete story, see Vishal Mangalwadi et al., *Burnt Alive: The Staines and the God They Loved* (Mumbai, India: GLS, 1999).

The Bible says that the fear of death is Satan's ultimate weapon to keep us in the slavery of evil. "Since the children have flesh and blood, he too shared in their humanity so that by his death he might destroy him who holds the power of death—that is, the devil—and free those who all their lives were held in slavery by their fear of death" (Heb. 2:14–15).

The medieval West used the fear of death as a weapon for centuries. During the twentieth century, highly educated Nazi Germany and the Soviet Union also used this fear extensively. There is no reason to think that a pagan America could not use it in the twenty-first century. Filmmakers such as Ben Stein have exposed the intolerance and intellectual totalitarianism of the "liberal" press, universities, courts, business houses, and entertainment industry. Therefore, we have to ask if there is a supernatural power that causes individuals and social institutions to become as brutal as they do.

I better understood the biblical teaching that sociopolitical evils have a supernatural dimension when I watched the Hindi film *Ardh Satya* (Half Truth). The film is about a police inspector in Bombay who tries to fight political/bureaucratic corruption. It shows that courage and integrity are only half-truths. When an honest man stands up against social evils, he destroys not the evil but himself. Evil in our social system is far stronger than a heroic police officer, a journalist, a social scientist, a civil rights activist, or a trade-union leader. Such people can do little about evil because they don't understand its true nature or power. The film laments the fact that we live in a system where evil is greater than good and that it rules. A similar point is made by some nonfiction documentaries. *Born Into Brothels* demonstrates that the well-intentioned activism of a resourceful and dedicated secular activist is too weak to make even a dent in the evils that are entrenched in a culture with an oppressive worldview and traditions.

I experienced firsthand the influence of evil on social institutions while serving the rural poor. The rulers in our area opposed our service to the poor because of heartless corruption, which was a key factor behind poverty. When the district authorities arrested thirty of us for bringing relief to poor peasants, we were told a proverb: our state gets three crops a year—the winter crop, the monsoon crop, and the relief crop. The last is always a bumper crop for politicians and civil servants; they get the lion's share of the money intended for relief for the poor.

If my experience in India has any relevance and if the biblical depiction of evil is correct, then it is not inconceivable that a large proportion of massive corporate bailout funds, meant to bring relief to toiling and struggling Americans, will simply become a bonanza to the corrupt and powerful in America. Of course, America is not India. At this moment honest and courageous people outnumber the corrupt in American politics, administration, and industry. But I have no doubt that America is seeing more and more corruption because supernatural evil is strengthening its grip over American institutions, and yet most Americans do not even think an evil force exists.

A rejection of the biblical, supernatural worldview does not make the secular world intellectually more sophisticated than believers who pray, "Thy kingdom come." It just makes it intellectually bankrupt. One only needs to view the latest eight-Oscar-winning (including "best film") *Slumdog Millionaire* to see the inability of the secular mind to understand socioeconomic evil. The film powerfully portrays the evils that dehumanize the "filthy" rich and the powerless poor in India, but it does not even pretend to explain how such evils can rule a democratic country. Neither the film nor its hero has any strategy to fight evil. In fact, the film has no hero. Viewers feel good only because blind luck helps the lead character win millions and his beloved. Even though *Slumdog Millionaire*'s portrayal of Indian slums is realistic, the story is unrealistic and romantic. Depressing films such as *City of Joy* and *Ardh Satya* (Half Truth) tell their stories more credibly.

The New Testament says that social evils are as powerful as they are because sometimes Satan takes control of this world's kingdoms. Without this supernatural worldview, it is impossible to understand adequately how sociopolitical authority can degenerate to the levels of cruelty and wickedness that it so often does.

How Does Satan Acquire His Rule?

Some Christians think that Satan's objective is to lead individual souls astray, but the book of Revelation reveals that Satan is out to "deceive the nations" (Rev. 20:3, 8). He "leads the whole world astray" (Rev. 12:9).

What is Satan's basic deception? Revelation says that the plan of Satan, the great dragon, is to control political power. The "dragon [Satan] gave the beast [the emperor] his power and his throne and great authority. . . . Men worshiped the dragon because he had given authority to the beast, and they also worshiped the beast" (Rev. 13:2, 4). It is the "beast"—that is, human rulers (Rev. 17:11)—that makes war against Christ and wants to govern in place of God. It was the authority and splendor of the oppressive political institutions of man that Satan claimed were his kingdom in Matthew 4:8–9.

The apostle Paul teaches in Romans 1:18–32 that the kingdom of Satan begins when we turn away from God's truth to believe satanic falsehood. When the mind is darkened, our behavior quickly becomes immoral. Sin then begins to rule in our bodies. Satan is able to corrupt our cultures and control social institutions because he is able to darken our minds first. Secular ideologies that deny God have to make the state the ultimate authority, the lord and only savior, and thus reject the first of the Ten Commandments, "You shall have no other gods before me" (Exod. 20:3). Satan uses false ideas to turn the state into an oppressive beast and rulers into wolves.

Prayer and Transformation

Daniel had acquired all the political power that a Jew could expect in the Babylonian and Medo-Persian empires. But he spent weeks in fasting and prayer for the rebuilding of Jerusalem because he knew that no amount of political power could help him triumph over the supernatural evil that held his people in bondage. God's miraculous intervention in answer to his prayers began the regeneration of his nation. That remarkable story is told in Daniel chapters six and nine.

The ninth chapter of Daniel tells us that in the first year of the Medo-Persian empire Daniel was reading the scrolls of Jeremiah's prophecies. Judah's rulers, which may have included Daniel's parents, had almost killed Jeremiah for treason because he had predicted that the Babylonians would destroy Jerusalem and its temple. Looking back, Daniel had good reasons to believe that Jeremiah was not only a genuine patriot but also a prophet who spoke the word of God. When Daniel read the prophecy in Jeremiah 25:11–14, which predicted that Jerusalem would be rebuilt after seventy years of Babylonian captivity, he realized that the prophecy referred to the very time in which he was living. So he began a period of fasting and prayer (Dan. 9:1–19). Could it be a coincidence that just then Daniel's bureaucratic rivals got the new king to issue an edict forbidding people to pray to any god other than the king (Dan. 6:1–9)? The edict was irrevocable. The lion's den was the punishment for violation.

Daniel did not think that the edict was coincidental; he knew that the physical (military) destruction of Jerusalem was first of all a spiritual affair. So he chose to persist in prayer at the risk of his life. Daniel was arrested, tied up, and thrown into the lion's den. The next morning, when the king discovered that some incredible supernatural force had prevented the lions from harming Daniel, he commanded that Daniel be brought up. The Scriptures leave it to us to imagine the conversation the astonished king must have had with Daniel. What the Scriptures do tell us is that the king was so astounded that he issued an immediate edict telling his people to worship the God of Daniel (Dan. 6:25–27). The empire went on to issue another edict encouraging the Jews to go back to Jerusalem to rebuild the temple of God (2 Chron. 36:23; Ezra 1:1–4).

At the time of Christ, that is, during the reign of the fourth beast of Daniel, the Jews were looking for the promised Messiah, the political deliverer foretold by Daniel. The disciples followed the Lord Jesus because he claimed to be ushering in the kingdom of God on earth. That is why he asked his disciples to pray, "Your kingdom come, your will be done on earth as it is in heaven" (Matt. 6:10). Jesus told his disciples that some demons cannot be cast out without fasting and prayer (Mark 9:29). I know that is true. I may know that God's truth is for me to love my wife or my neighbor, but that does not mean I will have the power to humble myself and pursue love. By listening to the devil (or my culture), I give the devil power over my heart. He enslaves me. My attitudes and behavior then hurt my family and me. The only way for me to find deliverance from the power of Satan is to humble myself before God and pray for the power of his Spirit.

This kingdom that Jesus began was something radically new, radically different from the kingdoms of the world—a kingdom of justice and peace. The kingdom of God begins when people submit themselves to the Word of God. Therefore, it has begun, but it will not be fully realized until Jesus comes again to reclaim God's authority over his creation.

America and the Word of God

Some Americans do not want America to be a "nation under God." They protest against American presidents such as Barack Obama putting their hand on the Bible to be sworn into office, and they do not want Christian pastors such as Rick Warren to pray at such ceremonies. For very good reasons, however, President Obama and American presidents before him have ignored people's protests. President Obama put his hand on Abraham Lincoln's Bible, publicly humbling himself before God. Why is this so?

Young Abraham Lincoln's worldview, moral imagination, and skill with words were shaped by the Bible and the books that expounded the Bible, such as Thomas Dilworth's *A New Guide to the English Tongue*, John Bunyan's *Pilgrim's Progress*, and Daniel Defoe's *Robinson Crusoe*. Later in life Lincoln was asked why he was able to resist temptations when someone offered him bribes. He replied that even as a president he could hear his mother reading aloud the biblical commands "Thou shalt not steal" and "Thou shalt not covet."

As an adult Lincoln doubted if the Bible was true. Naive rationalism of the nineteenth century made it hard for him to believe in miracles: how could Jesus have been born of a virgin? Science fiction didn't exist then; therefore, no skeptic could have imagined that cloning and virgin birth would be common phenomena in the twenty-first century. Skeptics assumed that the "laws of science" as they knew them at that time also bound God.

Even though rationalism confused his faith, Lincoln knew that God's Word, the Bible, was America's soul, the glue that bound slave owners and slavery haters into a common culture, the moral force that could transcend economic interests and bind a fractured nation into a common political union. Therefore, he read the Bible regularly and used it more than any other text for his personal growth and public service.

Contrary to what some secular professors say, Lincoln knew that the Bible was the true source of American democracy, justice, and integration. His definition of democracy as the "government of the people, for the people, by the people" came directly from the preface to the Wycliffe Bible.

The battle over slavery raised crucial questions: If majority vote is to govern America, what happens if the majority votes in favor of slavery? Does the majority have the right to be wrong?

Following the Bible, Lincoln's answer was an emphatic no. In order to remain just, united, and strong, America had to be a nation under God and his law. As Lord Acton was to note later, the tyranny of the majority could be infinitely worse than the tyranny of a despot. Minorities could not be safe unless the majorities were bound by God's law. Minorities do not receive their rights from a majority, citizens are not the property of the state, and slaves are not the properties of their owners. As John Locke had expounded the Bible, human beings owed their lives to their Creator and were endowed by him with inalienable rights of life, liberty, and happiness. Neither a monarch nor a majority had the right to take these away from anyone, including the slaves.

Lincoln knew that without the kingdom of God, without God's Word as a unifying force and a common standard of morality, every wave of fresh immigrants would replace warring Native American tribes with warring European cultures. This problem is as real today as it was in Lincoln's day.

The Kingdom of God and Human Equality

The Bible and its supernatural worldview wrote the principle of human equality into America's cultural DNA. The Declaration of Independence begins with the assertion: "We hold these truths to be self-evident, that all men are created equal." But Thomas Jefferson was wrong about one thing: human equality is not a self-evident, natural phenomenon; *inequality* is self-evident in nature and in society.

My ancestors were not dumb; to them inequality was obvious. They explained it with the ideas of karma and reincarnation, and they institutionalized it in caste and gender discrimination. Souls are born unequal, into different castes and sexes, because of their good or bad karma in previous lives. To be religious meant to respect these differences. An upper-caste person would be polluted if he touched a lower caste person, disowned if he ate with one, and maybe killed if he married one.

People like Jefferson thought that belief in equality could be grounded in the Enlightenment philosophy of universal reason and common sense. But what is called "common sense" differs in every culture. For instance, nearly all societies think it is common sense that women are inferior to men. When Jefferson and Thomas Paine talked about common sense, they were drawing upon a peculiar attempt of the Scottish Enlightenment to find an epistemology that could be a secular basis for ideas revealed in the Bible. The radical and God-given idea of human equality had so deeply penetrated American culture that it appeared self-evident to the founders.

Of course, most American atheists will tell you that they also believe in human equality. But that is only because the Bible wrote that notion into America's cultural DNA. If atheists were writing the Declaration of Independence, they would have to write something like, "We hold these truths to be self-evident: that all human beings have *evolved* equal, and are endowed *by natural selection* with certain unalienable rights." But that would be absurd. There is no observable, "natural" way in which all human beings are equal. Natural selection has never created political and social equality. Equality is a moral, theological, or supernatural idea that evolutionism can't support, because evolution is a theory created to explain inequality in nature.

God's Word wrote the principle of human equality into the American soul by its insistence that all human beings, male and female, are made in God's image. We have all descended from one set of parents, Adam and Eve, and therefore we are brothers and sisters. No race or group is inherently superior or inferior to any other. We are all equal because we are all sinners and because God loves us all equally. We are all equally valuable in the eyes of the supreme Valuer. We are all bound by, and protected by, the same supernatural moral law that originates from the same God. No one, not even the king, is exempt. This is the basis for political equality.

As we have seen in an earlier chapter, Jesus challenged the racism of his own culture by showing equal concern for the social outcasts—Gentiles, Samaritans, women, prostitutes, lepers. He taught, "Love your neighbor as yourself," and expanded the scope of "neighbor" to include everyone. He told his followers to make disciples from "every nation," for every race had an equal right to the kingdom of God. Later, some of Jesus' Jewish followers, called the Judaizers, tried to inject racial segregation back into the early church, but the apostle Paul fought against it. He argued, "There is neither Jew nor Greek, slave nor free, male nor female, for you are all one in Christ Jesus" (Gal. 3:28).

In the 1500s the German reformer Martin Luther discovered the truth of human equality in the New Testament doctrine of "the priesthood of all believers." The job of a housewife or a shoemaker was as sacred as the job of a priest. As translations in common vernacular and printing press technology spread the Bible throughout Europe, this idea spread with it. In the hands of public figures such as William Wilberforce, it led to the abolition of the British slave trade. In America it led to a civil war over the issue of slavery, then to women's suffrage and racial civil rights movements.

The Supernatural: The Source of Hope

The supernatural worldview—that God cares for this world and is establishing his kingdom on behalf of the righteous poor—made the United States the most optimistic nation on earth. North America was settled by people who believed that their special mandate was to live as citizens of God's kingdom in the New World. The first Great Awakening wrote hope for a better tomorrow into the very DNA of America.

However, *hope* is now beginning to be a part of America's past—in the worldview of America's founders. Cynicism and pessimism are replacing optimism, because America is following the tragic footsteps of Europe. In the nineteenth century, Europe secularized its Christian humanism and began the age of ideologies. Secular humanists thought that man was capable of creating Utopia without God. This false confidence led to ideologies such as Fascism, Nazism, and Communism and two world wars. The humanist hope blew up in mushroom clouds over Hiroshima and Nagasaki. Humanists finally realized that man was not as good as they had thought.

At an intellectual level, pessimism replaced optimism until the 1980s when the New Age became the first optimistic movement to be born in the West since the Second World War. The New Age did not put its hope in man. Its hope rested in UFOs, extraterrestrials, spirit-guides, meditation, Tantric or Gnostic sex, altered states of consciousness, and the constellation of Aquarius. It didn't take long for the New Age to become old, producing cynicism and despair.[4]

Day after day, ancient people saw the sun rise and set. Year after year, they saw spring followed by summer, autumn, winter, and spring again. From these and many other observable cycles in nature, they concluded that time and the cosmos were endless cycles. Human beings, societies, and the world itself are born, grow, decline, die, and are reborn. The metaphor of the Great Wheel is found in nearly every ancient culture. Things must always return to the way they were, so no real and permanent progress is possible. Fate has already determined the direction of history, and there is nothing anyone can do to change it. There is no metaphysical ground for hope: striving to improve the human condition is pointless. The author of Ecclesiastes summed up the wisdom born of human experience in the famous phrase, "There is nothing new under the sun."

The Greek and Roman religion of Stoicism taught the West that each of us is like a dog tied behind a moving wagon. You have no say in where fate is taking you; to be wise is to resign yourself to it rather than struggle in vain against it. Human existence is essentially one of suffering. The only thing you can do about it is to detach yourself from the things of this world and occupy yourself with the world beyond.

Indian thought is very similar to this traditional Western belief. The Buddha's first Noble Truth is that life is suffering: there is no point in trying to fight suffering; the best that you

4. See my book *When the New Age Gets Old: Looking for a Greater Spirituality* (Downers Grove, Ill.: InterVarsity Press, 1992).

can do is to meditate and seek a psychological nirvana, the bliss within, in an altered state of consciousness. This thinking leads to resignation, for we are locked into a cosmic cycle. Societies with such outlooks do not produce leaders with vision.

The Jews, however, had a very different experience of God, which shattered the traditional ancient worldview. As slaves in Egypt, they cried out to God because of their misery. God sent Moses to deliver them. Although they were unarmed, God rescued them from Pharaoh's mighty army. They saw God part the Red Sea, bring water out of a solid rock, and feed them in the wilderness for forty years. God, they realized, was not bound by nature. "I WILL BE WHAT I WILL BE,"[5] God said to Moses. He was not bound by time. God was free and wanted his children to be like him—also free. The covenant, the law, the Promised Land— these were new and permanent. The Wheel of Time would not carry the Israelites back to bondage.

Thus the Jewish Scriptures—the first and largest portion of the Bible—became the first source of the idea that time is not cyclical but linear. Time had a definite beginning, it will have a definite end, and every time in between is unique. This makes possible the idea of history. God created a world that is good, and although the world has been corrupted, it will be redeemed. Suffering is not an essential part of existence. Humans were not created to live in slums, but in Eden, which means "bliss." The Jews believed that God had promised, one day, to deliver them from their enemies and from the sinfulness of their own hearts. They believed this deliverance would come through a leader anointed by God, a Messiah. The prophet Isaiah says, "In faithfulness he [the Messiah] will bring forth justice; he will not falter or be discouraged till he establishes justice on earth. In his law the islands will put their hope" (Isa. 42:3–4).

This biblical belief that God is establishing his supernatural kingdom on earth is the source of Western hope.[6] Although

5. Exod. 3:14 NIV, alternative translation in footnote.
6. See chapter 13 for a more detailed discussion of hope.

secular despair has overtaken the West's biblical optimism, the fact is that hope—however anemic—survives as an aspect of the cultural DNA of the West. Obama tapped into this Bible-generated, underground cultural reservoir of hope, and that is why he won over more experienced and better connected rivals such as Hillary Clinton and John McCain. It will be a tragedy if Americans put their hope in a president rather than in the God who has been the source of their hope. The West can recover its philosophical basis for hope only if it turns back to the supernatural worldview of the Bible. That is why truth is the key to transformation.

EIGHT

His Truth

The Key to Transformation

Hen the pioneers of Western Protestant missions arrived in India, they established a college, which grew into Serampore University. Their leader, William Carey (1761–1834), a cobbler turned Bible translator, taught the Bible as well as languages, botany, horticulture, forestry, and astronomy.[1]

These Baptist missionaries had come to save souls. So why did they establish a university? Were they trying to soften the soil for converting Hindus and Muslims?

The missionaries were following the tradition set by the Protestant Reformers who were university professors and graduates. Martin Luther, the pioneer of the sixteenth century Reformation, was a professor at the University of Wittenberg. He insisted that

---

1. For information, see Vishal and Ruth Mangalwadi, *The Legacy of William Carey: A Model for Transforming a Culture* (Wheaton, Ill.: Crossway Books, 1999). To understand why the Protestant return to the Bible gave birth to modern science, see Peter Harrison, *The Bible, Protestantism, and the Rise of Natural Science* (Cambridge and New York: Cambridge University Press, 1998).

next to the reform of the church, the second most important need was to reform the university. He became the father of universal education—a key ideal of the modern era.

Following Luther and also French Reformer John Calvin, the Scottish Reformers put enormous money and effort into transforming Scotland into Europe's first educated nation. Soon the church turned Europe into history's first educated "continent." Geographically speaking, Europe is not a continent; the Bible made it a "continent" united by a worldview.

In this transformational process, bishop and educationist John Amos Comenius became a key player. He experienced the bitter fruit of Europe's Thirty Years' War of religious bigotry. That tragedy inspired his educational mission to create a new Europe through educating the younger generation. As a result, the phrase "educated person" became synonymous with a civilized, self-disciplined, moral, responsible citizen. This achievement became possible also because of the educational mission of the Roman Catholic Church galvanized by the Jesuits. Were the Roman Catholics merely competing with their Protestant rivals?

Not at all!

The Roman Catholic Church is the mother of Western education (Protestant and secular). Before the Reformation, practically all schools and universities were Roman Catholic.[2] They had no one to compete with, and since Europe was already "Christian," there was no need to soften Europe's soil for conversions. The educators (Roman Catholic and Protestant alike) were simply pursuing their religious calling to seek and impart knowledge. Most did not know they were laying the foundations of the modern world.

---

2. Back then, there was no such thing as secular education. Luther was the first to urge the state and merchants to support the church's educational efforts.

The Pursuit of Knowledge—a Divine Calling

This peculiar idea that the pursuit of knowledge is a divine calling came into Europe from the Bible via St. Augustine (AD 354–430).[3] As we saw in chapter 2, Augustine taught that God was a rational being and the human mind (not just the human "soul") was made in God's image. Therefore, our rationality was qualitatively different from the brain in other animals. God gave us a mind like his own so that we might know him and understand and govern his creation as his children. For Augustine this meant that according to the Bible, to be godly required us to cultivate our minds—the instrument of knowing God and his creation.

This Augustinian theological assumption enabled the West to put confidence in human logic, language, and rational knowledge (all the way from intuition and empirical observation to doctrines and creeds). Much before the birth of the modern age, the medieval Augustinian monasteries began doing something that became unique to Christianity. When a young man devoted his life to seek and to serve God, the monastery required him to spend years studying the Bible, languages, literature, logic, rhetoric, mathematics, music, theology, philosophy, and practical arts such as agriculture, animal husbandry, medicine, metallurgy, and technology. Thus, the monastery—which was an institution for cultivating "religious" life—began producing a peculiarly rational person, capable of researching; writing books; developing technology and science; developing capitalism; and developing complex, rational legal and political systems. The Bible became the ladder on which the West climbed the heights of its educational, technical, economic, political, and scientific excellence.[4]

3. The Greek rationalism had degenerated into skepticism, mysticism, and occultism long before Augustine, who taught Greek philosophy, became Christian.

4. This is elaborated in my forthcoming book *Must the Sun Set on the West? An Indian Explores the Soul of Western Civilization.* Some of the content is available on CDs. Visit www.VishalMangalwadi.com.

Tragically, during the eighteenth and nineteenth centuries an intellectual movement known as the Enlightenment separated the West's confidence in reason from its biblical foundations. The end result was that the twentieth century intellectuals awoke to a realization that the West no longer had any foundations for its earlier confidence in human reason. Secular rationalism collapsed into skepticism, cynicism, mysticism, and the occult. Universities that were built to help students find truth and become servants of God and neighbors turned (at best) into factories producing workers for a technocratic age. Public education became incapable of training civilized citizens.

Rational cynicism has now become the hallmark of secular universities. The West's popular culture is defined either by crass materialism or a nonrational, nonmoral, noncreedal spirituality of mysticism, UFOs, spirits, and the occult, which includes myths and meditation, drugs and divination, Yoga and Tantra, astrology and witchcraft, voodoo and Gnosticism. This has happened because the West has exchanged its worldview shaped by the Bible for a lie that the human mind is an accident of blind chance, no more valid than an animal brain.

In India, a result of Christian anti-intellectualism was that William Carey's successors at Serampore University handed over the faculties of arts and sciences to secular government. Christians confined themselves to teaching theology. The Christian mind disappeared from our intellectual landscape. Most of our information regarding history, philosophy, sociology, literature, politics, economy, law, psychology, and science started coming from secular, leftist, Hindu, and Neo-Buddhist interpreters. These biases were accepted as the truth, and young people growing up in Christian homes, schools, and colleges began to think that Christianity was a childish, Sunday-school-level faith.

This is tragic because these man-centered ideologies have completely corrupted our national life in India. Corruption has so permeated our national life that many have become cynical. Hopelessness is growing in spite of the economic growth of the last decade, which began after India was forced to turn from socialism to free-market principles. There is no doubt that as the West catches up with India's mystical spirituality, it will also catch up with our corruption and lose its freedoms.

Be that as it may, India's economic upturn is evidence that cynicism is unnecessary: decline is not inevitable. Like the partial healing of our economy, other facets of our national life can also be healed and regenerated.

A New Reformation?

The Protestant Reformation began when Martin Luther, an Augustinian monk, understood the meaning of a little phrase in the Bible: "the righteous will live by faith" (Roman 1:17; Gal. 3:11; Hab. 2:4). Those words[5] transformed Luther, enabling him to reject a religious culture that promoted corruption (e.g., the selling of indulgences) as the way of salvation. Luther's intellectual transformation began a social revolution that created the modern world. It snatched cultural power from the custodians of the older view and transferred it to a people who sought truth.

Today, a global reformation could begin if we understand a phrase in Isaiah 53:11:

> After the suffering of his soul,
>   he will see the light of life and be satisfied;
> *by his knowledge my righteous servant will justify many,*
>   and he will bear their iniquities.

---

5. Postmodernism has lost confidence in words because the West has rejected its logocentric worldview. Yet the fact is that human beings create culture and history because we speak. Words are creative because they presuppose imagination and freedom. Freedom means that our words can be true or false, liberating or deceiving, constructive or destructive. Our words can capture the invisible laws that regulate the cosmos because behind the cosmos are words—the Creator's words. Words create and transform.

Given the fact that the Protestant anti-intellectualism pre-dates secular anti-intellectualism by a century[6] the radically important question is: what does *knowledge* have to do with our justification?

Aren't we saved by faith alone?

To be saved means to know God. In John 17:3 the Lord Jesus says, "Now this is eternal life: that they may *know* you, the only true God, and Jesus Christ, whom you have sent." The apostle Paul explains in Colossians 2:3 that the Lord Jesus is the one "in whom are hidden all the treasures of wisdom and knowledge."

The existentialist philosopher Jean Paul Sartre realized that we could not know any finite thing unless we could relate it to an infinite reference point. Since man does not and cannot know God, Sartre concluded, man cannot know even himself. We cannot, for example, know the meaning and purpose of our own lives (unless the Creator tells us why he made us). No wonder a people that do not know God begin to worship creation (Gaia).[7] Since they do not know the Creator, they cannot know they are made in his image to rule, not worship, the creation.

My culture demonstrates that those who worship creation make themselves incapable of establishing their dominion over creation. Knowledge of God is not an abstract, otherworldly lux-ury. It is the starting point of drawing a map of reality (i.e., devel-oping a worldview) that explains reality, making it possible for us

6. This book is intended for Christian readers; therefore it is address-ing their concerns. In a lecture "From Da Vinci to Dan Brown: The Decline from Reason to Mysticism," I explained to a secular university how the Bible was the ladder which created intellectual giants such as Leonardo da Vinci and why myth-makers such as Dan Brown (author of *The Da Vinci Code*) are sinking into the perversion of sexual mysticism. For more information, see my eleven-part lecture series "Must the Sun Set on the West?" available from www.VishalMangalwadi.com.

7. For an explanation of "deep ecology," see my book *When the New Age Gets Old: Looking for a Greater Spirituality* (Downers Grove, Ill.: InterVarsity Press, 1992).

to live as we were meant to live.[8] Fear of God is the beginning of knowledge and wisdom (Job 28:28; Prov. 1:7).

In books such as *For the Glory of God* and *The Victory of Reason*, sociologist Rodney Stark explains why monotheism helped create modern Western civilization and became the most important source of "abundant" life that fallen history has ever seen. It is not the purpose of this chapter to explain how and why the biblical worldview developed universities and accumulated modern knowledge. For now it is enough to point out that we can know the truth because the infinite God has made himself known. Because believers know God, they can know themselves, know their neighbors, and understand their relationship to creation.

The Necessity of Knowing God

In Matthew 11:27 Jesus says, "No one *knows* the Father except the Son and those to whom the Son chooses to reveal him." In 1 John 5:20 the apostle John explains that the Lord Jesus did not come to this earth merely to die for our sins: "We know also that the Son of God has come and has given us *understanding*, so that we may *know* him who is *true* . . . his Son Jesus Christ. He is the *true* God and eternal life." Why is *knowledge* so necessary that God would incarnate as a man?

Adam and Eve were created to govern the earth. The kingdom of Satan began when they chose to doubt God and believe Satan. Just as the kingdom of Satan begins in our minds, so also the kingdom of God begins in our minds, when we choose to turn from our false ideas and believe God's word.

> Hear, O heavens! Listen, O earth!
>   For the LORD has spoken:
> "I reared children and brought them up,

8. For a discussion of idolatry, see my book *Missionary Conspiracy: Letters to a Postmodern Hindu* (New Delhi: Nivedit Good Books, 1996).

but they have rebelled against me.
The ox knows his master,
the donkey his owner's manger,
but Israel *does not know*,
my people *do not understand*."
Ah, sinful nation,
a people loaded with guilt,
a brood of evildoers,
children given to corruption!
They have forsaken the LORD. (Isa. 1:2–4)

They *know* nothing, they *understand* nothing;
their eyes are plastered over so they cannot see,
and their minds closed so they cannot *understand*.
No one stops to *think*,
no one has the *knowledge* or *understanding*. (Isa. 44:18–19)

Israel's watchmen are blind,
they all lack *knowledge*. . . .
They are shepherds who lack *understanding*. (Isa. 56:10–11)

My people are fools;
they *do not know* me.
They are senseless children;
they have *no understanding*.
They are skilled in doing evil;
they *know not* how to do good. (Jer. 4:22)

I thought, "These are only the poor;
they are foolish,
for they *do not know* the way of the LORD,
the requirements of their God.
So I will go to the leaders
and speak to them;
surely they *know* the way of the LORD,

the requirements of their God."
But with one accord they too had broken off the yoke
  and torn off the bonds. (Jer. 5:4–5)

Everyone is *senseless* and *without knowledge*. (Jer. 10:14)

The Lord Jesus agreed with Isaiah and Jeremiah:

This is why I speak to them in parables:
    Though seeing, they do not see;
        though hearing, they do not hear or *understand*.
In them is fulfilled the prophecy of Isaiah:
    "You will be ever hearing but never *understanding*;
        you will be ever seeing but never perceiving.
    For this people's heart has become calloused;
        they hardly hear with their ears,
        and they have closed their eyes.
    Otherwise they might see with their eyes,
        hear with their ears,
        understand with their hearts
    and turn, and I would heal them." (Matt. 13:13–15)

Woe to you experts in the law, because you have taken away
the key to *knowledge*. You yourselves have not entered, and
you have hindered those who were entering. (Luke 11:52)

The apostle Paul powerfully summarized the Old Testament
perspective on the source of pagan degeneration when he wrote:

The wrath of God is being revealed from heaven against all
the godlessness and wickedness of men who suppress the *truth*
by their wickedness, since what may be *known* about God is
plain to them . . . being *understood* from what has been made.
. . . For although they *knew* God, they neither glorified him
as God nor gave thanks to him, but their *thinking* became

futile and their foolish hearts were darkened. . . . They became *fools* and exchanged the glory of the immortal God for images made to look like mortal man and birds and animals and reptiles. . . . They exchanged the *truth* of God for a lie. . . . Since they did not think it worthwhile to retain the *knowledge* of God, he gave them over to a depraved *mind*, to do what ought not to be done. (Rom. 1:18–28)

You must no longer live as the Gentiles do, in the futility of their *thinking.* They are darkened in their *understanding* and separated from the life of God because of the *ignorance* that is in them due to the hardening of their hearts. (Eph. 4:17–18)

In the preceding verses Paul asserts the Old Testament view that the lack of knowledge and understanding result in a nation's destruction:

Therefore my people will go into exile
    for lack of *understanding.* (Isa. 5:13)

My people are destroyed from lack of *knowledge.* . . .
A people without *understanding* will come to ruin!
(Hosea 4:6, 14)

God's Promise to the Nations

The Lord promised to bless, heal, and save the nations by sending the Good Shepherd and good shepherds who are anointed by the Spirit of knowledge and wisdom.

The Spirit of the LORD will rest on him—
    the Spirit of *wisdom* and of *understanding,*
    the Spirit of counsel and of power,
    the Spirit of *knowledge* and of the fear of the LORD. . . .
They will neither harm nor destroy

on all my holy mountain,
for the earth will be full of the *knowledge* of the LORD
as the waters cover the sea. (Isa. 11:2, 9)

The mind of the rash will *know* and *understand*. (Isa. 32:4)

He will be the sure foundation for your times,
a rich store of salvation and *wisdom* and *knowledge*;
the fear of the LORD is the key to this treasure. (Isa. 33:6)

Then I will give you shepherds after my own heart, who will
lead you with *knowledge* and *understanding*. (Jer. 3:15)

I will give them a heart to *know* me, that I am the LORD.
They will be my people, and I will be their God, for they will
return to me with all their heart. (Jer. 24:7)

No longer will a man teach his neighbor,
or a man his brother, saying, *"Know* the LORD,"
because they will all *know* me,
from the least of them to the greatest,"
declares the LORD.
"For I will forgive their wickedness
and will remember their sins no more." (Jer. 31:34)

As predicted by Isaiah and Jeremiah, lack of knowledge and
understanding destroyed Israel. However, in the forty-eight chapters of the book of Ezekiel, the Lord repeated sixty-five times that
he intended to intervene in Israel's history in such a way that even
the dullest of them would know that he is the Lord.

Indeed, Israel's rebuilding began with Ezekiel's contemporary, Daniel, who was a man filled with a spirit of knowledge,
wisdom, and understanding (Dan. 1:17, 20; 4:9). Daniel knew
God as the one who gives *"wisdom* to the wise and *knowledge* to
the discerning. He reveals deep and hidden things; he *knows* what

lies in darkness" (Dan. 2:21–22). Daniel prophesied that "the people that do *know* their God shall be strong, and do exploits" (Dan. 11:32 KJV).

At the age of twelve, Jesus impressed the scholars in Jerusalem exactly as Daniel impressed Nebuchadnezzar. As Luke 2:47 tells us, "Everyone who heard him was amazed at his *understanding* and his answers." The Lord Jesus gave to his disciples "the *knowledge* of the secrets of the kingdom of heaven" (Matt. 13:11). He promised to give to his disciples "*words* and *wisdom* that none of your adversaries will be able to resist or contradict" (Luke 21:15).

Jesus fulfilled his promise. That is why Stephen was a man "full of the Spirit and *wisdom*" (Acts 6:3). His adversaries killed him because "they could not stand up against his *wisdom* or the Spirit by whom he spoke" (Acts 6:10).

The Importance of Knowing God's Truth

Why does God want his servants to be baptized with the Spirit of knowledge, wisdom, and understanding?

The Bible explains that while God plans to bless all the nations (Gen. 12:3; 18:18; 22:18; etc.), Satan is out to deceive the nations of the earth (Rev. 20:3, 8). The Lord Jesus came to set us free by giving us the knowledge of the truth. He said, "If you abide in my word, . . . you will *know the truth*, and the truth will set you free" (John 8:31–32 ESV).

Anti-intellectualism spread in evangelical churches partly because Reformation slogans such as "by faith alone" and "by Scripture alone" were misunderstood. In saying "by faith alone," the Reformers meant that salvation could not be earned by human religiosity. They knew that knowledge and understanding were preconditions of faith. Likewise, "by Scripture alone" meant that when tradition conflicted with Scripture, Christians were to abide by the Scriptures. The Reformers asserted the necessity of cultivating the mind and using reason in our search for truth. In his trial before the Diet of Worms (1522), Luther stated that he could not recant unless "the Scriptures and plain reason" convinced him.

Is salvation by faith alone? Jesus asked people to "repent and believe" (Mark 1:15). Repentance involves turning from what is false (e.g., idols) to what is true (see 1 Thess. 1:9). Jesus calls humanity to worship God in spirit as well as in truth (John 4:23). Paul asked Timothy to instruct his opponents gently "in the hope that God will grant them repentance leading them to a *knowledge of the truth*" (2 Tim. 2:25).

Anti-intellectualism became acceptable because many Protestants forgot that Jesus came not simply to take our souls to heaven but also to give us the knowledge of the truth:

[God] wants all men to be saved and to come to a *knowledge of the truth*. (1 Tim. 2:4)

[Christians are those] who believe and who *know the truth* . . . brought up in the truths of the faith. (1 Tim. 4:3, 6)

In embracing antirational mysticism, the secular world is reaping the consequences of the church's error—that of focusing on faith and the gifts of the Spirit and leaving the field of knowledge in the hands of unbelievers. This happened in part because some Christians were deceived by the secular idea that the human mind was a part of "the flesh." Therefore, they assumed that the mind had to be crucified.

However, the apostle Paul claimed, "I *know* whom I have believed" (2 Tim. 1:12). He declared that he was "an apostle of Jesus Christ for the faith of God's elect and the *knowledge of the truth*" (Titus 1:1). The letter to the Hebrews says Christians are those who "have received the *knowledge of the truth*" (Heb. 10:26). James commands us to ask God for wisdom (James 1:5). Peter says that knowledge is the source of grace, peace, godliness, and effectiveness:

> May grace and peace be multiplied to you in the *knowledge* of God and of Jesus our Lord. His divine power has granted to us all things that pertain to life and godliness, through the *knowledge* of him who called us. . . . Make every effort to supplement your faith with virtue, and virtue with *knowledge*. . . . These qualities . . . keep you from being ineffective or unfruitful in the *knowledge* of our Lord Jesus Christ. (2 Pet. 1:2–8 ESV)

The Renaissance and the Reformation created the modern world of inquiry, discovery, and knowledge because the Word of God taught medieval Christians (including the Reformers) that both our salvation and godliness required growing in knowledge:

> In him we have redemption through his blood . . . in accordance with the riches of God's grace that he lavished on us with *all wisdom and understanding*. And he *made known to us* the mystery of his will. (Eph. 1:7–9)

> Since the day we heard about you, we have not stopped praying for you and asking God to fill you with the *knowledge* of his will through all spiritual *wisdom* and *understanding*. And we pray this in order that you may live a life worthy of the Lord and may please him in every way: bearing fruit in every good work, growing in the *knowledge* of God. (Col. 1:9–10)

> My purpose is that they may be encouraged in heart and united in love, so that they may have the full riches of complete *understanding*, in order that they may *know* the mystery of God, namely, Christ. (Col. 2:2)

> I pray that you may be active in sharing your faith, so that you will have a full *understanding* of every good thing we have in Christ. (Philem. 1:6)

[Christ gives gifts to his church so that] we all reach unity in the faith and in the *knowledge* of the Son of God and become mature, attaining to the whole measure of the fullness of Christ. (Eph. 4:13)

And this is my prayer: that your love may abound more and more in *knowledge* and depth of *insight*. (Phil. 1:9)

[You] have put on the new self, which is being renewed in *knowledge* in the image of its Creator. (Col. 3:10)

Recovering the Pursuit of Wisdom

The Scriptures talk about *spiritual* understanding and wisdom because there is no such thing as *nonspiritual* wisdom and understanding. Humans have understanding because we are spiritual beings. By definition, machines, chemicals, and animals are incapable of understanding abstract concepts.

Knowing and fearing God is not an otherworldly, "spiritual" matter. It is the beginning of wisdom. It is the key to a healthy national life. When Judah was about to go into captivity, Jeremiah said to them: "'[King Josiah] defended the cause of the poor and needy, and so all went well. Is that not what it means to *know* me?' declares the LORD" (Jer. 22:16).

So what does this imply?

Isaiah 53:11 says that by his *knowledge* God's righteous servant will justify many. For a hundred years now the church has been growing in many nations (including America), yet the same nations are degenerating in many critical ways. This is because the church has been offering justification without the knowledge of truth. We have turned *salvation* into a shallow religious *experience* that *converts* but does not "make disciples of all nations" (Matt. 28:19).

The Lord Jesus, however, calls us to make people his apprentices, those who would learn from him and the Father:

Take my yoke upon you and *learn* from me, for I am gentle and humble in heart, and you will find rest for your souls. (Matt. 11:29)

It is written in the Prophets: 'They will all be taught by God.' Everyone who listens to the Father and *learns* from him comes to me. (John 6:45)

The Reformation transformed the West because it made Europeans learners, the Bible their textbook, and Jesus their supreme teacher. The choice before our generation is either to seek the knowledge of God once again or to slide into an abyss of pagan ignorance, corruption, and slavery. The Word of God commands us in Proverbs 4:5–8 to

Get wisdom, get understanding. . . .
Wisdom is supreme; therefore get wisdom.
    Though it cost all you have, get understanding.
Esteem her, and she will exalt you;
    embrace her, and she will honor you.

Recovery and pursuit of wisdom, understanding, and the knowledge of truth is the key to a new reformation because the postmodern intelligentsia knows that it does not know and cannot know the truth. Deception has to rely on force. It has to enslave, destroy. Intellectual and moral slavery is deceptively called "political correctness." This moral and semantic jugglery is similar to what pagans always do. For example, they try to make prostitution sacred by calling male and female prostitutes "gods" and "goddesses." While deceptive words enslave, the truth liberates. It empowers people by giving them genuine reasons to live and act in ways that are true, good, and beautiful. That is why the Ten Commandments begin by commanding us to believe and worship the one who is true.

Let's explore how God's moral truth is the only proper foundation for living.

NINE

His Law

Sin and Its Consequences

In 1977 a group of "low caste," "untouchable" young people invited me to their village because a minor flood had washed away their homes, crops, and cattle. They wanted me to start some relief and development projects. When I reached the village, they had just finished cremating a dead body and were bathing in the river. My friends showed me the pride of their village—a temple in the middle of the river, which they said was built a thousand years ago.

I asked them, "Why do you think you are so poor?"

"We work hard for ten or twenty years," they replied mournfully, "develop fields, build homes, and accumulate some capital. But then a flood comes and washes away everything, and we are reduced to zero."

"A thousand years ago," I reminded them, "our forefathers had the ability to build this temple in the middle of a river. It has withstood hundreds of floods. Did they have the ability back then to build houses on the banks of the river that could withstand floods?"

"Of course they did!" asserted my friends, pointing to the chief's stone house up on the highest point in the middle of the village. "That was built around the same time as this temple."

"Why didn't they build strong houses for themselves?" I asked my friends, but without waiting for their answer I went on to ask another question:

"A thousand years ago, our ancestors had the ability to build a temple in the middle of a river. It tells us of their engineering skills, their human organization, and the surplus time and the money they possessed. Do you think back then they had the ability to build a dam and canal system? Could they have said to the river, 'We love you, and we will make a home for you: please stay with us during summer months and flow through our fields. But for the rainy season we will make a different path for you through the jungles so that you don't have to go through our homes?'"

"Of course!" said my friends. "Our ancestors were as capable as anyone else in the world."

"So why did they make a temple instead of a dam? If they had made a dam, we would be richer than Switzerland, because in this climate we can take four crops a year. The Swiss have to work hard to get two crops."

My friends wondered where I was going with this, so I gave them a hint: "Did they make a temple because our ancestors feared and worshiped the river?"

"Yes, of course. The river is our mother. It gives us life. When it is angry, it brings death and destruction. If it wasn't for the river, our village wouldn't even exist. Therefore, we revere and worship the river as our goddess."

My friends, as you can tell, were very devout. They worshiped many gods, goddesses, and demons, but they also lived with chronic poverty. Over a period of time I helped them consider whether their poverty could be related to their beliefs and cultural values. I told them how God used Moses to transform a bunch of slaves into a mighty and prosperous nation we know as Israel. The God who set the Jews free from the slavery of Egypt also told them how they could both maintain this freedom and turn it into prosperity:

> So be careful to do what the LORD your God has commanded you; do not turn aside to the right or the left. Walk in all the way that the LORD your God has commanded you, so that you may live and prosper and prolong your days in the land that you will possess. (Deut. 5:32–33)

Naturally, some of our discussions centered on the Ten Commandments and why the first commandment focuses on worshiping in truth.

1. Worshiping in Truth

As God was leading the Israelites out of the grinding poverty of their slavery in Egypt and into the Promised Land, he spoke to them on Mount Sinai:

> I am the LORD your God, who brought you out of Egypt, out of the land of slavery. You shall have no other gods before me. (Exod. 20:2–3)

God was merely reminding the Israelites that they had experienced God. They already knew some truth about him, and therefore they needed to believe and worship the Truth. Believing what is not true, following false gods, would lead them back into slavery.

God, who redeemed the Israelites from oppressive slavery, who was taking them into a land flowing with milk and honey, told them that he is a moral God of justice and righteousness. False gods are different. I told my friends in the village that from 1972 to 1974 I traced the footsteps of many Americans and Europeans who had enthusiastically followed Hindu god-men. I wrote a book, *The World of the Gurus*, describing my discovery that many followers of these false gods and gurus found themselves trapped in immorality, slavery, and exploitation. Some were put off by what they saw; others joined the cults and learned the art of peddling occult knowledge, Tantra, meditation, and deceptive "enlightenment" to acquire power over their followers' fortunes and bodies.

The first commandment also reminded the Hebrews that God is not an abstract principle or impersonal force. He is a personal being, seeking to relate to human beings as precious persons— his own image. Those who do not know the truth about God cannot know the truth about man. That is why the Hindu sages described my friends as "low." Even in the West, those who reject God as the Creator are now forced to define human beings with reference to an ape or simply as a complex collection of molecules. They have no rational basis for treating humans differently than animals or machines. No wonder many Americans are now fooling around like monkeys with individuals they claim to love. As Western culture moves farther away from the Ten Commandments, this will only get worse. William Carey, the first British missionary to India, once saw a basket hanging from a tree. In it lay the body of an infant, half eaten by white ants and birds. He was shocked to learn that it was a common practice for parents to starve to death their unwanted infants in this way.

In the first commandment God defines both himself and man. My friends did not make stone houses for themselves because as "low caste" they were forced to live in mud houses in the vulnerable parts of the village. If they tried to make brick houses for themselves, they would be beaten or killed. They accepted their slavish status as low caste because they did not know the redeemer God.

What had been happening to these Indians for thousands of years, and happened to the God-denying nations of Germany and Russia in the twentieth century, could happen to Americans in the twenty-first century, because now some Americans do not want to be a nation under the Savior-God. They have to invent their own gods—the points of reference that will give meaning and moral values to them—which is exactly what God forbade in the second commandment.

2. Worship of Creation

God commanded the liberated slaves:

> You shall not make for yourself an idol in the form of anything in heaven above or on the earth beneath or in the waters below. You shall not bow down to them or worship them; for I, the LORD your God, am a jealous God, punishing the children for the sin of the fathers to the third and fourth generations of those who hate me, but showing love to a thousand generations of those who love me and keep my commandments. (Exod. 20:4–6)

My friends worshiped the river and therefore made themselves incapable of establishing dominion over it. They worshiped the cow and became incapable of manipulating or improving its breed. Some of them worshiped the "mountain god"; therefore they never looked under the mountain to see if there was copper or iron that they could mine, refine, and sell. No wonder they lived under poverty. The tragic consequences of these sins last for generations.[1] The tragedy is that now the advocates of "deep ecology" are urging Americans to worship Mother Earth as Gaia to save the Earth goddess.

God tells us not to worship nature because even though we are a part of creation, we are created in God's image to govern and manage the earth. I helped my friends understand that science and technology developed in the West because faith in a personal

---

1. I have discussed some of these consequences in a chapter "Idolatry—Essence and Consequence" in my book *Missionary Conspiracy: Letters to a Postmodern Hindu* (New Delhi: Nivedit Good Books, 1996).

Creator established the philosophical framework for belief in an objective, rational creation, whose laws could be discovered and harnessed by human rationality. Now Hollywood is replacing faith in a personal Creator with faith in chance or an impersonal "Force" (e.g., in Star Wars or Harry Potter), and the West is losing a concept of rational creation. The logic of such presupposition forces people to worship nature, seek magical powers, and consider the objective world as unreal, merely a projection of consciousness (*maya*).

Once upon a time, India made significant advances in science, mathematics, astronomy, architecture, arts, and grammar. But after it accepted the philosophy of non-dualism, or monism, called Advaita Vedanta, it began to look upon the world of science—of diversity or plurality—as the world of illusory maya, as a dream of Brahma (Universal Consciousness), a mirage from which we needed to be delivered.

Whoever makes your gods will also make your morality. He will then legislate a morality for you that suits his interests. My friends were enslaved as "untouchable" low-castes because they did not know the second commandment, which would have prevented them from allowing Brahmins to make gods for them. Now this is happening in the radical feminist movement in America. Clever women are creating imaginary goddesses for women and are harvesting worship, wealth, and sex for themselves.

God tells us not to make his image because he has already made his image, and that is your neighbor. If you want to love and serve God's image, it is your neighbor that you must love. Of course, that image of God has been marred by sin. That is why Jesus came as the visible image of the invisible God.

After my intervention in that village, my friends obtained bank loans and installed a lift-irrigation system; and once they had developed previously uncultivated lands, the upper-caste men beat them up and took over their lands! That is why the third commandment teaches us the fear of God.

3. The Fear of God

My friends and I discussed why our culture did not develop a humane justice system; why in our land wealth accrued in the hands of the powerful rather than those who worked creatively and diligently. Our consensus was that our culture lacked the third commandment.

Why do you think the president of the United States takes his oath of office in the name of God? And why do you think Americans testify in their secular courts in the name of God? Most people have forgotten that the answer is: Because of the third commandment.

> You shall not misuse the name of the LORD your God, for the LORD will not hold anyone guiltless who misuses his name (Exod. 20:7).

Anyone familiar with the current state of the American judicial system knows that it is not likely to survive another generation or two. As Americans cease fearing God, they no longer keep their vows and promises. Secular America is becoming a costly litigious society because godless people are also becoming unworthy of trust. In a society that does not fear God, the only way to establish justice will be to put everyone under constant surveillance. God watched over earlier generations; the godless generations will have to have Big Brother watching over them.

Gods of stone, wood, or metals neither save nor punish. The Hebrews as well as the Egyptians knew that the living God does both. The Hebrews went into slavery in Egypt because they sold their brother Joseph into slavery and lied to their father Jacob. When their descendants cried out to God for deliverance, he rescued them and entered into a covenant relationship with them as their God. The liberated Hebrews knew him as a living God. The living God wants to be our God and our Father. He gives us the right to use his name, to have all the privileges, authority, and power that come from his name. Unlike made-up gods and goddesses, he is not an impersonal, magical power that humans can manipulate for their advantages through magic, sorcery, rituals, offerings, or sacrifices. His name is not a mantra (sacred sound) like that of the demons, to be chanted for occult power or mystical experiences. The living God is a person. He is a holy God, a judge. Therefore, he is to be feared, respected, worshiped, and obeyed.

The Proverbs say, "The fear of the LORD is the beginning of wisdom" (9:10). A mind that fears God stays away from evil and loves truth and righteousness. Because it fears God, it ceases to fear man and the kingdoms of man. It also ceases to fear nature, but sees it as a mission field.

The first commandment, to have no gods other than the Savior God, deals with the state of our minds—whether we believe in truth or falsehood. The second and third commandments, which prohibit the worship of creation and exhort us to revere the living God, deal with the attitudes that result from our beliefs. It is not enough to believe in the Savior God; we must also walk in the fear of God.

Not taking the name of the Lord in vain implies a deep commitment to walk in integrity, with a sense of personal responsibility for our thoughts, words, and actions. The truth is that we are morally responsible creatures, thereby accountable to God. This fact demands that we should build our lives on the foundation of the fear of God. Why did atheism in the twentieth century lead to political totalitarianism, oppression, and poverty? Because, if there is no God, man is not accountable; he is not a sinner.

Societies that worship make-believe gods or refuse to worship the living God cannot have moral order and discipline that come from within. Order and discipline must be imposed by force. However, a free society must free up the time to cultivate inner moral discipline, which comes from the fear of God. That is the point of the fourth commandment.

4. The Blessing of Sabbath

My friends worked practically every day. They had festivals but no tradition of a weekly day of rest, when they could enjoy growing together as family and community in their knowledge, love, and fear of God. Well, to be exact, in our villages the weak worked every day, while the powerful worked only when they had to.

Liberty had tangible meaning for the Hebrew ex-slaves mainly because of the fourth commandment:

> Remember the Sabbath day by keeping it holy. Six days you shall labor and do all your work, but the seventh day is a Sabbath to the LORD your God. On it you shall not do any work, neither you, nor your son or daughter, nor your manservant or maidservant, nor your animals, nor the alien within your gates. (Exod. 20:8–10)

Sabbath means to take time away from work to build a godly community with your family and neighbors. Obviously, an individual or a nuclear family cannot harness the power of a river. That has to be a community effort, but community development fails unless cultures invest the time regularly to create community and keep it oiled and functioning. My friends had a temple, but a Hindu temple is very different from a church. It does not require people to observe Sabbath on a weekly basis to seek God together. Community comes into existence when people choose to put aside work, leisure, and private interests on a regular basis to gather together as whole families for worship, fellowship, and breaking bread.

Some people sin by not working diligently for six days, whereas others—because of greed, unbelief, or powerlessness—sin by working also on the day of rest and worship. Either way of breaking this command results in poverty. The necessity of work flows out of man's special position in the world as God's vice-regent, implied in the first three commandments. It is not enough to refrain from the worship of creation; the point is to establish wise and caring dominion over it. God put Adam in the Garden to "till it and keep it." Human fulfillment comes from work that is balanced by rest. Not to work is sin, but to be controlled by work is slavery.

My Indian culture had a different attitude toward work than the biblical cultures because our worldview made no distinction between creation and the Creator. On the one hand, this led to the worship of creation (e.g., the river), but on the other hand, if everything is divine, then in some way creation is unreal (maya) and a life of work is bondage. The human goal, or human salvation, requires those who can afford it to go into an ashram (*a-shram* = non-labor), away from a life of action into a life of meditation to find enlightenment—seeing the unreality of nature. Indians can work as hard as anyone else, and yet the work ethic of Indians working for the government is a handy subject for cartoonists. And the unfortunate fact is that many educated youth bribe to get government jobs precisely because they know that bureaucratic jobs mean secured salary, perks, and "extra income" (bribes) without much exertion.

Interestingly, during my visits to Hindu ashrams, I met Western pilgrims who rejected the biblical worldview and sought to acquire wealth and power through meditation, magic, occultism, spiritism, Yoga, and Tantra. Many Hollywood movies depict meditation and magic as more desirable sources of power than rational effort. The fourth commandment warns against an anti-work worldview because it is a source of poverty. "He who works his land will have abundant food, but the one who chases fantasies will have his fill of poverty" (Prov. 28:19).

However, work ceases to be meaningful and fulfilling if it is not seen as a part of the overall purpose of human life in relation to both creation and the Creator. If work is to be a vocation, a "call" that transcends drudgery, then it has to be seasoned with Sabbath rest. The Sabbath is not merely a physical or mental rejuvenation. The Sabbath is holy, and it is meant to service our hearts and minds with the divine perspective on life. Therefore, it is primarily a *spiritual* rejuvenation. Our spirits must govern our minds and bodies.

Whether work is the never-ending duties of a housewife washing dishes and mopping floors, or a watchman staying awake night after night, or the strenuous effort of an astronaut in space for months, the Lord's Sabbath can give meaning and inspiration to make labor not only tolerable but also a work of art that is pleasing and satisfying. By keeping the Sabbath to the Lord your God, you bring your life and work under God. The work then becomes a "call." It inspires the worker to persevere, to work for a cause higher than mere bread and butter.

Some people destroy the source of the community life in the West—the church—because they are opposed to "organized religion." They have little use for institutionalized Sabbath. It doesn't take much time to learn that those who cannot keep the Sabbath are not able to keep their families together either. That is the subject of the fifth commandment.

5. Honoring Parents

Community and economy depend upon the family. Given the fact that human beings are fallen, there are no perfect children and no perfect parents. Every child has plenty to complain about regarding his or her parents, but for good reasons morality often requires us to go against our fallen nature and do what we do not want to do. God commands:

> Honor your father and your mother, so that you may live long in the land the LORD your God is giving you. (Exod. 20:12)

Israel was a patriarchal, tribal society. The family was not merely a social unit but was also a civic, economic, military, and political entity. Therefore, this command implies that we honor our fathers and mothers and also that we learn to be law-abiding citizens, respecting all those in authority. We cannot exercise authority over creation without learning to honor those in authority over us. When we are given the authority to make decisions that affect others (such as our parents), we will make some decisions that are foolish, nasty, and even costly. If you are leading others in battle, you are likely to send your subordinates to their death. Being in charge, you may regret and mourn the way you must use your authority, yet your team would have no chance of surviving or winning if it did not respect and obey you.

The apostle Paul taught Christians living in Rome to pay taxes and to respect civic and political authorities (Rom. 13:1–7), even though he knew that the Roman empire was the fourth beast of Daniel 7:7. As per Nebuchadnezzar's dream, it was the empire of iron that was to be smashed to pieces by the stone of the kingdom of God (Dan. 2:34, 44–45). Paul asked Christians to honor those in authority because he had learned from experience that the grace of God was not absent from wicked, totalitarian kingdoms. The Jews would have killed Paul, had it not been for the Roman law which held that an accused had a right to defend himself before a judge as well as to make an appeal to higher authorities, up to the supreme court of Caesar himself. It is only by a life of consistent obedience that we earn the right to disobey human authority when such has to be done to obey the higher authority of God.

Pensions, retirement benefits, and other forms of social securities for the aged are to be welcomed as positive cultural developments. But when these measures become substitutes for the love and care of children for their parents, then instead of being expressions of respect for parents, they become an expression of the selfish individualism of a society that is bound to be as destructive to the family as is collectivism. The promise of *shalom*—that you may live long in the land—is dependent on the continuity of right relationships in the family.

Wisdom often comes from age and experience. Honoring parents is the necessary preparation for a life of useful work, which is taught in the fourth commandment. To dishonor parents or other authorities is sin; it leads to the chaos of conflicts and unhappiness. Respect and obedience for authority lead to order, peace, fruitfulness, and life.

When family is the business enterprise, it does not require any imagination to see how breaking the fifth commandment results in poverty. No enterprise can be profitable that does not cultivate respect for and obedience to superiors.

God says we must honor and obey those over us so that we "may live long in the land." One very important cause of the relative weakness of the economic life of socialist economies is that family-owned economic enterprises are seen as suspect, whereas artificial cooperatives, associations, or state-controlled public sector companies are promoted. More often than not, these latter ventures fail because they do not do justice to human factors in economic life. In contrast, even large multinational companies do better if a family spirit is injected into management.

But the command to "honor your father and mother" is not to be obeyed primarily because of its economic benefits. In fact, it is sinful to respect only those who have economic or intellectual power. Children may well have more knowledge or money than their parents, but that does not justify disrespect for poor or illiterate parents. If parents are to love and care for powerless, illiterate infants, then when children grow up, they should reciprocate respect and care for parents who may by then have become powerless. A society that does not care for parents will soon lose the rationale for caring for children too. Parents make it easier for children to respect them if they are faithful, forgiving, respectful, and loyal to each other.

To respect parents is to respect the source of one's life. That is the subject of the sixth commandment

6. Murder

My friends could not build stone houses for themselves because to build such houses would have meant to forfeit their lives. The upper-caste Hindus were not wicked; they were "moral"—for it was their "moral" duty to protect their religion. That included preventing a lower-caste person from trying to be an equal of an upper-caste person.[2] This highlights a simple difference between a biblical and every nonbiblical philosophy of government. In a nonbiblical system, say under a Pharaoh, an Israelite lived at the pleasure of the government. A Pharaoh could ask a midwife to kill a boy just because he was Hebrew, and it would be "moral" for her to obey her king. In biblical political philosophy, the government exists to protect a citizen's right to life. It is God who commanded:

You shall not murder. (Exod. 20:13)

This sixth commandment meant that even though David was a divinely anointed king, he had no right to take Uriah's life. Every human being has a God-given right to life, of which he or she cannot not be unjustly deprived.[3] God is pro-life. Jesus said he came to give life abundant.

Satan, however, is a murderer (John 8:44). As America becomes the kingdom of Satan, its government will assert ultimate authority over everyone's life. It has already given to parents the right to decide which child will live and which will be killed.[4] As care for the elderly becomes costly, the government will give to children the right to determine which parent will live and which must die. In a culture driven by money, it will be easy to forget that a human being is infinitely more important than capital.

After the Nazis were defeated, secular courts tried to prosecute the officers who had obeyed Hitler's orders to kill terminally

2. This is violation of *dharma*, i.e., divinely ordained purity of caste hierarchy.

3. This is the political philosophy stated in the United States Declaration of Independence.

4. The law that a person is guilty of double murder when he kills a woman he knows is pregnant acknowledges that at least a viable fetus is a human person.

sick patients and six million Jews. The Nazi defense was: "The government gave the order; we obeyed. Government's decree is the law. To disobey the law would have been morally wrong as well as personally dangerous." This defense is irrefutable—unless there really is a God, and his command, "You shall not kill," over-rules human authorities.

I went to the village to serve the poor, but *why* were my people so poor? It didn't take me long to learn that our area was ruled by dacoits (armed gangs of bandits). To have wealth meant to invite robbers. Our people preferred either to remain poor or to move out of the villages to the more secure environment of the cities. Those who saved a little chose not to invest it in a rural-based enterprise. Likewise, the commercial banks were reluctant to invest in perfectly viable projects in villages, because villages lacked the security of law and order. A society that cannot put the security of human life as its top priority cannot hope to rise above poverty. Therefore the commandment not to commit murder is fundamental for prosperity.

God's law offers protection not only for our life but also for our families. That is the purpose of the seventh commandment.

7. Adultery

While on a visit to Jamaica, I was told that this paradise lived in perpetual poverty because 85 percent of its children did not have legitimate fathers, and that this was a legacy of slavery. British slave owners encouraged their slaves to pursue sex, not love. The male slaves became stud bulls, breeding more slaves. They took no responsibility for the women they impregnated or the children they fathered. When sex is required to be an aid to love, a child has both his mother and father. The parents make sacrifices to ensure that their child does not suffer as a slave. That is one reason why God commanded the slaves he had liberated:

You shall not commit adultery. (Exod. 20:14)

As I discussed poverty with my friends, I said to them that their economic bullock cart moved slow because it was pulled by a single bull—the male. Their women were confined to house-hold chores. They agreed that rampant sexual immorality was the main reason for women's enslavement: "We cannot send our girls to the high school in the next village because we cannot trust our men to leave them alone. That's why they remain uneducated and unskilled. It takes a big dowry to marry them because they are economic liabilities."

Americans have become bolder about committing adultery because contraceptives and abortions are easily available. Does that mean the sexual revolution will not take its economic toll in the West? Women who are not sure of their husband's faithful-ness and commitment do not want to have children. Who will then pay for the Social Security checks and Medicare bills of the retired Americans?

The children of the immigrants?

Why should an immigrant go to the trouble of raising chil-dren to pay for you to retire on a golf course? Once hard-working immigrants have acquired enough voting strength, why shouldn't they vote away your Social Security, at least your Medicare? Why shouldn't they ask you to give up your right to life, just as you took away your children's right to life?

In chapter 1, I mentioned that in 1980 my wife and I were invited for a lecture tour of the Netherlands. On the first night our hosts put us up in a Christian hostel in the middle of the red-light district of Amsterdam. I had never seen anything like that. In my lectures that week, I often joked with my audience, "I thought I was coming from an underdeveloped country to a developed society. But on my first night here I learned that I have come from a culture that is about a thousand years ahead of yours. What you have in Amsterdam now, we had in our temples a millennium ago, and we know well where that road leads." The temple in the middle of the river was not built merely to worship the river; it was a tantric temple where priests and high-caste men organized ritual sex orgies to obtain mystical enlightenment. The novel *The Da Vinci Code* asks Christians to turn the Lord's Supper into a similar sexual ritual, and turn adultery into a religious exercise.

God's commandments protect our property just as they protect our life and our family.

8. Theft

My lower-caste friends created wealth, but not for themselves or their children. As I mentioned in chapter 1, just growing fruit trees could have eradicated their poverty. But it is not worth growing fruit if you cannot protect it from the upper castes, the feudal lords, or the bandits. And that is a form of slavery.

God delivered the Israelites from the slavery of Egypt and taught them that the only way to get out of the clutches of poverty was to obey the command:

You shall not steal. (Exod. 20:15)

This commandment implies that people have a right to the wealth they inherit or create. Security of life, family, and property creates the context in which economic development takes place. Citizens have a motivation to invent and create when they know that their state exists to protect their wealth for them and their children, and that their state will not rob them through unjust taxes. Citizens weaken their state's capacity to serve and protect them when they steal the taxes that belong to the community.

The Indian economy is trailing way behind China partly because thousands of billions of rupees have been hidden away by Indian politicians, civil servants, and business leaders in foreign banks as "black money." The politicians and bureaucrats have generated much of this money through illegal bribes on imports and exports, but much of the money is also generated by legitimate business, which is not brought into the country to evade taxes. The businessmen feel that the government will steal their money through unjust taxation, so they prefer to steal taxes from the government themselves. We have a joke: When a politician steals public property in the West, he goes to jail; when he steals it in India, he goes to the West—preferably to the Swiss banks. Some national leaders charge that the present situation is worse than the British Raj taking away to England the wealth that Indians had created.

One of the ways in which the business community stole the wealth of the ordinary people in biblical days was through "unjust weights and measures." Moses prohibited such theft in his law. The prophets denounced it as sin. But today many economies lower the value of their currency—in the name of "development"—as the simplest way of stealing the wealth of the people. Ultimately when people lose faith in the government's paper money, the country goes through the upheavals of bankruptcy. This practice of stealing by devaluing currency is the modern equivalent of using changeable weights and measures. It deters saving, and seriously hinders progress in poor countries. For example, a person who saves $100,000 to enable his child to start a commercial enterprise may find that by the time the child is ready, the value of his savings has gone down to, say, only $17,000. In contrast, a person who had taken a loan of $100,000 may find that it was very profitable to have been in debt, because the real value of his liability over the years has decreased on its own to only $17,000. It then becomes wiser to have liabilities than savings and investment. Americans are just learning that a society that prefers liabilities to savings makes itself vulnerable to poverty.

Since chapter 1 has already discussed the power of the eighth commandment to create the wealth and generosity of the Protestant nations, let us go on to notice that refraining from stealing is not enough: God told the Hebrews that their witness would have to be honest if they wanted to build a prosperous society.

9. Truth in Witness

> You shall not give false testimony against your neighbor.
> (Exod. 20:16)

My friends—whose lands were taken away by upper-caste men—did not go to the courts because they knew that while the feudal lords would have no problem getting witnesses, they themselves could not get one neighbor to witness truthfully.

A few years after that incident, some other farmers in a neighboring district cried to me (literally) that the transportation system (railways and trucks) had been so manipulated by some unscrupulous merchants that they were being forced to sell their potatoes at a price that did not cover even the cost of harvesting. So, along with some friends, I struggled to enable these farmers to solar-dry potatoes into wafers. We then ground the wafers into potato powder for the snack-food industry. One peasant farmer found this to be very profitable and urged me to allow him to install a grinding unit in his home. In theory, that would make it possible for us to sell potato powder at a cheaper price than anyone else in the world, because we could eliminate packing, transporting, and warehousing costs. However, the price of wheat flour was much cheaper than potato powder, and that presented a huge temptation to add wheat flour to the potato powder to make more money. In the end, dishonesty, litigation, corrupt courts, and untrustworthy witnesses drive business costs so high that the West is able to sell the powder to us much cheaper than we can sell it in our own country.

If the consequences of dishonesty on economic life were not bad enough, false witness goes further in destroying the judicial system itself. Atheist dictators such as Stalin made a mockery of justice by eliminating millions of opponents through sham judicial trials. In Hindu/secular countries such as India, which inherited a fair and independent judiciary from the British but not a culture built on the Ten Commandments, the ruling powers have used the judiciary to protect criminals and to harass and punish political opponents by resorting to false witnesses. It is common for the state to arrest social and religious workers on trumped-up charges. This is destroying the legitimacy of the state itself.

The ninth commandment is the branch on which the American judiciary is seated, and it is blindly sawing off that branch.

The tenth commandment takes the previous nine commandments from the external sphere—idolatry, murder, theft, adultery, etc.—to our inner attitude.

10. Content or Covetous

> You shall not covet your neighbor's house. You shall not covet your neighbor's wife, or his manservant or maidservant, his ox or donkey, or anything that belongs to your neighbor. (Exod. 20:17)

Our faith in God's goodness and love for us must result in contentment and thankfulness. Our respect for our neighbors and their property must mean that we work for what we want and need to have, instead of coveting what our neighbors have. I must create a house I can be proud of instead of coveting my neighbor's. I must work at loving my own wife to have happiness in my home.

Under the impact of Socialist thinking, many of our leaders in India and in some other Third World countries told us that we were poor because the Western world was exploiting us. The way out of poverty, therefore, was for us to get the West's money. All exploitations by the West, of course, must cease. But gradually I came to see that our own leaders were the greatest exploiters of our countries. Coveting our neighbor's wealth is an attitude that does not help. If I have a right to enjoy the wealth I create, so does my neighbor. Exploitation is a result of covetousness.

Not having a covetous disposition means contentment, thankfulness, and industriousness to earn what we want. Contentment means loving our neighbors enough to serve them and give to them. Covetousness results from a lack of faith in God and a lack of love for our neighbors. It robs us of contentment, peace, and social harmony—virtues that create the climate of a community's development. That is why covetousness is a destructive sin.

To be content also means to be thankful enough to worship the good God. The tenth commandment therefore takes us back to the first commandment—worshiping the God who has given us life and liberty; who has been kind enough to become our covenant King, revealing to us his laws of liberty and prosperity.

In a situation where you are not able to trust anyone, knowing that God is good becomes an enormous source of inner power—the power of faith, joy, contentment, thankfulness, and worship.

As a result of our conversations, my friends realized that God's law was a blessing that needed to revolutionize our culture. However, they also realized that each one of them was guilty of breaking practically every one of the Ten Commandments. This realization that we are all sinners made it exciting for me to discuss the transforming power of the gospel of God's forgiveness.

PART III

How Does the
Gospel Transform?

TEN

Evangelism

Heralding Truth

A society cannot be reformed unless it is first informed of what is wrong with it, what is right, and how to get the wrong put right. That is why Paul was appointed an apostle and a herald of truth (1 Tim. 2:7). Some societies permit action for reform; they are called "open" societies. These societies grant freedom to the citizens to oppose the evils of the rulers. They have institutionalized self-correcting mechanisms. But this is a relatively recent phenomenon in world history. Most societies even today are "closed." Insiders can hardly speak against the evils in their society, let alone do anything about them. Attacking socially approved sins in these societies is virtually impossible; even preaching takes enormous courage.

When centers of power have been taken over by corrupt vested interests or diabolical powers, a reform movement has to awaken and organize the common man to pray and to act. In other words, to bring about a fundamental change in the evil institutions of a society, we need a spiritual awakening as well as a mass movement. Preaching is the prerequisite for bringing forth repentance and building up a movement, and this can be undertaken by an individual.

In a closed society, preaching is often the only tool available to the reformers. For example, Jeremiah was given the task of reform. God said to him, "See, today I appoint you over nations and kingdoms to uproot and tear down, to destroy and overthrow, to build and to plant" (Jer. 1:10). What was Jeremiah's tool for reform? Nothing but preaching. God said to him, "You must go to everyone I send you to and say whatever I command you. Do not be afraid of them" (1:7–8).

The fact that a person is only preaching does not necessarily mean that he is not a reformer. John the Baptist was a lone voice preaching a new kingdom, but he triggered a movement of repentance from sin and seeking after the kingdom of God. By the time of Paul, the full-time preachers of the kingdom were numbered in scores. Ultimately it is ideas, not armies, that rule the world.

Social reform is usually a people movement that seeks to remove the evils of society and transform its unjust and oppressive values, ideals, practices, and institutions to be just, humane, and conducive to human fulfillment. A movement for social reform is based on

- a critical awareness in a society that the beliefs, values, practices, and institutions are fundamentally wrong;
- a hope that change is possible;
- a faith that a better alternative is in fact available;
- a leadership that is able to organize and mobilize the masses against the evil status quo.

Piecemeal social reform is possible. A group of people may see one particular social evil, repent of it, protest against it, and set right the injustice. But from a Christian point of view, evil is cosmic; it has a supernatural dimension. The conflict of good and evil is a conflict of two kingdoms—the kingdom of Satan versus the kingdom of God. Therefore an evangelist aims at wholistic, not piecemeal, reform. As St. Paul says, Christ's good news is that "the new has come!" (2 Cor. 5:17). The evangelist seeks to bring the kingdom of Satan under the righteous reign of God, even though he recognizes that until Christ returns all change is temporary, that the forces of evil will fight back and seek to corrupt the hearts and institutions of man.

The Truth Will Set You Free

The fact that the rule of Satan begins in our minds, when we choose to believe his deception, and culminates in the oppressive political institutions we build, means that untruth is the foundation of slavery. Proclamation of truth, therefore, is a basic means of setting people free from oppression and exploitation. Jesus said, "Then you will know the truth, and the truth will set you free" (John 8:32).

Often we fail to see that the oppressive and exploitative social structures survive not because of the strength of their institutions or their physical force, but by the spread of faith in these structures. People believe the falsehood and therefore allow themselves to be exploited.

I grew up in the city of Allahabad in the state of Uttar Pradesh in India. Millions of devout Hindus come there from all over India to bathe in the river Ganges. They know that the *Pandas* (priests) will loot them, but do their best to protect their money from the Pandas. Yet they usually return home with stories about the way they were cheated. Later they return to the Ganges and get looted again—and they continue coming. Why? Because they believe that the holy waters of the Ganges will wash away their sins and give salvation to the souls of their deceased relatives. Slavery is a matter of belief.

Christians at the time of Martin Luther knew that the papacy had become an exploitative establishment, yet they sustained it. Why? Because they were made to believe that the pope, as successor of St. Peter, held the keys to salvation.

Justification by faith is the heart of contemporary evangelistic preaching. It was also the heart of sixteenth century Reformation theology. Then, the doctrine of justification by faith created titanic sociopolitical reforms. Today it creates no ripples. Why?

Martin Luther had courageously added a significant word to the biblical teaching on salvation by faith, which gave this truth a cutting edge in the contemporary society. It was the word *alone*. "Justification by faith *alone*" consciously implied that the church's selling of indulgences for the salvation of the living and the dead was nothing but economic exploitation of the masses by a corrupt religio-political establishment. This doctrine meant that the work of Christ on the cross of Calvary was sufficient for human salvation and, therefore, the sacraments of the church were, in the final analysis, irrelevant for salvation. Thus, the entire army of priests, bishops, and even the pope, who saw their role as chiefly sacramental, were an unnecessary economic burden.

"Salvation by faith" and "the priesthood of all believers" were radical truths, not pious doctrines. These truths demanded that the pope and the whole priestly hierarchy be opposed because they had sucked Italy economically dry and were now threatening to rob Germany of its wealth.

Luther's preaching of justification by faith alone stirred up the masses because it offered spiritual as well as economic freedom. The masses are rarely moved by theological debates. It was not the theological truth that really stirred up the masses. It was the politico-economic implications of the truth, perceived by the ordinary people to be beneficial to them, which generated the mass movement for acceptance of the truth. In other words, evangelism in the sixteenth century attracted crowds partly because it freed nations from the yoke of oppression—because it was "good news to the poor" (Luke 4:18).

Paul's evangelism was exactly the same. Paul said to the Corinthians that when he visited them, he was determined to preach nothing "except Jesus Christ and him crucified" (1 Cor. 2:2). He preached nothing but Christology and soteriology, that is, the doctrines of Christ and of salvation through the cross. We need to look at these two doctrines of Paul to understand how evangelism set people free from the slavery of oppressive Jewish and Roman systems.

Paul's Doctrine of Salvation

Paul's preaching of salvation through Christ's death on the cross is summed up in two major themes in his epistles: grace versus law and faith versus works.

Paul preached, taught, and debated that man can be saved not by works of the law, but by faith in the grace of Christ. Paul taught that by faith in the atoning death of Christ, man can find forgiveness from sin and reconciliation with God. This, according to Paul, meant that there was no further need for circumcision, animal sacrifices, and observance of Jewish rituals or special days. Under the traditions the Jews had added to the Mosaic Law, man had to spend much money to earn salvation; now it was available freely. Believers no longer needed to live under the yoke of the law. This simple but revolutionary message undercut, in one fine stroke, the entire edifice of the exploitative Jewish structure.

Jesus said that he had come to set the captives free (Luke 4:18); Paul was showing how that was accomplished through Christ's death. The Jews who went to the temple in Jerusalem to offer sacrifices knew that it was a "den of robbers" (Matt. 21:13). Yet they patronized the temple and allowed themselves to be exploited by a corrupt establishment. Why? Because they believed they could be saved only through observance of the law. By declaring that man cannot be saved by the law but only by faith in the sacrifice of Christ, Paul was destroying the very foundations of the exploitative religious establishment. Naturally, the Jewish leaders were threatened by this preaching and, as we shall see, they persecuted Paul because of the threat his message was to their whole system.

Paul may have learned the basics of his theology from Stephen, who taught that the temple in Jerusalem was not the heavenly reality. It was portrayed so by the leaders who had a vested interest in religious establishment. Stephen said that God gave Moses the vision of the heavenly reality, and Moses made a shadow of the heavenly reality in the form of a mobile tabernacle. After Israel settled down, David wanted to build a temple, but because David was a man of war God allowed only his son Solomon to build it. That, Stephen argued, meant that the temple was not the ultimate sacred place of meeting with God. In any case, Stephen continued, God made it plain even in the Old Testament that he who created the heavens and earth does not dwell in temples built by human hands. (See Acts 6 and 7.) This was a message that undercut the vested interest of the Jewish leaders in motivating people to keep patronizing the temple. Predictably, this teaching brought about violent retaliation.

After his conversion, Paul preached Stephen's message with greater clarity and depth. The author of the epistle to the Hebrews best summed up this message, that the work of Christ had made the exploitative religious legalism redundant. He wrote, "By calling this covenant 'new,' he [God] has made the first one obsolete; and what is obsolete and aging will soon disappear" (Heb. 8:13).

Paul was an evangelist because he preached salvation by grace. And his preaching was seen as good news because it freed his audience from their slavery to the law. When the Jewish converts sought to bring the law back into the church, Paul fought them, arguing that if that happened grace would be futile and Christians would be back in slavery. It was Paul's determined fight which finally made Peter declare in the Jerusalem council that religious legalism was a yoke on the necks of the Gentile disciples that neither the Jews nor their fathers had been able to bear (Acts 15:10). Paul's preaching of salvation was thus a message of social reform, of freedom from a yoke.

The late Dr. Bhimrao Ambedkar, the greatest leader of the untouchables in India, understood this same basic technique of social reform that Paul used. That is why he preached "conversion" as the answer to the social evil of the caste system. It is unfortunately true that Buddhism, to which he led his disciples, has turned out to be a blind alley, but it remains true that one can try different options to reform a society:

One can accept the basic structure of the society (e.g., the Hindu caste system) and seek to minimize inherent injustices by law (as the government of India has tried to do for the past six decades). But Ambedkar, who wrote much of India's constitution, knew that this approach could not transform the situation fundamentally.

Therefore, a second option is to refuse to accept the basic structure of an unjust society and seek to change the people on top who are responsible for injustices. But it is almost impossible to change the people on top merely by preaching, because they are usually happy with the status quo. As Jesus said, in essence, it's easier for a camel to go through the eye of a needle than for a beneficiary of the kingdom of Satan to enter the kingdom of God. The oppressive, exploitative system is favorable to the people on top; therefore they do not want change. So one may be tempted to use either violent or nonviolent force to overthrow the oppressors. It may be possible to overthrow the government by seizing or killing a few or a few hundred people, but what can one do if the oppressors number literally hundreds of thousands, or if they are too powerful to be overthrown by force? In any case, as we saw in the chapter on God's law, it takes much more than a revolution to create a just government.

The third option, then, is to change the oppressed. One can refuse to accept the basic unjust structure of society and reform the system by changing the oppressed. For example, if the untouchables cannot change the high-caste oppressors, their only option is to change themselves. This change has to be at two levels. First, they have to be set free from mental or ideological slavery. They have to cease believing that they are born "untouchables" because of the karma (actions) of their past lives, or that blessings in future lives depend on fulfilling the duties of their present status of slavery. They are held in slavery by faith in a falsehood, and truth alone can set them free from this mentality of slavery.

Second, they have to opt out of the socio-religious system (i.e., cease to be Hindus) in order to cease being untouchables. They have to discard dehumanizing, oppressive, and exploitative lies on the one hand, and on the other hand accept a new worldview that all human beings share the dignity of being made in God's image. They need to belong to a community that practices this truth and helps them find their intrinsic dignity by becoming God's children.

Oppressive systems survive by propagating falsehood. Evangelism liberates by spreading truth, that is, by undercutting the intellectual foundations of an exploitative system and by creating an alternative social structure that helps people live out the truth.

Paul's Doctrine of Christ

For Paul, "preaching the good news" and "preaching Christ" were synonymous: the Messiah was Paul's good news. Much of Paul's theology is therefore Christology. Paul's gospel is that Jesus is the Christ; the heart of his message is the crucified, risen, exalted, and soon-returning Christ.

Paul preached that Jesus, who was humiliated on the cross, has now been exalted over all rulers, powers, authorities, and dominions of this age as well as of the age to come. This same Jesus, who is going to return soon to set up his kingdom, will destroy the man of sin, the evil ruler who sets himself above God. Paul's Christology was thus a political gospel. Jesus was presented as "King of kings" and "Lord of lords." Jesus, not Caesar, was the one before whom every knee would bow and whom every tongue would confess to be Lord.

In his Christology, Paul was not comparing or contrasting Christ with the deities of the prevalent religious sects. As in Nebuchadnezzar's dream, the Messiah was the alternative to the emperor and the religio-political ideology of the day. The gospel was formulated against the background of the imperial faith as the answer to the exploitative empire. Jesus was not another or more powerful god, but the only God. He, according to Paul, was the ruler, the final authority, the judge, the king—the Lord.

In a society where the "dragon" has deceived people into worshiping the beast, Caesar becomes the lord, and statism the official creed. When the state is the ultimate, the final reality, the absolute, or the lord, it becomes the exploiter, the source of most social evils and oppression. In such a setting, preaching about a Lord who, as a shepherd or savior, is above the state is exciting news. As Canon Michael Green has said, "If Jesus was going to return as triumphant Son of Man in the clouds of heaven . . . then clearly here was the final winding-up of history for which they were all waiting; here was the break-in of the theocracy and the defeat of the impious Romans. This surely must have been a factor in the immediate growth of Christianity from its cradle in Jerusalem."[1]

It is true that many preachers of Christology teach Jesus' divinity and "saviorhood" but fail to preach Jesus' kingship. Most Christians therefore understand how "Jesus saves" is good news but fail to see how "Jesus is Lord" is also good news. But the wise men who came looking for the baby Jesus in Jerusalem were looking for a king and not specifically for a savior. Why? Because they were disillusioned with the beastly kings and kingdoms of this world.

What were the kingdoms of this world?

Brutal!

Immediately after the visit of the wise men, King Herod ordered the massacre of all boys in and around Bethlehem who were under two! There was nothing the parents could do to protect the lives of their infants. In such a milieu the news that the Messiah—a new king—was born, was indeed good news.

In the Roman world of the first century, the message that "the kingdom of heaven is at hand" received such a massive response,

1. Michael Green, *Evangelism in the Early Church*, rev. ed. (Grand Rapids: Eerdmans, 2004), 157.

in spite of brutal opposition from the state, because it was presented to a people who believed the prophecy of Daniel. As we saw in chapter 7, Daniel had taught that at the time of the fourth empire (after the Babylonian, Persian, and Greek empires) the God of heaven would raise up his kingdom. The evangelism during New Testament times meant that the vision of Nebuchadnezzar—that during the era of the kingdom of iron, a stone uncut with human hands will smash and destroy the dazzling statue of precious metals (human kingdoms) and itself become a mighty mountain—was about to be fulfilled.

The original New Testament hearers and readers were living in the fourth empire, in the oppressive kingdom of the beast, in the darkness of despair and death. Therefore, the message that the kingdom of heaven has come, that Jesus is the Christ, naturally stirred up hope and excitement—as well as determined opposition.

Just as Paul's preaching of salvation as a free gift of God through faith in the cross of Christ undercut Jewish theology and set people free from the yoke of slavery to the Jewish Establishment, Paul's preaching of Jesus as Lord undercut the intellectual foundations of Roman imperialism and destroyed political totalitarianism. The common man's excitement at the realization that Jesus was King was most visible on the first Palm Sunday, when Jesus entered Jerusalem on a colt with a crowd following him and shouting, "Blessed is the King of Israel!" (John 12:13).

Many Jews believed Paul's gospel, but their leaders persecuted Paul for destroying their entire system through his preaching of the cross (Acts 21:28). The Romans persecuted him for destroying their imperialism by his preaching of Jesus as Lord. For example, in Thessalonica, when Paul preached, "This Jesus I am proclaiming to you is the Christ" (Acts 17:3), his opponents understood him as "defying Caesar's decrees, saying that there is another king, one called Jesus" (17:7). Did they misunderstand Paul? If it were a matter of misunderstanding a spiritual king as a political threat, then Paul and the other apostles could have easily corrected that misunderstanding. In fact, they would have avoided preaching Jesus as *Christ* and concentrated on preaching him only as the savior. But they did not compromise their preaching. They knew Jesus as "the ruler of the kings of the earth" (Rev. 1:5) and preached him as such. In fact, they believed that Christians would rule over the nations of the earth (Rev. 2:26–27). It was natural that such preaching would result in persecution.

We Wrestle "Not Against Flesh and Blood"

Some Christians may find it hard to accept this insight into Paul's Christology. They might argue that Paul himself said, "Our struggle is not against flesh and blood" (Eph. 6:12). How can Paul then be concerned with political reform?

Paul did say our struggle is not against flesh and blood, but added in the same verse that we struggle "against the rulers, against the authorities, against the powers of this dark world *and* against the spiritual forces of evil in the heavenly realms." Paul did wrestle with evil spirits—the spiritual forces of evil in the heavenly realms. But much of his time was spent in struggling against the rulers and authorities of this dark world—who were humans. It was not the evil spirits who beheaded John the Baptist, crucified Jesus, stoned Stephen, or persecuted Paul. The church was and is pitched against the rulers and authorities of this dark world—against those in positions of power and authority, who prefer darkness over light. And it is also true that there are spiritual forces of evil over these human rulers.

I can understand why Christians living in open societies fail to understand Paul's oblique language of "powers and principalities." But they ought to understand that Paul was not living in an open society with freedom of speech guaranteed. In fact, when he wrote the letter to the Ephesians he was under arrest, with perhaps a Roman guard reading what he wrote or listening to what he dictated. How could he say openly that he was wrestling against the totalitarianism of Caesar?

In one of our villages, a high-caste man beat an untouchable man to death. He ordered the body to be cremated that night before the police could come or a postmortem could be done. The untouchables were terrorized. Since they had to live in that village, they could not oppose the wicked village chief openly. They only whispered to us against the "rulers of this dark world," in an oblique language very similar to Paul's.

Evangelism and Political Freedom

Evangelists did not think of political freedom in negative terms of the overthrow of the Roman or Jewish establishments. They understood and preached political freedom primarily in terms of submission of human kings to the rule of God. This is significant because history has not been able to come up with a better understanding of political freedom than this.

There are many nations even today whose understanding of political freedom is no more than skin-deep. Not in a metaphorical sense, but literally. For an average Indian, for example, political freedom is when the white colonial rulers leave, and brown, black, or yellow natives take over the rule. Most often this color-of-skin definition of political freedom means worse oppression and tyranny. One does not need to prove the emptiness of this definition. In almost any nation that has attained "political freedom" since the Second World War, the new rulers are happy with their freedom, but the ruled are usually more oppressed and exploited than before. The color-of-skin political freedom generally means freedom for the new governors, not necessarily the governed.

Only where the freedom is understood as the rule of law is there some freedom for the governed. A people are free only to the degree to which the powers of their government are limited by law. There is only one test of political freedom: are the rulers under the law or above the law? If any of the human rulers are above the law, then that is rule of rulers, not the rule of law. Potentially that is a dictatorship, not a free country.

Rule of the human rulers is not freedom. Rule of law is. This raises the fundamental question: is the ultimate source of law human or divine? If the law is entirely human, then those who have the power to make the law have the power to change it too, and thus they are above the law. Genuine freedom is impossible in societies that have only human law.

Only if absolute law comes from beyond man can it be binding on all men. Only before a transcendent law can there be a genuine equality of all men. Kings and prisoners alike can be equal before the law if the law itself is above the king. Transcendent law presupposes a transcendent Lawgiver. If there is no just Ruler above the kings of the earth, if he has not given his law to men, then political freedom or rule of law is a sheer illusion, a mirage that is impossible to attain. Man is condemned forever to live under the rule of "might is right," whether the might be of a few or of the majority. The concept of the rule of law becomes a superstition without faith in a just Ruler above the human rulers.

Today, both at state and federal levels, the executive and legislative wings of the American government are using "activist" judges to promote their ideological agenda because it is harder for voters to vote out or impeach judges. Some judges are enjoying the authority to override God's law. But these judges do not realize that they are being used. The judiciary has no power of its own; it depends on whoever controls the police or the army. Therefore, every nation that rejects God and becomes a nation under man makes judges servants of the executive. Sooner rather than later the judges and the people have to lose their freedoms and live under the bayonet.

Proclaiming Jesus as "the ruler of the kings of the earth" was and is the only genuine way of establishing politically free societies. In this sense, evangelism does not overthrow the existing political kingdoms, but by bringing kings under a transcendental law it curtails the arbitrary freedom of the kings and thereby increases the political freedom of the ruled.

Political freedom is determined not primarily by whether or not the king himself is Christian, but by whether or not he is under the law of God. Political freedom will increase in proportion to the submission of the rulers to the transcendent law in their public lives.

Was Paul fighting a corrupt political establishment? No, if fighting is understood militarily, but yes, if it is understood evangelistically. He was witnessing uncompromisingly that Jesus, not Caesar, is Lord. Christ chose Paul precisely for such political evangelism. God said to Ananias, "This man is my chosen instrument to carry my name before the Gentiles and their kings" (Acts 9:15). For Paul evangelism results in sociopolitical transformation because it brings the kings of this world under the rule of Christ. Bringing totalitarian human rulers under the authority of a transcendent law is the highest definition of political freedom that history has seen.

The New Testament teaching regarding the second coming of Christ and the final judgment of man reinforces the perspective outlined above. The doctrine of the final judgment of man affirms the great significance and responsibility of each individual. What each individual does with his or her life is important to God. But this doctrine also establishes the equality of every man, whether high or low, before the law of God. Paul says to the slave owners that they should treat their slaves in the light of the fact that both they and their slaves have a common master "in heaven, and there is no favoritism with him" (Eph. 6:9).

The same applies to the human rulers and the ruled, judges and accused prisoners. There is an ultimate equality of all men before the law of God. This is a radical Christian basis for political freedom now on this earth. When an evangelist tells the kings of this earth that they, too, have a king and judge over them, before whom they are as much accountable as any other man, the evangelist curtails the totalitarian powers of the human rulers and demands that they act justly. That is what political reform or freedom ultimately means.

From this perspective, the doctrines of the second coming and the final judgment do not give us the right to assume that the world will go from bad to worse, making reform impossible. On the contrary, these doctrines demand that our evangelism results in curtailing the oppressive totalitarian powers of the human rulers. The kings, presidents, and prime ministers of the earth should be brought under the rule of Christ. That is evangelism, and that is also political freedom: curtailing and limiting the power of the state over the individual, demanding that the laws of the state be just in light of the justice and righteousness of God.

Evangelism frees the powerless individual. It threatens powerful vested interests because it transforms cultures and limits the power of government by making Christ the ruler of the kings of the earth. Proclaiming the kingship of Christ requires supernatural power. To that subject, therefore, we must now turn.

ELEVEN

The Holy Spirit

The Spirit of Truth and Power

Ruth and I have been married for thirty-four years. We love
each other and irritate each other. We have empowered each
other as well as wounded each other. About twenty years ago,
whenever I acted mean, Ruth resorted to reading a book called
Get Rid of Him. (She lost that book about ten years ago, but I'm
still around her.) These years of marriage have taught me that
love is a gift of grace, a fruit of the Spirit. Chemistry is incapable
of sustaining love and marriage.

We will return to the subject of personal transformation, but
allow me to begin with the subject of societal transformation.

Just before his ascension Jesus said to his disciples, "You will
receive power when the Holy Spirit comes on you; and you will
be my witnesses" (Acts 1:8). Superhuman power is needed for
witness if it means calling not just ordinary individuals but rulers themselves to acknowledge Jesus as Lord, to repent from their
evil ways, and to reform. God said to the prophet Ezekiel that
he was sending him not to a people who would respond to his
preaching in great numbers but to a people who would not listen

because they were "hardened and obstinate." Therefore God said, "I will make your forehead like the hardest stone, harder than flint. Do not be afraid of them" (Ezek. 3:7–9).

Jesus' promise of power came in response to the disciples' question, "Lord, are you at this time going to restore the kingdom to Israel?" (Acts 1:6). Jesus said that their attitude should not be to know the time and merely wait for God to usher in his kingdom. Rather, their job was to go into the world and, filled with divine power, boldly witness to the kingship of Jesus, bringing the world into subjection to the authority and rule of God (see Acts 1:8; Matt. 28:18–20). That is evangelism. That is also the reform of a rebellious and corrupt humanity.

After the disciples were baptized with the Holy Spirit, Peter, quoting the prophet Joel, said that the result of the outpouring of the Holy Spirit would be that young men would see visions, old men would dream dreams, and all God's men and women would prophesy (Acts 2:17–18). In the Old Testament, Joel painted that grand picture of what the restoration of Israel would look like. Restoration was not merely deliverance from foreign rulers and an abundance of food and wine (Joel 2:18–22). It was also an outpouring of God's Spirit and a great outburst of inspired, healthy, and positive creativity manifesting itself in a quality of life and godly culture that brings praise to God (Joel 2:26–29).

In a stagnant and enslaved society, old men do not dream dreams; they mourn for bygone glories. Young men are not inspired by visions of hope for the future; they resign themselves to live with the present static reality of despair and gloom. The creative springs of life dry up, and there is no song of praise in the hearts of slaves. People perish because there is no prophetic vision. No one speaks for justice and truth with the freedom and authority of God. Not only the masses but also the mighty bow before evil and prefer discreet silence.

Israel had been a stagnant, enslaved society till the day of Pentecost. Individuals like John the Baptist and Jesus had been murdered, but no one had the courage to speak for justice and truth. The outpouring of the Holy Spirit made the difference between death and life. An ordinary man like Peter became like a mighty prophet of old. With the thundering authority of divine courage, he confronted Israel with their cowardice and cruelty in crucifying Christ. That was powerful, prophetic witness to the truth. With the coming of the breath of God, the dry bones had come to life and had become a mighty army (see Ezek. 37:1–14).

Power through the Spirit of Knowledge

Jesus promised the power of the Holy Spirit to his disciples in order to make them witnesses. Who is a witness, one who has power or one who knows? Confusion on this point has meant that in some circles Christian spirituality has changed from "knowing God" to "having power."

A witness is a person who knows. The apostles were eyewitnesses to Jesus Christ because, they said, they had known him "the whole time the Lord Jesus went in and out among us, beginning from John's baptism to the time when Jesus was taken up from us" (Acts 1:21–22). The apostle John authenticates the apostles' right to be witnesses to Jesus Christ on the grounds that they knew what they were talking about:

> That which was from the beginning, which we have heard, which we have seen with our eyes, which we looked at and our hands have touched—this we proclaim concerning the Word of life. The life appeared; we have seen it and testify to it, and we proclaim to you the eternal life, which was with the Father and has appeared to us. We proclaim to you what we have seen and heard. (1 John 1:1–3)

Why is reform needed? What destroys a nation or a civilization? In chapter 8 we noted that "people are destroyed from lack of knowledge" (Hosea 4:6) and "a people without understanding will come to ruin" (Hosea 4:14). Because God wants to

bless ignorant nations, he promised to anoint his servant with the
Spirit of knowledge:

> The Spirit of the LORD will rest on him—
>> the Spirit of wisdom and of understanding,
>> the Spirit of counsel and of power,
>> the Spirit of knowledge and of the fear of the LORD.
> (Isa. 11:2)

God gives the Spirit of understanding to his servants because he
plans to fill the earth with the knowledge of God as the waters
cover the sea (Isa. 11:9).

Knowledge, as we said earlier, is necessary if one is to be a
witness. But knowledge alone is not enough. Suppose you witness a murder committed by a gang of drug dealers who have
powerful political and police connections. Could you stand in a
witness box and testify that this gang (similar to a gang of chief
priests, Herods, and Pilates) killed an innocent man? You may
know and believe the truth, but daring to be a witness requires
power, especially if your witness is aimed at uprooting a wicked
and brutal power structure wedded to oppression and injustice.
A radical witness that goes to the root issues of injustices in a
society is a prophetic witness.

Gift of the Spirit: Prophecy

The New Testament talks of many gifts and the manifold fruit
of the Holy Spirit in the lives of believers. We need to look at
one gift, prophecy, and one fruit, love, to see how the power of
the Holy Spirit is essential for social reform. The New Testament
church considered prophecy to be more important than the other
gifts of the Holy Spirit because prophecy is the reforming witness
to the truth of God (Rev. 11:3; 19:10).

Today, the terms *prophecy* and *evangelism* are often kept distinct. That distinction may have academic value, but in real

life prophecy and evangelism are not separate. For example, in 1 Corinthians 14, where Paul exhorts believers to seek the gift of prophecy, he says that if an unbeliever walks into a Christian meeting where everybody is prophesying, "he will be convinced by all that he is a sinner...and the secrets of his heart will be laid bare. So he will fall down and worship God" (vv. 24–25). Thus prophesying and evangelizing are not necessarily distinct activities. An evangelistic message from God is a prophetic message.

In the New Testament sense, such a message is usually called *evangelistic* rather than *prophetic* because the emphasis of this message is on the good news of forgiveness, rather than judgment, as was often the case in Old Testament prophecy. Forgiveness has value because judgment means punishment.

A prophet is an evangelist who proclaims God's promise of forgiveness and salvation in place of a well-deserved judgment. Therefore, when the New Testament asks us to seek the gift of prophecy, it asks us to be evangelists. A prophet calls for repentance from immoral behavior and also from untrue beliefs as a precondition for forgiveness. One reason the church is so ineffective today is that even though we do speak against personal sin, we choose not to challenge the falsehood that our society believes in. In India we find evangelists preaching against smoking and drinking, but we rarely find someone preaching against idolatry. Yet false belief is the foundation of many a human misery. If our message does not touch the miseries of the common man, it does not appear to many to be good news. The Holy Spirit gives us the power to be a reforming witness because he gives us the gift of prophecy, which includes the power to judge and protest against the evils of the kingdom of Satan.

The Power to Judge and Protest

Proclaiming Jesus as the king of heaven does not generally result in persecution. But when we start proclaiming Jesus as the ruler of the kings of the earth, we invite trouble. Because then we automatically judge the world around us by the yardstick of his justice and righteousness and demand that his will ought to be done on earth as it is in heaven.

It takes enormous power and discernment to judge the powers and principalities that are committed to corruption and cruelty. But that is what Peter, empowered by the Holy Spirit, was doing in his sermon on the day of Pentecost. He charged his audience with the sin of cruel murder: "You, with the help of wicked men, put him [Jesus] to death by nailing him to the cross" (Acts 2:23). And again, "Therefore let all Israel be assured of this: God has made this Jesus, whom you crucified, both Lord and Christ" (2:36). The Bible records that "with many other words he [Peter] warned them, and he pleaded with them, 'Save yourselves from this corrupt generation'" (2:40). That was prophetic evangelism.

Peter's prophetic evangelism judged a specific sin which, in fact, revealed the extent of blind, naked, unashamed cruelty to which that society had degenerated. Peter also judged the fear, cowardice, and blindness of the masses which allowed corrupt rulers to kill a good, innocent man, whom the people themselves acknowledged as a prophet from God. This fearful cowardice that permitted evil to reign was one of the main causes of the injustice in their corrupt society.

Peter's exhortation to "save yourselves from this corrupt generation" was not merely a message of repentance from private sins. It was a continuation of the theme of the kingdom of Satan versus the kingdom of God started by John the Baptist. Proclamation of Jesus as the Christ was a proclamation of his kingship, of the beginning of the renewal of Israel, of the start of the kingdom of God.

The crucifixion of a righteous man symbolized the degeneration of a whole society. That symbol was what Peter attacked. In those statements, made at the risk of his life, Peter was judging the evils of his day, protesting against them publicly and calling for repentance and change. His accusations were so pointed and so directly against the unjust, official stance of the state (that

Jesus was a criminal) that his hearers had no option but to repent or to kill him. That was prophetic evangelism at its best.

This kind of witness obviously calls for great power, and one major aspect of the power of the Holy Spirit is the power to judge the world.

When the apostle Paul said, "For the kingdom of God is not a matter of talk but of power" (1 Cor. 4:20), what did he mean? The context clearly means the power to judge, the power to "whip" (4:21). Paul confronted the sin of adultery in the church at Corinth. He said the church ought to have the power to judge the adulterer: "When you are assembled in the name of our Lord Jesus and I am with you in spirit, and the power of our Lord Jesus is present, hand this man over to Satan, so that the sinful nature may be destroyed" (1 Cor. 5:4–5). The Christians at Corinth were taken up by the gifts of the Holy Spirit, especially the gift of tongues. Paul told them that the power of the kingdom is not manifested in words alone but in the authority to judge and punish sin temporally for the sake of eternal salvation. Many Christians in America are becoming promiscuous like the Corinthians because church leaders lack the power to confront sin.

In India, our problem is financial corruption. Christian officers in the government of India and in the business world are often respected for their integrity and ethical standards, but the same cannot always be said about some of the leaders of churches and Christian institutions. And even church leaders who do have personal integrity do not always seem to have the power to judge the sin within the church. But is this power to be exercised only within the church? Paul goes on to say in the same context that the saints will judge the world (1 Cor. 6:2).

Are we going to judge the world only after Christ returns?

In the judicial sense of the word *judgment* (which carries with it the authority to punish), the saints will judge the world after Jesus returns (1 Cor. 5:9–12; Rev. 2:26–27; 20:4–6). But in the moral and prophetic sense of the word *judgment*, our task begins when we are empowered by the Holy Spirit. Jesus said, "When he [the Spirit] comes, he will convict the world of guilt in regard to sin and righteousness and judgment" (John 16:8). How will the Spirit convict the world? Obviously through the Spirit-filled believers.

But if we judge the sin of the world, the world is bound to persecute us. Jesus was not killed because he showed people the way to heaven. He said that the world "hates me because I testify that what it does is evil" (John 7:7). We must witness or testify not merely about who Jesus is but also about what the world is. The Bible says that we must expose the works of darkness (Eph. 5:11). We need power to do that because when we judge the world, the world retaliates by judging us. Stephen was stoned to death because he said to the Jews in Jerusalem:

> You stiff-necked people, with uncircumcised hearts and ears! You are just like your fathers: You always resist the Holy Spirit! Was there ever a prophet your fathers did not persecute? They even killed those who predicted the coming of the Righteous One. And now you have betrayed and murdered him. (Acts 7:51–52)

That is prophetic witness, and it requires power from above.

Usually even the mighty men of this world are too weak to stand as witnesses against the evils of their contemporary powers and principalities. They consider compromise to be wisdom. The violent "Cartoon Controversy" that erupted in Denmark in 2006 exposed the cowardice of the cultural elite. In 2004 the author of a children's book requested several artists to help illustrate his educational book on the prophet Mohammed. In his book he said nothing critical about Mohammed; it was a straightforward description meant for school use. He wanted illustrations because all children's books are illustrated. The first artist refused because Muslims had recently killed the Dutch filmmaker Theo van Gogh for making a film depicting the plight of Muslim women. (Van Gogh was shot eight times, then stabbed. His throat was cut, and two knives were left in his body, one of which attached a five-page note.) The second artist declined to illustrate the book because, he said, Muslims had just beaten up a professor in Norway for reading some verses of Koran to his non-Muslim students. A third artist refused the job because he didn't know what Muslims might do to him!

During a dinner, the frustrated author expressed his amazement at this loss of courage in the artistic community, which brags about its freedom of expression. That conversation inspired an article, which in turn inspired a newspaper to invite forty cartoonists to present their perceptions of Mohammed. Only fourteen artists, three of which were on the newspaper's staff, had the courage to draw Mohammed. The Muslim community responded by organizing violent and murderous protests around the world, further bullying the European press into submission.

What would happen if an American paper exposed that the commercial success of a politically well-connected billionaire was built on corruption that hurt the community, and then the publisher's wife and daughter disappeared mysteriously? The publisher might publish a second story and lose his son in an automobile accident. What if he decided to publish a follow-up story, only to find that his press was set on fire that same night by an "employee's negligence." Would the press in that city have the courage to plan another negative story about the billionaire? Or would the press rather express its artistic courage by attacking Christ and ridiculing religion—the very forces that created the prophetic press?[1] The Puritans created the free press because they took up their cross as prophets. Secularism that rejects the Holy Spirit has no power to take up its cross to bear prophetic witness to truth. It cannot sustain the freedom of the press.

God's holiness means that he hates evil. His hatred is expressed in two ways: he saves men from sin and he also judges

---

1. For a brief history of the press, see Vishal Mangalwadi, *India: The Grand Experiment* (Surrey, UK: Pippa Rann Books, 1997).

sin. Salvation and judgment are the inseparable sides of the same coin: God's holiness and hatred of evil. The church as Christ's body is meant to be both an agent of salvation and an agent of God's justice. The loss of this balanced perspective has robbed the church of her dynamism to transform society. Protestantism no longer protests against evil, because it sees itself merely as a channel of God's salvation and not of God's justice. What does it mean for Jesus to be the ruler of the kings of the earth if he does not judge them? What good is it if his Spirit does not empower those whom he fills to pronounce prophetic judgment?

After his resurrection Jesus said, "All authority in heaven and on earth has been given to me" (Matt. 28:18). Paul said that the Head of the church is already seated on the throne above all powers, principalities, and rulers of this world (Eph. 1:20–23). This means that Christ's body has to carry out his instructions and orders. The church is Christ's mouthpiece. And to be a prophet means to be the mouthpiece of God (Exod. 4:14–16).

This loss of perspective, which separates prophecy from evangelism, which preaches salvation without proclaiming repentance and justice, reduces the church to a rudderless boat floating at the mercy of social currents, some of which are ghastly in their cruelty and injustice. Some church leaders, for example, are enthusiastic to perform marriages for homosexuals but too timid to oppose the annual murder of sixty million babies through abortion. Today we seek the patronage of the Pharaoh in order to preach to the enslaved people. We do not dare to witness to Pharaoh himself.

But the tragedy is that when we cease to be the voice for justice, we also become ineffective as channels of salvation. When we are not breaking the yoke of oppression, we have no "good news for the poor" either. The poor masses consider us irrelevant, and our critics legitimately dismiss us as giving "opium" and not spreading the good news. Martin Luther's preaching on justification by faith alone was a judgment of an Establishment that had become corrupt. That is why it required enormous power, and that is why it resulted in such great reform and many conversions. Paul's preaching of Jesus and his cross, as we saw in chapter 10, was the judgment of Jewish and Roman exploitative Establishments. That is why Paul was seen as an opponent of the Jewish law, of the enslaving temple worship and traditions. No wonder he needed power from above for such preaching. Such witness has to be stamped with one's blood. It has to be a cross-bearing witness.

The tragedy of the contemporary church is that those Christians who rightly stress the necessity of the work of the Holy Spirit in our lives are often mistaken about the purpose of God's gift of the Holy Spirit to the church. They mistake *signs* to be the reality itself. They seem to think that the Holy Spirit is given primarily to empower us to do miracles. But God said:

> I will put my Spirit on him [my servant]
> > and he will bring justice to the nations. . . .
> A bruised reed he will not break,
> > and a smoldering wick he will not snuff out.
> In faithfulness he will bring forth justice;
> > he will not falter or be discouraged
> till he establishes justice on earth. (Isa. 42:1–4).

It is a great folly to dismiss this as "the Old Covenant." The Lord Jesus himself said: "The Spirit of the Lord is on me, because he has anointed me . . . to proclaim freedom for the prisoners and recovery of sight for the blind, to release the oppressed" (Luke 4:18).

Miracles are signs of the kingdom; justice and righteousness are its contents (see Ps. 45:6–7).

The Power for Cross-Bearing

Jesus, who commissioned his disciples to go out as his witnesses, called them to a life of cross-bearing. The disciples were willing to drink the cup—the passion and humiliation of the cross—that Jesus drank (Matt. 20:22), but they did not have the power to do so. Jesus said that their spirits were willing but the flesh was weak (Matt. 26:41).

Jerusalem had crucified Jesus because he claimed to be her legitimate king. For one to reassert in Jerusalem within two months of his murder that Christ was indeed the king, was to woo death. How could the disciples, who had earlier fled from persecution, bear witness to Jesus' kingship without receiving strength that came from beyond themselves? For such a witness they needed more than the power of oratory, the power of tongues, and the power to perform miracles. The disciples were able to perform miracles long before they were baptized with the Holy Spirit on the day of Pentecost, but they were too weak to face persecution (Matt. 10:1; Luke 10:17). What they needed was the courage to confront their corrupt and cruel society with its sin, call it to repentance, and take the consequences of such a confrontation, namely, persecution.

This was precisely the transformation that the baptism of the Holy Spirit brought about in the disciples. When the Jewish leaders who had killed Jesus and arrested the apostles came face to face with the courage of "unschooled, ordinary men" like Peter and John, "they were astonished" (Acts 4:13). The leaders imprisoned, threatened, and flogged the apostles, warning them not to speak in the name of Jesus. But the disciples had the strength to disregard the warnings, rejoice in persecution, and deliberately choose to disobey the state. This is evangelism.

This is also civil disobedience. By disobeying the state, the disciples affirmed that there was a law and a lawgiver higher than the state. They affirmed that the present leadership was unjust, immoral, and unworthy of obedience. By their disobedience they proclaimed they had a new king, that they were subjects of the government of God. Their willingness to suffer and die was a testimony to their certain knowledge and faith in the resurrection. Such a cross-bearing affirmation of the sovereignty of God is political freedom, just as its opposite, Fascism, is "the practical and violent resistance to transcendence."[2]

Cross-bearing is the original version of civil disobedience. It is a Christian's submission to the higher law of God, a deliberate rejection of the immoral laws of the state, and a joyful acceptance of the consequences of the stand.

Cross-bearing is not easy, and that is why before his arrest in Gethsemane Jesus asked his disciples to "watch and pray so that you will not fall into temptation" (Matt. 26:41). One needs power for cross-bearing witness. That is why Paul prayed for the Colossians that they might be "strengthened with all power . . . so that you may have great endurance and patience" (Col. 1:11). Paul asked Timothy to "be strong in the grace that is in Christ Jesus. . . . Endure hardship with us like a good soldier of Christ Jesus" (2 Tim. 2:1, 3).

Thus the power for prophetic evangelism is the power to bear a courageous witness to the truth and accept persecution from those who are committed to suppress the truth with unrighteousness.

Willingly to choose suffering and self-sacrifice for the sake of righteousness is to walk the way of the cross. It is to engage in a moral and spiritual conflict with the powers and principalities. You stand for truth; they stand for oppression. They stand with the sword; you stand with the cross, the symbol of self-sacrifice. Cross-bearing means power because choosing suffering presupposes fearlessness. The kingdom of Satan is the reign of terror (Heb. 2:14–15). For scientists, historians, and scholars seeking to maintain intellectual integrity, American "Liberalism" can be just as totalitarian and intimidating as Fascism or Communism. Its doctrine of "political correctness" already stifles liberty. And we know that social evils blossom in the oppressive kingdom of Satan because people are too afraid to resist them at personal cost.

2. Ernst Nolte, quoted in Gene Edward Veith Jr., *Fascism: Modern and Postmodern* (New Delhi: Nivedit Good Books, 2000), 46.

If we oppose the corruption of powers and principalities, we are threatened, harassed, persecuted, or ultimately killed. That is how oppressive societies perpetuate their injustice. The way of the cross does not mean accepting injustices. It means refusing to accept what is unjust and taking the consequences of that stand, even if it results in death.

Glancing through the Gospels, one sees that Jesus emphatically taught his followers not to fear those who could kill the body. This fearless willingness to suffer is a prerequisite to prophetic evangelism. God said to Jeremiah:

> Get yourself ready! Stand up and say to them whatever I command you. Do not be terrified by them, or I will terrify you before them. Today I made you a fortified city . . . to stand against the whole land—against the kings of Judah, its officials, its priests and the people of the land. They will fight against you but will not overcome you. (Jer. 1:17–19)

Such scriptures made the Protestant Reformation possible by inspiring Martin Luther and his followers to sing:

> Let goods and kindred go, this mortal life also;
> The body they may kill: God's truth abideth still,
> His kingdom is forever.

The Power for Loving Service

A fearless prophet defying the state, preaching both judgment and repentance and facing persecution, creates the image of a rough and rugged man. But Jesus had asked Peter to take loving care of his tender lambs, to feed and protect them (John 21:15–17). The kingdom of God is for the meek and the lowly (Matt. 5:3–5). God in his kingdom has

> scattered those who are proud in their inmost thoughts.
> He has brought down rulers from their thrones

but has lifted up the humble.
He has filled the hungry with good things
but has sent the rich away empty. (Luke 1:51–53)

The disciples, like normal human beings, were looking for themselves in the kingdom of God (Matt. 18:1; 20:20–23). Their favorite topic of debate was "Who is the greatest among us?" But the power of the Holy Spirit was not for anyone's self-glorification; it was for serving others, especially the powerless.

Jesus continuously taught his disciples that to be great they had to humble themselves and be transformed into servants. He tried to teach them that the kingdom of Satan was for the big, but the kingdom of God was for the little children, the nobodies. This verbal teaching was not enough. Jesus also gave them object lessons by blessing the children and by becoming a servant himself and washing the disciples' feet. But teaching and examples were not enough. The disciples needed power to become servants. They needed the power to see that the great dreams of the restoration of Israel had meaning only if the powerless people had a place in those dreams.

It takes great vision and power to become a servant in a selfish, exploitative society. That is what the baptism of the Holy Spirit achieved in the disciples. Their eyes were opened to see the needs around them and to respond to those human needs with tenderness and with the Holy Spirit's resourcefulness. Earlier they had seen the lame man at the beautiful gate as a beggar, but now they saw him with eyes of compassion, as a human being in need of something more than money. Their love for him was the fruit of the Holy Spirit in them (Gal. 5:22). Christlike compassion and character are what the Holy Spirit produces in those who seek him. Transforming our inner life is the primary work of the Holy Spirit in all believers. By the Spirit's power we first become witnesses; then we are able to give credible witness.

The Holy Spirit not only gave the apostles the power to have compassion for the insignificant crippled beggar. He also empowered them to heal the beggar, to meet his need.

We cannot belittle the supernatural gifts of healing, casting out demons, and performing miracles. I have seen these miracles take place in answer to my own prayers as well as those of others who have the gift of healing. But we must remember that the power of performing miracles was not a result of the baptism of the Holy Spirit. The apostles and the seventy disciples were given that gift long before Pentecost. What the baptism of the Holy Spirit did for them was to make them servants. Earlier the seventy (or seventy-two) had exulted in their power to perform miracles (Luke 10:17). Now they exalted Christ, as his servants. They not only healed the sick and cast out demons; they also looked after the widows, the orphans, the poor, and the drought-stricken (Acts 4:32–35; 6:1; 2 Cor. 8–9; etc.).

A prophetic judgment against oppression, cruelty, and exploitation in our society can have no meaning if it is not backed by our own life of service and the care of the powerless lambs. But our service also has little effectiveness if it is not seen against the background of our overall Christlike compassion for humanity.

We have seen in chapter 6 that Christ's compassion was not some sentimental pity or charity. It grew out of a prophetic insight into the social evils of his day. Jesus saw the crowds as harassed and helpless sheep, whose shepherds had turned into wolves. He was moved enough to cry, outraged enough to condemn, and concerned enough to identify himself with them so fully as to lay down his life for them. That is compassionate service. Naturally, it calls for supernatural power—the power to deny ourselves, take up our cross, and follow the Good Shepherd.

There is no dearth of Christian service today. But because much of it is service without prophetic compassion, it is powerless to bring about a radical change in individuals and society. To be a Good Samaritan has eternal value in itself, but it is not the highest ideal of Christian service. It is only the beginning. A concern for the wounded and robbed man must lead us on to a prophetic judgment of the systems that violate the rights, dignity, and values of human beings made in God's image.

Our service will have a cutting edge when it is seen against the background of our overall concern for man. A prophetic judgment of all that dehumanizes man in our society gives meaning and power to our service toward those wounded and crushed by the same society. But in order to be credible, our prophetic words must be backed by service, by a practical affirmation of the value of man. A prophet may stand outside society, but a servant gets inside and dirties his hands. For a prophet to have his message heard, he has to become a prophet-servant.

Such service which grows out of a prophetic compassion brings one power because it makes one a good shepherd. Jesus had compassion for the crowds partly because the Jewish political, economic, civic, and religious leaders, who should have been shepherds to the people, had instead become wolves (Matt. 9:36). The crowds sought Jesus because they were looking for a shepherd, a new leader. Jesus, therefore, sent his disciples to preach, to serve, and to become shepherds to those lost sheep (Matt. 10:6–8, 16). Jesus' mission was to become the Chief Shepherd, to take over leadership from the wolves.

The role of a shepherd, community leader, or reformer has social power. Jesus used that power as a deterrent against his arrest (Luke 20:19). He had been to the temple many times and was no doubt indignant at its corruption. But he did not challenge it until he had a crowd behind him, shouting his praises. The chief priests and soldiers were afraid to arrest him, for they feared the crowds would take to rioting (see, for example, Matt. 21:46). John the Baptist had remained a prophet, so although Herod had to think twice, it was comparatively easy to arrest and kill him (see Matt. 14:5). But Jesus had gone on to become a shepherd by being a servant, and his flock was a powerful deterrent against his arrest.

It was the same with the sixteenth-century Reformers. Martin Luther would have been arrested and killed as soon as the Reformation began, had his service not built up a powerful popular opinion in his favor. When Karl von Miltitz, a Saxon nobleman and chamberlain in the papal court, was sent by the pope to secure the support of Frederick the Wise (the Duke of Saxony) against Luther, he realized as he traveled through Germany that public opinion was so strongly in favor of Luther that even if he had an army at his command, he could not take Luther to Rome. The people did not stand up for Luther (or Jesus) just because he was a saint, a great preacher, or a theologian, but because they could see that Luther's stand against the Roman exploitation was in their own interest.

Service is the legitimate means of acquiring the power to lead. Service done with prophetic compassion makes one a shepherd, the de facto leader of the community.

Jesus asked Peter to take care of his sheep. The Holy Spirit empowered Peter for that service. Paul made it clear in 1 Corinthians 12 that the power and gifts of the Holy Spirit are for service to others. "There are different kinds of service," he said, "but the same God. . . . To each one the manifestation of the Spirit is given for the common good" (vv. 5–7). That is why love—the fruit of the Spirit—is the greatest power we must seek (1 Cor. 13).

Prayer: The Source of Power

The Holy Spirit empowers us for prophetic, compassionate evangelism in response to prayer. The power comes from prayer because prayer puts us in touch with God.

In the Garden of Gethsemane, just before his arrest, Jesus asked his disciples to pray so that they might have the power to withstand opposition. They did not pray; thus they fled before the threat of persecution. Before his ascension, Jesus again asked his disciples to pray. This time they did, and they were filled with the Holy Spirit and with power to serve, to suffer, and to turn the world upside down (i.e., reform) with their prophetic preaching.

A theology of power has to begin with God, who is all-powerful. When Zerubbabel, Joshua the high priest, Ezra, and

Nehemiah faced the task of restoration and rebuilding, they were told by God, "Not by might nor by power, but by my Spirit" the great mountain shall be removed (Zech. 4:6). Nehemiah had to build with a sword in his hand, but the Bible makes it clear that his faith rested not in the power of the sword but in God. If there was ever a man of prayer, he was one. His power for great reforms came from prayer.

Dependence on God and the use of service, suffering, the sword, or wise strategies are not mutually exclusive. It is like taking medicine and praying for healing. Of course, some people do not even take medicines because they find it inconsistent with faith.

My question to them is: "Why do you pick up a wrench or a screwdriver to repair your bicycle when it breaks? Don't you believe that God can fix it? Why don't you just pray?"

They inevitably reply, "Because a bicycle is a machine."

But the body is also a machine, as is the universe. Just as a man can work on a bicycle, so can man work on the human body and in the physical universe. Because man is made in God's image, his actions have significance. We must not belittle man's God-given abilities and significance. But we must also remember that just as a machine is open to human intervention, so is it open to divine intervention. God can and does work in the universe, in a human body, and in a machine like a bicycle. Four times I have seen a scooter and a car run on prayer!

Because the universe is open to God's intervention, prayer has meaning and significance. Both prayer and wise strategies are necessary for world-transforming witness. Man forgets prayer only at his own peril.

One night the chief of a village, Karri, came to our community to ask if any of us knew sorcery. A snake had bitten a Brahmin woman, Ramkali. The sorcerers had been called and were casting spells when Ramkali became unconscious. Then the government doctor who was there gave her intravenous glucose, because he didn't have antivenin. Her condition became more critical. Now, as she was dying, her friends were running around looking for witch doctors.

I said to the chief, "We don't know sorcery, but we can pray."

He said, "Please come and at least pray."

One Muslim seeker and three of us Christians went to pray. We knelt around Ramkali's bed. Over fifty people, including the doctor, watched us as we prayed for this virtually dead woman. In less than ten minutes, as we opened our eyes, she did too! On the third day she walked to our home three miles away to thank us and the living God who answers prayers.

I know that prayer is a Christian's source of power because I have seen the power of prayer in our struggle with the government, police, politicians, power structures of villages, gangs, and bandits. For months the highest police officer of Chattarpur had been threatening to kill me. For at least one year a politician of the ruling party and another of the Communist party schemed ways to murder me. But through the power of prayer, we were able to withstand all this. We have the power of prayer in bringing hardened people to repentance and in moving believers to share their wealth with the needy at great personal cost.

I believe in human planning, strategy, and action because human beings are significant. We affect not only machines but society and history as well. But I also believe in prayer because God is almighty. He acts in the mechanical universe as well as in the hearts of believers and unbelievers. I believe in prayer because God is the author and finisher of history; therefore prayer for reformation, prayer for change in society, has meaning. Some of the greatest reforms in biblical history came when men like Daniel and Nehemiah prayed (see Dan. 9 and Neh. 1).

Sometimes prayer is the only solution when we are faced with natural, social, or spiritual problems that are beyond human wisdom and strength, because prayer releases the power of God. It is necessary that we stand in the supernatural power of the Holy Spirit, because the battle between good and evil ultimately is supernatural. Modern man ignores the diabolic, supernatural dimensions of evil and is therefore unable to understand or to deal with the social dimensions of evil.

Praying is trusting God. The Bible says that faith is what ultimately overcomes the world (1 John 5:5). Faith is power because it produces hope and generates action in a stagnant society. Faith is power because it produces patience and perseverance. Faith is power because it gives staying ability in the midst of opposition—the ability to stand, to serve, to fight, to suffer, to die, and to overcome. Supremely, trusting or praying releases power because our dependence on God moves him to act.

The Holy Spirit came upon the disciples when a hundred and twenty of them knit their hearts together in prayer. Though they were many, by sharing one Spirit they became "one body"—a church.

TWELVE

The Church

The Pillar of Truth

The seeds of false ideas grow into unjust, harmful social relationships and produce suffering. The Lord Jesus and his Spirit created the church as a means of nurturing people into liberating truths that promote loving relationships. The apostle Paul said that the church was intended to be a pillar and foundation of truth (1 Tim. 3:15). That makes church a threat to those who have vested interests in false and oppressive ideas.

Chronic, intergenerational poverty is often a product of oppressive, exploitative economic relations. The Proverbs say, "A poor man's field may produce abundant food, but injustice sweeps it away" (13:23). The church was meant to be an antidote to poverty because it was meant to be a community bound by self-sacrificing love. Evangelism that does not take church planting seriously usually springs from a theology that does not take the social dimensions of sin and salvation seriously.

The Mission of Christ and the Necessity of the Church

Was it necessary for Jesus and his Spirit to organize the disciples into a church? To answer this we will look at three things: Jesus' perception of himself, his perception of people, and his conception of the church.

First, Jesus proved he was the Messiah by pointing to his mission to the weak and the poor. When John the Baptist sent his disciples to find out whether Jesus was indeed the Christ, the Lord responded by exhibiting his compassion for the needy, saying, "Go back and report to John what you have seen and heard: The blind receive sight, the lame walk, those who have leprosy are cured, the deaf hear, the dead are raised, and the good news is preached to the poor" (Luke 7:22). According to Luke, when Jesus first claimed to be the Messiah, he supported this claim with a prophecy of Isaiah:

> The Spirit of the Lord is on me,
>   because he has anointed me
>   to preach good news to the poor.
> He has sent me to proclaim freedom for the prisoners
>   and recovery of sight for the blind,
> to release the oppressed,
>   to proclaim the year of the Lord's favor. (Luke 4:18–19)

Second, Jesus did not see people merely as souls to be saved from hell. He saw them as sheep without a shepherd, "harassed and helpless" (Matt. 9:36); as sheep in need of deliverance from the wolves (Matt. 10:16); as oppressed men, "weary and burdened," who needed rest, or *shalom* (Matt. 11:28). Jesus' claim to kingship rested on the fact that he was the "ruler who [would] be the shepherd of . . . Israel" (Matt. 2:6).

Third, Jesus said that he was sent "to the lost sheep of Israel" (Matt. 15:24), to gather them into the fold like the good shepherd who leaves the ninety-nine and goes after the one sheep that is lost (Matt. 18:12–14). He sent out his disciples to do the same, to work as under-shepherds, to gather the harassed sheep into an *ecclesia*, the church. "As the Father has sent me," said Jesus, "I am sending you" (John 20:21). Why was he sending them? To take care of the sheep, who were (and are) at the mercy of wolves. "Feed my lambs," he gently pleaded with Simon Peter. "Take care of my sheep. ... Feed my sheep" (John 21:15–17).

The Church as a Power Structure

To many observers the church appears as nothing more than a harmless worshiping, witnessing, and serving community. If that were so, would the early church have invited the persecution it did? Would it have needed the supernatural power that we discussed in the previous chapter? Why did Jesus use the word *ecclesia* to describe the community he was intending to create? In his study *New Testament Words*, William Barclay describes the picture Jesus would have conjured up in the minds of his audience by using the word *church*:

> The *ecclesia* was the convened assembly of the people (in Greek City States). It consisted of all the citizens of the city who had not lost their civic rights. Apart from the fact that its decisions must conform to the laws of the State, its powers were to all intents and purposes unlimited. It elected and dismissed magistrates and directed the policy of the city. It declared wars, made peace, contracted treaties and arranged alliances. It elected generals and other military officers. It assigned troops to different campaigns and dispatched them from the city. It was ultimately responsible for the conduct of all military operations. It raised and allocated funds. Two things are interesting to note: first, all its meetings began with prayer and a sacrifice. Second, it was a true democracy. Its two great watchwords were "equality" (*isonomia*) and "freedom" (*eleutheria*). It was an assembly where everyone had an equal right and an equal duty to take part.[1]

1. William Barclay, *New Testament Words* (London: SCM Press, 1964), 68–69.

Barclay tells us that *ecclesia* described a power structure. Did Jesus understand "church" in that way?

In the very first usage of the word *ecclesia*, Jesus envisaged a community in conflict. He said to Simon, "And I tell you that you are Peter, and on this rock I will build my church, and the gates of Hades will not overcome it" (Matt. 16:18). Jesus had no doubt that just as he was going to the cross, his church was going to be a social structure in conflict with the forces of death. Why? Because in an oppressive society, if a group stands up to take care of the lambs, it automatically stands up against the wolves. The wolves are bound to fight the good shepherd. They have to do their best to destroy the ecclesia if the ecclesia dares to protect the sheep.

The church was not meant to be an army that attacks evil, oppressive social structures. It was to be a community that cares for the harassed and helpless sheep. But, unlike many Christians, Christ had no romantic vision of peaceful service. He knew that one couldn't serve the sheep realistically without infuriating the vested interests: the wolves. Therefore, because conflict was inevitable, the church had to be a powerful structure, a community that could withstand the very forces of Hades itself. It had to be a community that had the power to take up its cross, to follow its master.

The Church as the Antidote to Social Evils

Perhaps the themes of this chapter are best summed up in Ezekiel 34, which deals with the following facts:

1. Poverty is a product of unjust relation. At the time of Ezekiel's writing, poverty in Judah was a product of unjust economic relationships:

The word of the LORD came to me: "Son of man, prophesy against the shepherds of Israel; prophesy and say to them:

'This is what the Sovereign LORD says: Woe to the shepherds of Israel who only take care of themselves! Should not shepherds take care of the flock? You eat the curds, clothe yourselves with the wool and slaughter the choice animals, but you do not take care of the flock. You have not strengthened the weak or healed the sick or bound up the injured. You have not brought back the strays or searched for the lost. You have ruled them harshly and brutally. . . .

"'As for you, my flock, this is what the Sovereign LORD says: I will judge between one sheep and another, and between rams and goats. Is it not enough for you to feed on the good pasture? Must you also trample the rest of your pasture with your feet? Is it not enough for you to drink clear water? Must you also muddy the rest with your feet? Must my flock feed on what you have trampled and drink what you have muddied with your feet?

"'Therefore this is what the Sovereign LORD says to them: See, I myself will judge between the fat sheep and the lean sheep.'" (Ezek. 34:1–4; 17–20).

2. The ingathering of sheep is an answer to poverty. The shepherding role of the Messiah was seen in his care for the weak and the hungry sheep:

"'For this is what the Sovereign LORD says: I myself will search for my sheep and look after them. As a shepherd looks after his scattered flock when he is with them, so will I look after my sheep. I will rescue them from all the places where they were scattered. . . . I myself will tend my sheep and have them lie down, declares the Sovereign LORD.'" (Ezek. 34:11–12, 15)

3. The kingship of Christ is defined as "shepherd-hood." One of the Messiah's primary answers to socioeconomic problems was to gather the harassed sheep into his flock:

"'I myself will tend my sheep and have them lie down, declares the Sovereign LORD. I will search for the lost and bring back the strays. I will bind up the injured and strengthen the weak, but the sleek and the strong I will destroy. I will shepherd the flock with justice. . . . I will place over them one shepherd, my servant David, and he will tend them; he will tend them and be their shepherd. I the LORD will be their God, and my servant David will be prince among them. . . .

"'I will provide for them a land renowned for its crops, and they will no longer be victims of famine in the land or bear the scorn of the nations. Then they will know that I, the LORD their God, am with them and that they, the house of Israel, are my people. . . . You my sheep, the sheep of my pasture, are people, and I am your God.'" (Ezek. 34:15–16, 23–24, 29–31)

Contemporary Image of the Church

Looking at much of the contemporary church, one can be justi-fied in dismissing the view that the church is the antidote to pov-erty. Shamefully, we must confess that very often the institutional church has been the cause or means of perpetuating injustice and poverty. One ecumenical theologian, who is on the payroll of a church-related institution and is concerned about poverty, argued in a conference that the greatest sacrifice the church can make for the poor is to sacrifice itself, that is, get out of existence! I have no quarrel with such theologians, because they are talking about the existing image and reality of a decadent part of the church.

The problem with these theologians begins when they seem to dismiss the very concept of church as irrelevant to the struggle against injustice and for the weak. At that point it seems that the economists understand the need for human organization to com-bat poverty better than the theologians. For example, in his book *Poverty and Development* C. T. Kurien, a leftist economist, says that development in India is possible only through a conscious and deliberate mass movement:

> A mass movement can be effected only through organizing for action and through various forms of new institutions. . . . Such institutions also serve as new centers of power however limited their density may be to begin with. What is significant is that they form a new basis of power—the power of an informed and organized people as contrasted with property power, for instance. The building up of such a new power base is necessary to bring about a separation between property power and political power which so often tend to merge.[2]

Many people fail to see the relevance of the church in the question of social evils such as chronic poverty because progress is judged in terms such as *quantity of production*. Therefore the problem of poverty is seen as a problem of technology: lack of technical know-how, tools, capital, or material resources. Knowledge, tools, and resources are indeed important, but their lack is not the basic problem—certainly not in rural India. A Western agriculturist who worked for years in India trying to fight poverty at the grass-roots level with appropriate technology, ultimately gave up in despair. He said to me, "If the problems were technological, we could have solved them, because we have all the technical answers. But the problem is different. My training and background do not enable me even to understand the problem of poverty in India."

One of the basic causes of poverty is the concentration of political power in the hands of those who are also economically and socially powerful. Hinduism gives religious sanction to this concentration of power, which is almost consistently used for oppression. The top leadership of the nation also uses (and

2. C. T. Kurien, *Poverty and Development* (Madras: CLS, 1974), 24.

thereby reinforces) this hold on the existing power structures for gathering votes. Much of the church development also works to strengthen the existing leadership,[3] but few consciously stand up to empower the oppressed—though that is precisely what Jesus did.

In the book of Acts we see that Jerusalem, like any other pilgrim center, attracted the poor, orphans, widows, beggars, priests, and others. These poor were attracted to the church because it was a center of power that cared for the weak, in contrast to the Jewish temple. Once they came into the church, they were no longer poor, because the believers shared their wealth with each other very liberally. "There were no needy persons among them," the New Testament says. "For from time to time those who owned lands or houses sold them, brought the money from the sales and put it at the apostles' feet, and it was distributed to anyone as he had need" (Acts 4:34–35).

This care for the powerless did not come about only after Pentecost. It was part of the ministry of Christ's ecclesia during his life. It was not just the twelve apostles whose needs were met by the common purse of Christ's community. When blind beggars, such as the ones at Jericho, received their sight, the Gospels say that "they received their sight and followed" Jesus (Matt. 20:34). The beggars no longer begged but lived as a part of the community of disciples.

When Jesus called disciples to follow him, he offered to look after their material needs too. They did not need to go back to their jobs, such as fishing. Even the rich young ruler was asked to give away all his wealth to the poor and follow Jesus (Luke 18:22), meaning that for his needs he must trust Jesus and his community, not his own material resources. The incident at the Lord's Supper makes it clear that care for the poor was a routine function of Christ's community. When Jesus told Judas, "What

3. For years World Vision, for example, insisted on working through the "existing power structures."

you are about to do, do quickly," his disciples thought that "since Judas had charge of the money, . . . Jesus was telling him . . . to give something to the poor" (John 13:27–29). Earlier, when Mary anointed Jesus' feet with expensive perfume, Judas asked, "Why wasn't this perfume sold and the money given to the poor?" (John 12:5).

This care of the poor continued after Christ's ascension. Paul says that the church leadership had specifically asked him to take care of the poor, which he was doing anyway (Gal. 2:10). The church was a power structure intended to care for the powerless. Jesus compared the church to a small seed that grows into a mighty tree, "so that the birds of the air come and perch in its branches" (Matt. 13:32).

In contrast to the Jewish Establishment, where political and economic power had become concentrated in the same hands, the New Testament church was a counterbalancing center of power. C. T. Kurien said that India needed "a new basis of power—the power of an informed and organized people as contrasted with property power."[4] To build up an ecclesia in poor societies, such as an Indian village where the present social organization (caste) favors the powerful, is to build up a new power base, which automatically threatens the concentration of political and economic power. However, it is important for us not to be carried away by the Marxist presuppositions of writers such as Mr. Kurien. The church of Jesus Christ must welcome the rich as much as the poor. Before the wealth can be distributed, it has to be created. Those who create wealth and share it with others will have their reward in heaven (Matt. 19:21).

The evangelists who go out preaching the good news, in obedience to their Lord, are often unaware of the social implications of conversion and church planting. Their opponents, however, understand much better the threat that the church represents, which is why they oppose evangelism and church planting. Today

4. C. T. Kurien, *Poverty and Development* (Madras: CLS, 1974), 24.

in India, the most serious opposition to evangelism, conversion, and church planting comes from those Hindu organizations such as the Rashtriya Swayamsevak Sangh (RSS) and Vishwa Hindu Parishad (VHP), which are committed to reestablishing political control of the nation in the hands of the high-caste Hindus—those who already have the economic and social power. These organizations understand the political threat a growing church represents. The RSS is self-consciously built on the teachings of the German thinkers who created Nazism. These thinkers understood well the threat Christianity presents to every ideology of domination of some by the others. For example, Friedrich Nietzsche, one of the most influential German thinkers, wrote in *Twilight of the Idols*: "Christianity, rooted in Judaism and only understandable as having grown from this soil, represents the *counter-movement* to any morality of breeding, of pedigree, of privilege: it is the *anti-Aryan* religion *par excellence*."[5]

To appreciate the breadth of Jesus' vision of ecclesia, it will be helpful to look afresh at his statement in Matthew 16:18, "I tell you that you are Peter, and on this rock I will build my church, and the gates of Hades will not overcome it."

Church: a community in conflict with the forces of death

We have already noticed that in this statement Jesus implied that the church will be a community in conflict with the forces of death because it will be a channel of life to the little lambs, which are harassed and helpless without a shepherd.

Church: a community of servants, not a collection of heroes

The disciples dreamed of the day when satanic political institutions would be overthrown and they would sit on the thrones next to Jesus. They had joined Christ for a great revolution. Therefore, when some mothers brought their little children to Jesus so

5. Friedrich Nietzsche, *Twilight of the Idols*, trans. Duncan Large (Oxford and New York: Oxford University Press, 1998), 35. (Italics in original.)

that he might bless them, the disciples got upset. They probably said, "Why do you make our Master weary by these petty petitions of yours? Don't you see the great mission for which we need to conserve our energies?"

Jesus rebuked the disciples. "Let the little children come to me," he said, "for the kingdom of heaven belongs to such as these" (Matt. 19:14). The great people are already having a good time in the kingdom of Satan; they don't need the kingdom of God. If the kingdom of God means nothing for these little ones, it means nothing at all.

After Peter's confession of Jesus as the Messiah in Matthew 16:16, Jesus began to teach his disciples "that he must go to Jerusalem and suffer many things at the hands of the elders, chief priests and teachers of the law, and that he must be killed" (Matt. 16:21). This upset Peter so much that he began to rebuke Jesus.

Peter may have said, "What do you mean you are going to die? Are we fools that we have left our wives and work to follow you, and you want to end up on a cross? Our families have allowed us to follow you because one day they expect to see us on the throne with you. You can't desert us like that."

Jesus responded to Peter with a severe rebuke: "Get behind me, Satan!" (16:23).

Just because Peter acknowledged Jesus as king, he did not qualify to become a hero in Christ's ecclesia. He was called to become a servant, a shepherd to the helpless sheep, and to lay down his life for the lambs. Jesus said, "If anyone would come after me, he must deny himself and take up his cross and follow me. For whoever wants to save his life will lose it, but whoever loses his life for me will find it" (16:24–25).

Jesus implied that the structure which can withstand the forces of death will not be a collection of heroes but a community of love, an ecclesia, where leaders are willing to lay down their lives for one another. That was Christ's vision of the church.

The New Testament writers devote much space in their epistles to exhort us to be a church, a body, a temple in which God can dwell through his Spirit, because there is a context of love and holiness which results in our mutual submission to one another.

Church: a community built on a victorious faith

"On this rock," said Jesus, "I will build my church. . . . I will give you the keys of the kingdom of heaven; whatever you bind on earth will be bound in heaven, and whatever you loose on earth, will be loosed in heaven" (Matt. 16:18–19).

Chairman Mao taught that political power comes from the barrel of a gun. Jesus said to Peter that his knowledge and faith that Jesus is "the Christ, the Son of the living God" were the rock upon which Christ's victorious ecclesia would be built.

While the angel was describing to Daniel the brutal power of the kingdom of Satan, he conceded that strength of arms would not be able to withstand the power of wickedness. "But," the angel says, "the people that know their God shall be strong, and do exploits" (Dan. 11:32 ASV)—or, as the New International Version puts it, "The people who know their God will firmly resist him [the evil ruler]."

The apostle John says, "This is the victory that has overcome the world, even our faith. Who is it that overcomes the world? Only he who believes that Jesus is the Son of God" (1 John 5:4–5). The church is a community that cares for the weak, but it is built on a victorious faith in a supernatural Messiah. The battle for social reform requires a transcendental faith.

Church: a dwelling place of God

Our world is filled with evil because it has become the kingdom of Satan. Jesus is changing the world by establishing the church as the house of God in the midst of the Satan's kingdom. The church is God's new community in a fallen world, a channel of life and liberty. It is described as God's "temple," "household," "bride," and "body," of which Christ is the head. It is created to be the showpiece of God's work of redemption, through which the manifold wisdom of God is exhibited to the rulers and authorities in the natural and the supernatural realms (Eph. 3:10).

Church: the tangible evidence of the hope of the new kingdom

Christ's promise to Peter that upon the truth that Peter confessed he would build his church, "and the gates of Hades will not overcome it" (Matt. 16:18), implies that the church is the key to the hope of the new kingdom. It is to be the tangible evidence that Jesus has ushered in a new kingdom; a new community built on truth; a community that cares for others with self-sacrificing love; a community which overcomes sinful, alienating social divides, such as Jews versus Gentiles, masters versus slaves, men versus women.

The apostle Paul says that the church is

> the mystery of Christ, which was not made known to men in other generations as it has now been revealed by the Spirit to God's holy apostles and prophets. This mystery is that through the gospel the Gentiles are heirs together with Israel, members together of one body, and sharers together in the promise in Christ Jesus. (Eph. 3:4–6)

Paul was excited about the church, the great mystery of God, because the church is the "unsearchable riches of Christ . . . in God" (Eph. 3:8–9).

In a caste-ridden country such as India, the church can become a matter of excitement if it is seen to be uniting "untouchables" and the "high caste" into one body. The same applies to other countries where human beings are sharply divided according to race, color, economic status, gender, etc. These alienations are the results of sin, features of the kingdom of Satan. Salvation includes becoming one body by overcoming the sin that separates.

An Unfinished Story

In 1980, as a result of the work of our service, three small worshiping congregations had sprung up, consisting exclusively of non-Christians who had put their trust in Christ. In one village, five families, led by my father, used to meet for worship. Dhanni, a semiliterate man who came to Christ from an untouchable background, was one of them. When he was a child, a high-caste Hindu had forcibly taken his family land. In 1974, while Dhanni was still a Hindu, he started a court case against the man who had taken his land by force. The case did not go far, because no one in the village was willing to come forward as a witness in support of Dhanni. This was because twenty-five families had grabbed the little plots that had been given to over a hundred families. The twenty-five families were more powerful than the hundred families, so the poor could not even give witness for one another.

The church was a new factor in that oppressive situation. Dhanni shared his problem with other Christians, and they prayed about it. They felt that the case should be reopened. After some time, the church discovered that legally the land still belonged to Dhanni; he just needed the courage to cultivate it. The prayer and moral support of the little church gave him the courage to venture out and repossess his land. Another believer, Sajju, from the same village offered to plow the land for Dhanni with our tractor. The high-caste man's family stood by with their axes, abusing us and threatening to murder Sajju. However, because they feared that the other church members would bear witness in court, they did not take any step.

The next day they said, "You have plowed the land, but we will sow it." That night Sajju took the tractor and sowed the field himself. The high-caste Hindus were infuriated.

They called a meeting of the high-castes from nearly thirty villages to discuss what to do with these Christians. The high-caste man who had grabbed Dhanni's land argued convincingly that it was not a matter of one man and his land but of thousands of acres belonging to thousands of low-castes. He said, "If one of these untouchables succeeded in getting his land back with the help of the Christians, you can be sure that thousands of them will become Christians and we shall lose our land." Those who participated in the meeting vowed with *Ganga Jal* (water of the river Ganges) that they would chase the Christians away from their areas. They understood the threat that the church posed, merely by virtue of its commitment to stand with one of its weak members.

My father was threatened, "You tell your son not to meddle in our affairs, otherwise the consequences for you will be bad." We prayed and felt that it was worth the consequences. If we failed, we failed. But if we succeeded, then it could open up floodgates of justice for thousands of oppressed and thousands of acres of land.

My wife and I were leaving for a lectures-cum-study trip to Europe for three months. The night before we left, three men entered my father's farmhouse. They beat up him and my step-mother, tied them up, and looted the house. Then one of them threatened to gouge out my father's eyes with a knife. He didn't do so because my father promised to empty out his bank account the following day and give them his life's savings.

My father came to see us in the morning. He was worried that the men might have come to us after leaving them. He did not say a word about the incident, but as we left for the airport he excused himself and went to the bank to draw out the money.

My father had to flee from the village and take temporary shelter in the city. He was shattered. Two days later, two Hindu neighbors of Sajju were murdered over a land dispute. This shook Sajju. Then Dhanni was threatened with murder. A little later my aunt and her husband were brutally murdered in their own home in Chattarpur, where my father was staying. This last epi-sode apparently did not have anything to do with our struggle, but the cumulative impact of it all was that the little church was thoroughly demoralized. Under pressure, Dhanni agreed to "sell" the land to the high-caste man. The high-caste man's illegal pos-session was legalized for a paltry sum of three hundred rupees.

My father took a loan from our organization and helped Dhanni buy another plot of land in the same village. It was a witness to the church's care and commitment to the oppressed, even though it was also an admission of powerlessness and fail-ure. Dhanni is still there cultivating. For the moment the church stands disintegrated. It is a reminder of Moses' abortive attempt in Egypt to free the Israelites. By himself Moses was too weak to stand against the forces of Hades; he was forced to flee. But that was not the end of the story. Moses met with God. He was transformed into a prophet, and he returned and liberated the Jews in the power of God.

The above story has not ended yet. Dhanni has land of his own, with an irrigation well. The bank financed him to buy an electric pump. He worked hard but could not feed his family by farming alone. Although his girls were getting free education in a Christian boarding school, he couldn't pay for their travel from home to school, so he withdrew them from the school. He sold firewood to make a little extra money, but he was still forced to borrow just to eat.

However, the high-caste man who had grabbed Dhanni's land and had my father nearly killed became our friend. A couple of years later he spent a whole day in one of our spiritual retreats with Dhanni and Sajju, listening to the gospel. He knows that even though we disapprove of what he did, we love him and are concerned about the fact that he, too, is enslaved and exploited by the religio-politico-economic system in which he lives. He knows we understand that he, too, is not making ends meet and is therefore forced to exploit his neighbors, laborers, cattle, land, forest, and his own children. He now knows that the Christians are as much concerned for his salvation as for Dhanni's. Everyone in the area knows that even though the Christian community is small and physically powerless, it is a community that possesses life- and culture-transforming beliefs and spirit.

I do not know how that story will end, but these experiences contributed to my understanding that the problems of poverty, where they are rooted *not* in a lack of resources and skills but in unjust relationships, are better dealt with by God's NGO (nongovernmental organization) than by secular NGOs. The church is an NGO that God has built. While our secular NGOs bring people together for brief periods, for specific programs, God's NGO brings people together in a lifelong relationship. In a church, people do not come together because of economic interests. They come because they know that they are sinners and need to get right with God and with one another. They come into God's church because they are disappointed with men and, therefore, want to put their hope in God.

Having looked at our failure, let's turn our gaze upon the hope that God offers.

THIRTEEN

Hope

He's Making All Things New

The Christians of William Carey's generation[1] believed that the darkness would not overcome the light (John 1:5) and that a little leaven of the gospel would transform the whole dough (Matt. 13:33). Their hope inspired them to resist evils. Today much of the church suffers from an eschatological paralysis: it believes that even though we keep launching new projects to spread the light, the darkness will keep growing, turning the world from bad to worse. This pessimism robs us of much of the motivation to challenge evils around us.

The terrible "success" of Fascism, Nazism, and Communism in the twentieth century, plus two world wars, destroyed the secular hope for the future of mankind as it is. As a result the Western church began to read the Scriptures with the pessimistic outlook of its culture and baptized it with biblical verses and

1. See Vishal and Ruth Mangalwadi, *The Legacy of William Carey: A Model for Transforming a Culture* (Wheaton, Ill.: Crossway Books, 1999).

dispensational theology. It looked forward to the destruction of "The Late Great Planet Earth" instead of seeking to reform it.

Biblical Christians of the earlier era had hope for man and his planet because they believed that, far from abandoning this world, God, who is faithful to his word and his creation, had made a covenant with this planet. The eternal, infinite God had personally entered the finite, space-time world of fallen man with his salvation. The kingdom of God had broken into the kingdoms of this world, and the gates of Hades would not overcome it (Matt. 16:18). For them Christian hope was not only beyond history, but also within it.

Does the Bible give a valid basis for hope in history?

A Realist's Case Against Hope

If you were to visit Bundelkhand, the area where I served, some of my critics would tell you, "If Vishal is starting a project, it is bound to fail." There is a good case for their assessment. My record of many failures is a very real reason for me to be pessimistic about my future efforts. Various factors are responsible for my failures, and some of them lie outside my control. But without question, some of the causes lie in my own limitations, ignorance, and sinfulness. So, when my finiteness, foolishness, and sinfulness have been conclusively established, how can I reasonably hope that my efforts or the efforts of other finite and sinful men will create a better future in the kingdom of Satan?

Some other critics would tell you that "Vishal is a good fellow, and reasonably capable, but he has not been able to find good coworkers. Everyone he trusts lets him down. So his rate of success is very little compared to his investment and efforts." Correct again! Any number of resourceful and gifted people can testify that many or all of their efforts have come to nothing because of the personal limitations or selfishness of their colleagues and successors. Given the quality of local manpower that even the Red Cross or World Vision has to work with, can anyone realistically have any hope for the future of chronically poor, warring cultures? "None whatsoever" is the assessment of some who have observed our efforts.

Other critics of mine, who are more sympathetic, would say to you, "The soil here is very bad; you can't do anything with it." Meaning: "The people you are seeking to serve have themselves become so bad that they will use their benefactors as long as they can, and then they will abuse them. They will never support them at personal cost. And because benefactors cannot achieve much without the active, sacrificial support of the local people, there is no hope." True again! Some soils produce much fruit, others nothing. The worst soils demand the best efforts and yet tend to give you only disappointments. The cynics are not necessarily those who have not tried, but often those who have tried hard and failed.

My well-wishers in the area may say to you, "Vishal has done here what no one else has. But the powers that rule this area have a deeply entrenched vested interest in the status quo. They are cruel and well armed. They will not allow a center of power to emerge in their territory that changes the system to the advantage of 'the weary and the heavy-laden.' The chief minister of the state himself depends on these powers and principalities. Therefore, in some of the villages the government itself has not been able to open schools for forty years, as education will undermine the present power equations. In many villages where schools have opened, the teachers survive only because they agree not to educate the children from low-caste families. So, if the government can do nothing, what can these unarmed social workers achieve? They have burned down Vishal's community once, and if he becomes a threat to the existing power structures, they will not hesitate in eliminating him." Indeed, what hope can one have for a society where wickedness rules?

Even if I were not as foolish and sinful as I am; if my coworkers were better than I in every respect; if the people I am seeking to serve were fearless, self-sacrificing participants in my efforts;

and if the power structures at local, state, and national levels were supportive of actions for development—shall I succeed? Shall I then have a basis for being an optimist? Wouldn't an earthquake, a famine, an epidemic, a flood, a war, climate change, or a comet wipe away all that I create?

Viewed from the macro level, how can I have any confidence that the coming decades will not produce a dictator or a nuclear war? Wouldn't all our labors then be in vain? Isn't it foolish to be optimistic about the future, given the track record of mankind in recent and past history? Add to this list the new man-made environmental hazards from acid rain and deforestation (destroying the lungs of the world) to chlorofluorocarbons (CFCs) and the thinning of the ozone layer in the stratosphere (making organic life on this planet vulnerable to the sun's harmful ultraviolet radiation, the so-called greenhouse effect), and you have an almost irrefutable case against hope.

The Christian Case for Hope

Peter had every right to be cynical that morning. He had labored the whole night and caught no fish. He was irritated and tired. He wanted to go home and sleep, if possible without being seen by his family, who were waiting for the fish so that one member could start cooking the day's meal while another went to sell the catch. But Jesus enters the scene of failure and asks Peter to lend him the boat to serve as a pulpit for a while. Peter consents, partly because it gives him an excuse to delay the moment of embarrassment, of reaching his expectant family without fish.

After his sermon, Jesus asks Peter to take the boat into the deep and cast his net just once more. Perhaps Jesus wanted to pay for his use of the boat, but he also wanted to show that in spite of Peter's own failures there was hope with God.

"What does this carpenter/preacher know about fishing?" would have been the natural response of Peter's professional pride. Peter knew that the fish in this area only came to the surface at night; they could not be caught in the daylight. Yet Peter says, "Master, I have worked hard the whole night. I have failed repeatedly and therefore I have lost hope, but I will obey you." In that single attempt of obedience Peter caught two boatloads of fish. Divine intervention gives success in a situation of repeated failure.

The crowd had been with Jesus for three days. Their food was gone, and they were hungry. Jesus asks his disciples to feed the five thousand men, plus women and children. "How?" they wonder. A little boy then surrenders his five loaves and two fish to Jesus. These are blessed and broken. Multitudes are satisfied because divine intervention multiplies the meager sacrifice that man can offer.

The master of the wedding banquet was panicking because the wine was finished; what a disgrace it would be to send the guests away unsatisfied! Jesus' mother pleads for his intervention, and she tells the servants to obey him. They fill the jars with water. Divine intervention transforms the water of human effort into a choice wine.

Jesus could have asked Peter to close his eyes for a moment and filled his boat with fish; he could have filled the disciples' baskets with a meal or the jars at Cana with wine—all miraculously materialized. But instead he required the physical efforts of casting the net again, a boy's sacrifice of his own food, the human obedience of filling the jars with water. In a situation of hopelessness it was human efforts of obedience and faith that were blessed with success. While it is right to look at my failures realistically, it is wrong not to trust and obey. With Jesus there is hope in spite of my failures.

Jesus knew he could not trust the crowd which said it trusted him (John 2:24). But could he entrust his mission to his disciples? Weren't they totally selfish in their ambitions to sit at his right and his left? Weren't they worldly in their values when they rebuked the mothers who brought their children to Jesus for his blessings? Weren't they carnal when they debated who was the greatest among them? Weren't they too weak in their flesh to stay awake with him in his moment of trial in Gethsemane, and too timid to confess him before a girl in the high priest's home? Didn't one of them betray him for thirty pieces of silver, while others fled to save their lives when he faced the cross? Indeed, the material Jesus had to work with inspired no hope. Yet he knew that these same, weak, good-for-nothing men could receive power when the Holy Spirit came upon them, and then they could turn the world upside down. Because God's power is available to weak men and women, there is hope.

Jesus knew well that the sheep would not lay down their lives for their shepherd. It is the shepherd's responsibility to lay down his life for their sake. He knew that the sheep would all be scattered when the shepherd was slain (Matt. 26:31). Woe unto us if we seek to serve the sheep in the hope of some returns from them. The Scriptures say, "Cursed is the one who trusts in man" (Jer. 17:5). How can the sheep, who cannot save themselves, save the shepherd? Yet, if the shepherd truly loves them and is willing to lay down his life for them, they will follow him (John 10:15). A grain of wheat will abide alone until it falls to the ground and dies. "But if it dies," Jesus said, "it produces many seeds." (John 12:24). So while it is true that one cannot have hope if he looks to his coworkers or the beneficiaries of his service, yet faith in God and willingness to obey unto death provide solid foundations for hope.

In our conflicts with powers and principalities, I have lost many coworkers because they looked too closely at the power of the wickedness they were up against. The strength and cruelty of the enemy overwhelmed them; some chose to join what appeared to them to be the stronger side, while others left the battlefield.

These coworkers have always reminded me of Saruman in J. R. R. Tolkien's trilogy, *The Lord of the Rings*. Saruman was a mighty wizard and knew that he should not look at the crystal ball–like *palantír*, but he did and saw the evil eye. When he saw the awesome power of wickedness, he became terrified and joined the evil side. In contrast, Gandalf, another wizard, refused to look at the stone. He kept his sight focused on the power of truth. The little hobbits have been my favorite heroes. Oblivious to the power of wickedness and the great perils that awaited them at every turn, their only concern was to obey their call; so they kept walking in the midst of fearsome dangers, protected by unseen forces. That is a beautiful picture of Christian warfare. A person who looks too closely at principalities and powers will be frightened. He will have no reasonable basis for hope, just as ten of the twelve spies that Moses sent to scout the Promised Land concluded that they could not possibly win. It takes a Joshua to conquer the Promised Land, because he looks not at the power of the enemy but at the commander of the armies of the Lord (see Josh. 5:13–15), and therefore is willing just to walk around the impenetrable walls of Jericho and by faith raise the shouts of praise and victory (Josh. 6).

The inevitability of death, whether through old age or nuclear holocaust, is the ultimate logical cause for pessimism. Death and decay make all human endeavors futile, even absurd. As we noted in chapter 7, fear of death is the ultimate weapon of the kingdom of Satan (Heb. 2:14–15). If you threaten the rule of wickedness in a social system, the maximum it can do to protect itself is to eliminate you. By his death and resurrection, however, Jesus has destroyed Satan's final weapon. He was not only raised from the dead but was exalted to the highest position of authority in the universe. "All authority," said Jesus, "in heaven and on earth has been given to me" (Matt. 28:18). His victory over death in history is the ultimate foundation of resurrection, the Bible says: God will destroy death, the last enemy (1 Cor. 15:26). And we will rise with him to eternal life. Not only human beings but also "the creation itself will be liberated from its bondage to decay and brought into the glorious freedom of the children of God" (Rom. 8:21).

Jesus, who rose bodily from the dead, who ascended into heaven and is exalted above all principalities and powers, is coming back to earth to judge and to rule. This gives the final basis for hope to a Christian. But it is tragic that in our age this doctrine of hope—the second coming of Christ—has been read with the pessimistic outlook of the secular world and turned into the final basis for "Christian" pessimism.

A Hindu views God as Creator (Brahma), Sustainer (Vishnu), and Destroyer (Shiva). But the Bible presents God as Creator, Savior, and Judge—not destroyer. A judge in the Bible is someone who punishes the wicked and establishes justice on earth. That is a message of hope for a person who chooses to suffer for the sake of righteousness in an age where wickedness is the way to prosper.

In Revelation chapter 6, John sees the souls of the martyrs who ask God, "How long . . . until you judge the inhabitants of the earth and avenge our blood?" (v. 10). Is it in vain, they ask, that we chose the path of righteousness, refused to compromise with evil, and lost our heads? Was it worth sacrificing our families, properties, pleasures, and lives for truth?

They are assured that it was all worth it because God will visit the earth in judgment. The Scriptures say that Jesus will return with the fire of judgment:

> The present heavens and earth are reserved for fire, being kept for the day of judgment and destruction of ungodly men. . . .
>
> But the day of the Lord will come like a thief. The heavens will disappear with a roar; the elements will be destroyed by fire, and the earth and everything in it will be laid bare [i.e., found]. . . .
>
> But in keeping with his promise we are looking forward to a new heaven and a new earth, the home of righteousness. (2 Pet. 3:7, 10, 13)

This passage, which is meant to give a warning to the wicked and hope to the saints, has been read by many Christians in such a way that it takes away all hope for the social and physical world in history.

We need to realize, first of all, that the background of Peter's teaching here is the prophecy of Malachi: "Then suddenly the Lord you are seeking will come to his temple. . . . But who can endure the day of his coming? Who can stand when he appears? For he will be like a refiner's fire or a launderer's soap. He will sit as a refiner and purifier of silver" (Mal. 3:1–3). The fire this scripture is talking about is a refiner's fire, which burns up the dross and purifies the silver. The fire is for "the destruction of the ungodly men" and "the elements." The word *elements* does not refer to the elements of physical earth, the building blocks of our planet. The Greek for *elements* that Peter uses is *stoicheia*, which is also used in Galatians 4:3 and 9 where it is translated as "basic principles of the world" and "those weak and miserable principles," and in Colossians 2:8 and 20 where it is translated as "basic principles of the world" which are "hollow and deceptive philosophy, which depends on human tradition" and enslaves people. The word *elements* thus refers not to the elements of modern chemistry but to the elements of Greek thought, which even has a connotation of stars and spirits of astrology that control men. Thus, according to Peter, the fire of the Lord will burn up the "ungodly men" and their enslaving religious principles that result in wickedness and hostility to God.

Some versions of the Bible do translate 2 Peter 3:10 as "the elements will be destroyed by fire, and the earth and everything in it will be *burned up*." Most modern English translations, however, correctly use the phrase "laid bare," or the more literal translation "found," instead of "burned up." This is correct because "found" is the literal meaning of the Greek word *heurethesetai* (from *heurisko*, "to find") used by Peter, according to the Sinaiticus and Vaticanus manuscripts of Greek Bible. The word *found* in the phrase "earth will be found" is the same word joyously used in the parable of the prodigal son—"my son was lost but is now found"—and in the parable which says that the kingdom of God is like a man who found a pearl of great value. So what Peter is saying in 2 Peter 3:10 is not that the earth will be burned up, but that the ungodly men and the basic teachings of the world that hold this world in captivity to sin and death will be burned up and the earth will be refined and restored to its original status.

This interpretation of 2 Peter 3:10 is the consistent way of interpreting the text in its context. In 2 Peter chapters 2 and 3, Peter relates the coming judgment with fire to the previous judgment with fire, which was not in the Hindu sense of destruction of the world but in the sense of judgment that purifies. And in concluding his teaching on this subject, Peter uses the word *heurethenai* (from the same root *heurisko*, "to find") in the sense of being refined and found: "Since everything will be destroyed in this way, what kind of people ought you to be? . . . Since you are looking forward to this [as a positive hope], make every effort to be *found* spotless, blameless and at peace with him" (2 Pet. 3:11, 14).

This positive view of the future is also taught by Paul in Romans 8:19–21:

> The creation waits in eager expectation for the sons of God to be revealed. For the creation was subjected to frustration, not by its own choice, but by the will of the one who subjected it, in hope that the creation itself will be liberated from its bondage to decay and brought into the glorious freedom of the children of God.

Peter does not contradict Paul's teachings in his second epistle, but confirms them:

> Bear in mind that our Lord's patience [in delaying judgment] means salvation, just as our dear brother Paul also wrote to you with the wisdom that God gave him. He writes the same way in all his letters, speaking in them of these matters. His letters contain some things that are hard to understand which ignorant and unstable people distort, as they do the other Scriptures, to their own destruction. (2 Pet. 3:15–16)

The translation of 2 Peter 3:10b as the earth will be "found" is also in harmony with 3:13, which says that we are looking forward to a new earth. The word "new" is not from the Greek *neos*, which means "brand new," but from *kainos*, which means "renewed." All that was created as "good" will be retained and restored.[2]

This earth will not disappear but will be given to the meek as their inheritance (Matt. 5:5). We shall not live in heaven forever; the mansions that Jesus is preparing in heaven (John 14:2) will come down to earth (Rev. 21:2). We shall not live as disembodied spirits; the dead shall rise again with glorified, nonperishable bodies (1 Cor. 15:51–55). And God himself will dwell on earth with his saints (John 14:23; Rev. 21:3). The physical creation will not disappear, but:

> The wilderness and dry land shall be glad,
>   the desert shall rejoice and blossom;
> like the crocus it shall blossom abundantly,
>   and rejoice with joy and singing. (Isa. 35:1–2 RSV)

Nor will the animals be absent in the new earth:

> The wolf shall dwell with the lamb,
>   and the leopard shall lie down with the kid,
> and the calf and the lion and the fatling together;
>   and a little child shall lead them. . . .
> The sucking child shall play over the hole of the asp,
>   and the weaned child shall put his hand on the adder's den.
> (Isa. 11:6, 8 RSV)

It is not the souls of the saints that will live with Jesus but the nations of this world:

---

2. For a detailed Bible study on this subject, please see Dr. Wim Rietkerk's book, *The Future Great Planet Earth* (Mussoorie, India: Nivedit Good Books, 1989).

He shall judge between the nations,
    and shall decide for many peoples;
and they shall beat their swords into plowshares,
    and their spears into pruning hooks;
nation shall not lift up sword against nation,
    neither shall they learn war any more. (Isa. 2:4 RSV)

On the other hand, in the new earth "the nations will walk by its [God's city's] light, and the kings of the earth will bring their splendor into it. On no day will its gates ever be shut, for there will be no night there. The glory and honor of the nations will be brought into it" (Rev. 21:24–26). The city of God will have a river of the water of life, and on each side of the river there will be the tree of life: "And the leaves of the tree are for the healing of the nations. No longer will there be any curse" (Rev. 22:2–3).

There is hope for this planet, including for its deserts and trees, because our Creator is faithful to his creation. He remembers his covenant not to destroy it:

Then God said to Noah and to his sons with him: "I now establish my covenant with you and with your descendants after you and with every living creature that was with you— the birds, the livestock and all the wild animals, all those that came out of the ark with you—every living creature on earth. I establish my covenant with you: Never again will all life be cut off by the waters of a flood; never again will there be a flood to destroy the earth." (Gen. 9:8–11)

The late Dr. Francis Schaeffer often used to say, "Man is lost, but he is not zero." Hinduism makes Self (God) the only reality, and both man (self) and the physical world zero, that is, *maya*, a projection of universal consciousness, like a dream that can be both created and destroyed. Much of modern scientific thought also reduces man to zero—a mere machine or animal.

The behavioral school of psychology denies that man is a person who makes real choices. Man, according to them, is no different from a machine, where everything is determined by external causes. Likewise, the view that the universe is not the work of a personal creator but a product of random chance and impersonal energy, makes the physical world zero. The Christian view, on the other hand, is that the physical universe and man are both works of a personal Creator who declared them to be good and is faithful to his creation. This fact puts great value on both man and the earth.

Man is not zero, but he is a sinner. The earth is not zero, but it is cursed because of man's sin. God is not a destroyer but a judge, who will punish sin and destroy all the consequences of sin because he seeks to redeem his creation. This is a message of great hope for the future of this earth. Not only the earth but, as Paul says, even believers will go through the refiner's fire:

> If any man builds on this foundation using gold, silver, costly stones, wood, hay or straw, his work will be shown for what it is, because the Day will bring it to light. It will be revealed with fire, and the fire will test the quality of each man's work. If what he has built survives, he will receive his reward. If it is burned up, he will suffer loss; he himself will be saved, but only as one escaping through the flames. (1 Cor. 3:12–15)

That the fire of God will consume all that is sinful in me and in the world is not a message of doom but a message of hope, which should make me work to build things that will last for eternity. The fact that our works of beauty and value will be refined and will last must cause us to thank God:

> We give thanks to you, Lord God Almighty,
>   the One who is and who was,
> because you have taken your great power

and have begun to reign.
The nations were angry;
    and your wrath has come.
The time has come for judging the dead,
    and for rewarding your servants the prophets
and your saints and those who reverence your name,
    both small and great—
and for destroying those who destroy the earth.
(Rev. 11:17–18)

The Significance of Human Action

The Christian's hope for a better future rests not on his own record of success but on Christ's victory in history over sin, Satan, and death, and on his promise to return as judge and ruler.

Does that make human action insignificant and irrelevant? No, because the purpose of God's saving action is to restore man's dominion on earth. The consequence of Adam's sin was that man who was meant to be the ruler became a slave on earth, not only to Satan and sin, but to nature as well. The earth began to grow thorns and thistles, and man had to eat of the sweat of his brow. In his struggle with nature, man ultimately lost, died, and became dust. Physical creation won over its ruler—man. Death became the master. But by defeating death and giving eternal life to those who repent and believe, God is restoring to man his authority over the world. Jesus did not come to take our souls to a nonmaterial, eternal heaven; he came to restore the kingdom to us. Saints do go to heaven when they die, but they wait there to return with Christ to rule on this earth; heaven is a waiting room until the great restoration. The purpose of salvation is to make us kings and priests or, as Peter puts it, the "royal priesthood" (1 Pet. 2:9). Man is given the task to rule. Although we lost the kingdom and became slaves, Jesus saves us from sin and gives us his authority to rule.

The elders and the heavenly creatures sing to the lamb of God:

> You are worthy to take the scroll
>   and to open its seals,
> because you were slain,
>   and with your blood you purchased men for God
>   from every tribe and language and people and nation.
> You have made them to be a kingdom and priests to serve
>   our God,
>   and they will reign on the earth. (Rev. 5:9–10)

Our future is not to worship God in heaven through eternity but to reign on earth. Paul says that we who were dead in trespasses and sins have already been raised to life and made to sit with Christ in a position of authority to do good works (Eph. 2:1–10). A believer, therefore, has the responsibility to exercise his authority in his situation. As my friend Chandrakant Shourie has pointed out: When Israel stood before the Red Sea, the angel of the Lord, who was going ahead of them, went behind them to protect them from Pharaoh's army. The angel in a pillar of fire would not let them go back, but in front of them was the sea. They were trapped. God did not ask the angel to divide the sea. Moses was asked to raise the rod over the sea. The rod of authority was placed in man's hand; man had to act in obedience and faith. It could be that Moses had to hold the rod over the sea the whole night, for it says: "Then Moses stretched out his hand over the sea, and all that night the LORD drove the sea back with a strong east wind and turned it into dry land. The waters were divided, and the Israelites went through the sea on dry ground" (Exod. 14:21–22).

God is the one who delivers us from slavery, but he has given the rod of authority to human beings. We have to act in obedience of faith if we want to see God's power to deliver.

Witnesses, Not Revolutionaries

If God is the deliverer, then man is primarily a witness to divine deliverance, not the savior himself. To be a witness, however, does not mean to live on a "spiritual" plane removed from the realities of daily life. To bear witness to the kingship of Christ is to pick a fight with the prince of death, who wishes to keep this world in bondage to decay.

After Jesus' resurrection the disciples asked him, "Lord, are you at this time going to restore the kingdom to Israel?" (Acts 1:6). They had seen themselves as failures: earlier they had promised to fight for Christ's kingdom; now they knew they couldn't. If the kingdom was going to come, it had to be the Lord's action: "Are *you* at this time going to restore the kingdom?" It is tragic that the Christians who take our future hope most seriously often choose to spend their time trying to figure out the time of Christ's arrival instead of seeking to become witnesses of his kingship.

Jesus replies, "It is not your job to sit back and try to figure out the timetable of my return. I know you do not have the power to challenge the kingdom of Satan. But you will receive power when the Holy Spirit has come upon you. Then you will have a role to play. You will go out with my authority to the uttermost parts of the world and bear transforming witness to my kingship."

PART IV

How Can I Participate?

Corruption and the Culture of the Cross

In most places and times it has been very difficult for the "small man" to get his case heard. The judge (and, doubtless, one or two of his underlings) has to be bribed. If you can't afford to "oil his palm" your case will never reach court. Our judges do not receive bribes. (We probably take this blessing too much for granted; it will not remain with us automatically).

—C. S. Lewis in *Reflections on the Psalms*

In the 1990s I preached the substance of this appendix in a worship service in Romania. I was amazed by the number of people who lined up to thank me. One man gestured toward his pregnant wife and said, "Our baby is due in a month. No Romanian doctor will deliver our baby without a hefty bribe. After hearing you, I think I should give my money not to a white-coat robber but to someone who may die without medical care. We should plan for a home delivery."

Later I was speaking at a youth rally and a church elder brought me a formal request from the elders board: "Please do not speak about corruption. This topic is too sensitive here. Just preach the gospel."

C. S. Lewis was right when he said that the post-Christian West takes bribery-free society for granted. It is an amazing blessing, a fruit of the gospel. That fruit will not last much longer, since the roots have been dug out. The Western church has already lost the battle against sexual corruption; it is completely unprepared for the battle against economic corruption. The Romanian evangelicals saw no connection between the gospel and freedom from bribery because the American evangelicals who discipled them thought that the gospel was about going to heaven and had nothing to do with God's kingdom on earth. They didn't know that it was the gospel that transformed America.

American evangelicalism has little to say about corruption because for a few generations now corruption has not been a common problem for average Americans. However, it is a major issue all over the world and will increasingly become a concern in the West because (a) the West is like a computer from which the anti-virus program, the gospel, has been uninstalled, and (b) the West is not merely *connected* to but increasingly *dependent* on a world that rewards corruption. Corruption is a highly infectious and debilitating disease. I hope my Western readers will bear with my illustrations drawn from my own (Indian) culture.

Corruption Is Curable

The gospel has cured corruption without dictatorial government, without Islamic or Marxist systems of instant and brutal justice.

The British rule began in Bengal in 1757 with Robert Clive and his council members taking huge bribes from the puppet he installed as the Nawab. The officers of the British East India Company had come to India to make money. Their leaders' bribe-taking encouraged the Company staff to turn their government into "a gang of public robbers" (Lord Macaulay). Later, when the

British Parliament put pressure on Clive and he tried to curb corruption, two hundred British officers ganged up to eliminate him. He was saved by the loyalty of his Indian soldiers. Once Clive's iron hand was removed, the British rule in India degenerated into what Macaulay called "the rule of an evil genie." British corruption destroyed Bengal's economy and became a factor in the death of several million people in the famine of 1769–70.

Amazingly, the cross of Jesus Christ did what an army general could not do: following the Wesleyan revival in England, the British evangelicals transformed their government in India. In 1947 independent India and Pakistan received clean, although not perfect, administrations.

What the gospel did for England and India once, it can do again.

The question is, why do most Christians in non-Protestant cultures participate in corruption without any sense of guilt? When the bride of Christ compromises with evils and begins to live as the mistress of Satan, it produces death. The call to stand up against corruption is simply a call to the church to be the bride of Christ, to bring forth the fruit of the Spirit, to give birth to a quality of holiness that is beyond natural human ability.

I. Corruption: Its Character and Consequences

Is the battle against corruption worth fighting? A devout evangelical leader in India told me he would neither take nor give a bribe for his personal convenience. "However," he said, "I run an orphanage. My children cannot get water unless I bribe. For their sake, I have no other option."

I replied, "The least I must say is that you are rewriting the Scriptures. Jesus said, 'I am the good shepherd. The good shepherd lays down his life for the sheep' (John 10:11). You are implying that 'a good shepherd gives bribes for his sheep.' Don't your children need more than water? It is great to build an orphanage, but for their sake don't you also need to build a nation in which they are able to get a job without bribing and to live with integrity, dignity, and pride?"

1. Corruption turns every institution upside down

The Ganges and Yamuna, premier rivers of northern India, come down to the plains from the Himalayan glaciers on both sides of Dehradun. Between the two great rivers are dozens of water springs and waterfalls, and some of the water runs right through the city. Should Dehradun then ever lack water?

The water supply does not depend on the mercy of the monsoon; the rivers are snow-fed. The water does not have to be pumped into Dehradun; it needs merely to be filtered and piped. Yet, a few summers ago, some of my friends had to spend Rs. 30,000 (the equivalent of a staff member's annual salary) in bribes to get water for their summer programs.

This is why: There is no water in the taps, so my friends go to the waterworks department and pay the required fee for a tanker to haul water. The tanker does not turn up. They go back to complain. The boss calls up the driver and abuses him in front of them. The driver explains that he was on his way when he had a flat tire. By the time the tire was repaired, it was time to deliver water to the local politician! The boss tells my friends to go home, assuring that the tanker will follow. As they are getting into their car, an elderly guard catches up with them. "You seem to be new here," he whispers. "Complaining won't help. The tanker never delivers water unless appeased. Don't be fooled by the boss's drama—even the gods above get their share."

Why is there a water shortage in Dehradun every summer, just when you need water the most? The answer is simple: If there is water in your taps, the political bosses, the managers, and the staff at the water department get only their salaries. When you don't have water, they get salaries plus huge bribes. Thus, ensuring that your taps don't have water is one of the interests of the water department.

Likewise, during the socialist phase of our economy, it was the interest of the telecom department to make sure that you didn't get the phone you paid for. What serves the interest of the schoolteachers? To ensure that your child does not do well in the class. You need to hire the teacher to tutor your child after school hours.

What serves the interest of the public works department and their contractors? What serves the interest of the electricity department? What does a police officer in need of money want in his area—crime or no crime?

Why don't the investigating agencies succeed in prosecuting the corrupt officials? Prosecutors will get much more than salaries if the culprits are allowed to go. What would the press gain if it kept a story alive in public memory by dogged perseverance? Journalists and editors gain more if they make only sufficient noise to shame the culprits into appeasing them with bribes.

Corruption turns every institution from servant into master. Corrupt societies don't produce institutions such as a free press or independent judiciary to safeguard the liberties of the "small man."

2. Corruption enslaves and destroys by undermining the value of work and individual merit

Some years ago, India was shaken by the news of a politician in New Delhi who murdered his wife and burned her body in the outdoor tandoor (oven) of a five-star hotel—a public place within walking distance of the Parliament House! It was reported that he had been using his wife to appease top members of the Congress Party to get himself into Parliament. He began to suspect that his wife might use sex not to make *him* our nation's leader but to become one herself.

If a budding politician knows that it is not a track record of social service, not a vision for the nation, but sexual bribes that will make him the parliamentary candidate for the Gandhi-Nehru (Congress) party, why should he bother developing personal merit? What must an employee (say, an army officer) do to get his promotion? What would be the most effective way for a PhD student to get her doctorate?

Corruption ensures that our nation will only have mediocre men and women as leaders, educators, and administrators. Those who value merit and hard work prefer to find personal fulfillment by building up nations that still put a premium on such values.

Christianity turned Western democracy into meritocracy that promoted competition in excellence because righteousness implied placing competence above connections. Rulers were shepherds who appointed officers on the basis of merit. Thanks to the Bible, modern Western democracy became a system that made nepotism submit to measurable standards of ability and performance.

Secularism without the Bible has perverted all this in India; it has created a "democratic" culture that enables a person to attain advantages, opportunities, contracts, offices, and promotions on the basis of caste and family connections, influence, money, conspiracies, and force. Post-Christian secularism is doing exactly the same thing to Western democracy: in the United States, a governor has just been impeached for trying to sell to the highest bidder the Senate seat that President Obama vacated. His job was to nominate the most competent public servant to that position.

3. Corruption is antithetical to freedom

The Asian Development Bank estimates that corruption pushes up the price of Indian goods and services by 20 to 100 percent. This is why China is able to export much more than India. Corruption makes us economically so noncompetitive that many experts are willing to trade our freedom for a curb on corruption. They feel that India should emulate the Chinese model of political authoritarianism because dictatorship means that one has to bribe fewer rulers.

Corruption is the antithesis of the idea of a free (noncoercive) economy, which grew out of the European Reformation's return to a biblical spirituality. If I give you my book and take your money in exchange, that is not robbery, because I return value for value in a free (noncoercive) exchange of value. Corruption, in contrast, involves abusing one's power to harass, coerce, or deceive others (individuals, institutions, or the state) to acquire value (money, service, goods, ideas, time, property, or honor) without returning proportionate value to them.

4. Corruption violates our dignity as human beings

Nothing has violated the dignity of the "sovereign" (citizen) of the Indian Republic more than the corruption of the Indian state. A small grocer in a village in northwestern India had a monthly income of Rs. 1200. The village chief, the contractor of the red sandstone mines, was the richest man of the village. The grocer asked the chief's son first to pay a long-pending debt of Rs. 120 (less than three dollars) before taking another pack of cigarettes on credit. The son returned with his father and brother, who kidnapped the grocer and beat him. They put a thick needle through his nose, tied a string to it, and paraded him through the village saying, "You must know that you are only a beast. You must live as a beast."

Was this an isolated incident? Every officer and politician who extorts bribes from helpless citizens makes exactly the same statement, every day, in every city in India. When you are forced to bribe, you cease being a free citizen. You accept the status of a domesticated beast, working and earning for others, not for yourself.

5. Corruption grows as a cancerous malignancy

You are constructing a building. You have bought the material, hired the architect, the equipment, the masons, and the laborers. Now you need water; every minute without water is a loss. A bribe will bring the water, but the problem is that your willingness to bribe one department raises the expectations of every other department. After all, you also need the services of the sanitary department, the electricity department, and the telephone department. Compromising in one sphere saps your moral energy to take on the other departments. And since you had to spend your hard-earned money in bribing, you naturally want to recover it when you have the opportunity, whether it is through taking bribes, commissions, or gifts, or through misusing official property, time, or money. Corruption thus spreads into all areas of life, so that not just our politicians but also our prophets (the press) and the parish priests (including some denominational bishops) are corrupted.

Corruption also grows in what it demands. If people can lay their hands on your pocket, they will eventually lay them on your daughters, wives, and on your person too. It is not unusual for the police, for example, to begin by taking commissions from criminals, then become bold enough to demand money from the victims who lodge a report. Then, in order to extract bribes, they lock up innocent people. Finally, if they don't get bribes, they murder young men in fake "encounters," calling the men "terrorists."

6. Corruption hurts the poor and brutalizes our character

The "powerful" find a corrupt society to be a boon; the honest people, on the other hand, perceive that honest hard work is a disadvantage. The people who honestly pay their electricity bills discover that they are also paying for those dishonest neighbors who bribe the employees of the electricity department and steal electricity. The poor learn that the bribes blind the eyes of the rulers and judges to their disadvantage. They cannot get justice on the basis of the righteousness of their cause. A poor student cannot get into a technical college or find a job on the basis of his hard work and ability. When the scales are tilted unfairly in favor of the affluent, the disadvantaged begin to detest the system.

As Romanian Christians testified, corruption brutalizes national character. Once a doctor has extracted his pound of flesh from a helpless patient, what do you think the nurse will do? Unless she is committed to following a self-sacrificing Savior, she will follow in the footsteps of the surgeon. Then the nursing attendant, the ward maid, and the janitor will follow, turning corruption into a culture. Patients better pay the bribes, otherwise those who came with one disease may return with the germs of ten more.

7. *Corruption is an antinational activity and a sin against God*

Corruption compromises our national security. Corrupt officials sell military secrets. When military officials buy expensive weapons in exchange for personal kickbacks, they buy substandard products, risking the lives of our soldiers and the security of our nation. Bribery puts love for money or power above love for one's neighbor.

One could argue that a person's enlightened self-interest is inseparable from his national interest. But a corrupt person says, "Why should I allow you to define my interest?" Be that as it may, corruption has to be opposed because it is sin. Sin is rebellion against God before it is offense against man, nature, or nation. Corruption violates at least two of the Ten Commandments: God says, "You shall not covet . . . anything that belongs to your neighbor" (Exod. 20:17), yet all corruption is rooted in covetousness. Corruption also violates the command, "You shall not steal" (Exod. 20:15).

II. Corruption: Its Causes

1. *Roots of corruption go deeper than politico-economic systems*

Socialism played a big role in corrupting Indian government; it expanded the government too rapidly. More officers had to be recruited than could be trained in the high moral tradition of the British-trained Indian Civil Service.[1] Socialism gave power

---

1. A big budget by a new government in America will also mean a sudden increase in the number of government-run projects and employees. Hiring too many staff quickly to complete time-bound projects makes it difficult to train new staff—especially in terms of their character.

to petty officials which they were able to abuse. Because corruption has flourished more in socialist societies than in capitalistic societies, some people think that capitalism will moralize our government. That is wishful thinking.

Capitalism limits state power, reducing the opportunity for bribe-taking. When private companies are free to compete with each other, customers do not have to bribe. Private schools, for example, usually teach better. But as America is now learning, capitalism encourages pursuit of self-interest; therefore, in itself it is anything but a moralizing ideology. In order to remain moral and succeed, the capitalist economic system needs a cultural force—a church, a scripture, an education system—that continuously nurtures the moral muscles of a society.

Many micro-level religious monasteries, orders, and communities operate effectively without private property, on strict socialist principles. They demonstrate that, with proper spirituality, even socialism can work, at least on a small scale. The Lord Jesus said, "No one can serve two masters. Either he will hate the one and love the other, or he will be devoted to one and despise the other. You cannot serve both God and Money" (Matt. 6:24).

2. Corruption is rooted in covetousness

Why are we Indians able to break the tenth commandment, "You shall not covet," without a sense of guilt? One reason is that our culture understands evil in terms of karma, or action. Covetousness is not a deed (karma) but an attitude. It is an attitude reflecting a lack of knowledge about God, a lack of faith in our loving and caring heavenly Father, a lack of contentment and gratitude. Sin, thus, is internal—in our hearts—before it manifests in outward deeds.

Secularism is creating the same problem for the West. It replaces morality (God's commandments) with human legislation. Governments cannot legislate against inner attitudes such as covetousness. The law cannot teach "godliness with contentment" (1 Tim. 6:6).

3. Covetousness is magnified by modern materialistic consumerism

Consumption is not unspiritual. The problem is with *materialistic* consumerism, which evaluates life by the things that you possess. Our primary love must be for God and for our neighbor. We must judge every society by how it treats God's image—people. Corruption abuses people. Materialistic consumerism feeds our greed and blinds our eyes. Instead of serving people, we try to squeeze out their wealth for ourselves. Karl Marx's fear that capitalism would create hell was not baseless.

4. Corruption is rooted in the unbiblical idea that power is a passport to personal privilege

N. T. Rama Rao was an actor who played mythical gods in Telugu films, and his popularity catapulted him into the chief ministership of Andhra Pradesh. He, more than any other politician, brought astrology back into public life in India. Rama Rao alienated his senior colleagues when he began to govern, as though he was not a team leader but a god. His party split, and he lost his position and power. The electorate punished those who had stabbed him politically and voted him back into power a second time. Soon after becoming chief minister, Rama Rao summoned the legislators of his party, washed his feet in a basin of water, and made them drink it as an oath of loyalty to him. But in no time his autocratic ways split the party again.

After Rama Rao became the chief minister for the third time, he stopped going to office because his astrologers and Vastu Shastries told him that the previous calamities had occurred because the entrance to his office faced a direction where the stars were inauspicious for him. Nine residential houses had to be demolished, and a new road and gate built, before he would go to his office. Within a few months of these new arrangements, his son and son-in-law led a revolt against him. They successfully ousted him from office, and he died of a heart attack. His astrologers explained that this calamity overtook him because there are ten planets, and the astrologers knew only nine. They had taken care to appease each of the nine. "This tragedy," they said, "is the influence of the tenth planet."

Sometime after this event I was speaking in a public meeting in Hyderabad. I said, "Rama Rao's misfortune may have been caused by the gods that have favored the ambitious rebels—but why should the gods be inauspicious to Rama Rao? Wasn't he doing good for his people? He sold rice cheaply to the poor; he banned alcohol; he promised saris to poor girls when they marry. The downtrodden people loved him and voted for him. Why, then, should gods be inauspicious to him?" The answer, of course, was that our gods do not have to have a reason to be cross with us. It is their nature to harass and oppress innocent citizens to extort appeasement from them.

During the nineteenth century, British evangelicals succeeded in transforming England and their government in India because they believed in a different God. Their God used his power not to oppress and extort, but to serve, to wash the feet of his disciples, and to give his own life on the cross of Calvary to deliver us from the power of sin.

5. Corruption is facilitated by our moral relativism

For Indian philosophers the distinction between good and evil is temporal and unreal, not absolute. In God, good and evil merge into oneness. Because no divinely ordained moral law exists, there is no sin and no final judgment. Morality has to be *defined* by the priest and *enforced* by the rulers. What is moral for a man is different from what is moral for a woman, and what is immoral for a subject may be moral for a ruler.

Charles Grant, who played the most important role in starting the moral transformation of the British rule in India, witnessed the practical outworking of the philosophy of moral relativism. In the 1770s and early 1780s, he saw hordes of hundreds and thousands of *sannyasis* (religious ascetics and priests) who came into Malda, in Bengal, to loot and plunder. Grant was amazed that the Indian soldiers in the British army refused to fight against these religious robbers because to oppose *sannyasis* was sacrilegious. Grant began the campaign for giving to India a philosophical basis for moral absolutes. This mission aimed at a religio-philosophical/moral transformation of India via evangelization. It was Grant's campaign that succeeded in his friend William Wilberforce's parliamentary victory in 1813 for missions and education. The tragedy is that England herself is now accepting the moral relativism that destroyed India.

6. *Corruption thrives when we cease to fear God*

The Bible serves as an effective antidote to corruption because it tells us that God is holy and is our ultimate judge. He punishes sin. My people did not fear God because they were taught that they are God. The secular West has ceased to fear God because it is being taught that either there is no God or that he will not judge sinners. The Scriptures say, "The fear of the LORD is the beginning of wisdom" (Prov. 9:10). Corruption creeps in when we deny God. Psalm 14:1 says:

> The fool says in his heart,
> 　"There is no God."
> They are corrupt, their deeds are vile;
> 　there is no one who does good.

7. *Most cultures provide no incentive to fight corruption*

In the 1820s a twenty-year-old Christian civil servant, Charles Trevelyan, arrived in India without a godfather in the British East India Company or in British Parliament. He was posted under the veteran British Resident in Delhi and saw how corrupt his boss was. He was warned that if he opposed the corruption, he would ruin his career and risk his life since everyone did what his boss was doing. Yet he risked his career and his life to expose his boss and his Company's corruption. Trevelyan went on to turn the pioneering educational efforts of William Carey, Raja Ram Mohun Roy, and Alexander Duff into the education revolution

of the nineteenth century. He argued courageously and successfully that English education must prepare India for her political
freedom.

India became an independent secular democracy in 1947. In
the last sixty years corruption has grown exponentially, but we
have not seen secular or Hindu civil servants take heroic personal risks to fight corruption. Why? Trevelyan fought corruption in public life not because he wanted to be a hero but because
the Lord Jesus had freed him from sin in his own heart. He had
become a public servant because he was Christ's servant. He did
not come to India seeking fortune for himself; he came seeking
Christ's kingdom of righteousness. He knew that he was called to
take up his cross, whether or not he saw good triumph over evil
in his life. Christ's resurrection had assured him that ultimately
the darkness would not overcome the light. Neither Hinduism
nor secularism inspires such faith and willingness to suffer for
righteousness.

III. Corruption and the Culture of the Cross

1. The cross and culture

Communists thought that armed revolutions would transform nations but found that revolutions do not equal reform, just
like weeding does not equal gardening. Roots of corruption go
deeper than individual leaders and regimes. Dethroning leaders
or smashing "the system" rarely does lasting good. Evil is rooted
in our hearts and minds (Mark 7:21). Ultimately it is our inner
life—our assumptions, values, worldview, desires, emotion, and
attitudes—as well as our relationships, that need to be transformed. The Communists could not create the utopia that they
had hoped for, because different belief systems produce different
results.

The cross is the emblem of a Christian culture. It began to
transform England with the generation that wrote the Magna
Carta (1215). Henry de Bracton, England's most famous judge in

that period, expounded the meaning of the cross. He argued that the cross implies that God wants justice and mercy, not brute force, to rule on earth. God could have used his power to destroy Satan and his works, said de Bracton, but he used the cross to defeat Satan. Among other things, the cross symbolizes the means God uses to redeem mankind from sin, including corruption.

Because of this understanding of the cross, Christian cultures evolved differently than Islamic cultures, where corruption can be dealt with only by brute force. A few years ago Imran Khan, Pakistan's star cricketer-turned-politician, formed a political party and ran for office. During the elections he pledged that if his party were voted to power, as the prime minister he would hang corrupt people on poles in public squares! Islam tends to respond to evil in this way because it does not know the Savior who himself was hanged on the pole to regenerate us.

2. The cross and morals

Moral law is observable neither in the universe nor in society. What happens to a politician who murders his rivals and enemies? If he is powerful enough and brutal enough, in many countries he will become king, president for life, or a military dictator. The more people he kills, the more powerful he becomes. How can his people then believe that "you shall not kill" is a real moral law that transcends human legislation? If it is a real moral law, then shouldn't there be consequences for breaking it?

This intellectual problem, which the academic world has faced during the last century or so, is not unique. It was an acute problem for the Jewish prophets in the Old Testament too. They saw visions and prophesied that God would uphold his moral law and punish the wicked—but nothing happened! The people began to mock God and his prophets: "He [God] will do nothing! No harm will come to us; we will never see sword or famine. The prophets are but wind and the word is not in them" (Jer. 5:12–13). The mockery turned into a proverb: "The days go by and every vision comes to nothing" (Ezek. 12:22). Naturally, the people began to doubt that God even existed. Corruption, consequently, grew and crushed the poor and the weak because God did not seem to intervene. The righteous suffered and began to wonder aloud if it was useless to be righteous. They had no intellectual basis for persisting in moral uprightness which brought only misery:

> But as for me, my feet had almost slipped [into sin]. . . .
> For I envied the arrogant
>   when I saw the prosperity of the wicked. . . .
> From their callous hearts comes iniquity;
>   the evil conceits of their minds know no limits.
> They scoff, and speak with malice;
>   in their arrogance they threaten oppression. . . .
> Surely in vain have I kept my heart pure;
>   in vain have I washed my hands in innocence.
> (Ps. 73:2–13)

Prophets took their people's complaints to God: "Why don't you see? Why don't you do something about the all-pervasive violence, wickedness, corruption, and injustice?" (see Hab. 1:2–4). God responded by saying he was going to uphold his moral law. He was going to bring the Babylonians to punish his corrupt people. These Babylonians, God said, would execute his judgment upon Judah's wickedness. This judgment, because it had been repeatedly predicted by several prophets, was going to serve as empirical evidence that God does uphold his law; he does punish sin.

The prophets now had a second problem on their hands. If the all-knowing and all-powerful God really holds us accountable, and if he would actually uphold his moral law and punish the guilty, then what hope could mankind have? How could God judge sinners and also fulfill his promises to bless their nation and make it a blessing to all the nations of the earth?

God revealed to the prophet Isaiah how he was going to resolve this problem. Seven hundred years before Jesus actually went to the cross, God said to Isaiah that the Messiah would take the punishment of his nation's (and the world's) sin upon himself:

> But he was pierced for our transgressions,
>   he was crushed for our iniquities;
> the punishment that brought us peace was upon him,
>   and by his wounds we are healed . . .
>   and the LORD has laid on him the iniquity of us all.
> (Isa. 53:5–6)

As Jesus hung upon the cross, it was not the justice of mankind that was displayed. Both his judges, Pilate and Herod, admitted that Jesus had committed no offense that called for his execution. Everyone knew that Jesus was being crucified because of the envy, jealousy, fears, and hypocrisy of the socioreligious and political leaders of his day. What hung on the cross was the greed of his betrayer, the lies of false witnesses, and the moral cowardice of the masses, the disciples, and the governor who could not resist injustice and oppression. What hung upon the cross was the brutality, oppression, and terror upon which the kingdoms of this world, the kingdom of Satan, have been founded.

Christ's resurrection is a proof that God rewards righteousness with the resurrected life.

The cross resolves the philosophical dilemma of the Hebrew prophets. God *is* holy. Moral law *is* real. God *will* judge (and *has* judged) sin. But the holy God does not need to destroy sinners, for Jesus Christ has taken the sin of the world upon himself. Forgiveness *is* possible. Our conscience need not condemn us, for our Judge offers forgiveness. Thanks to the cross of Christ, we now have a firm basis—empirical, historical, and philosophical—for affirming moral absolutes, without that same moral law condemning us.

The cross is not another religious idea. It is good news—the gospel. It is the only available force that can withstand and push back the storm of moral relativism that is coming upon the secular world. Without the cross, the world has no foundations whatsoever for affirming moral absolutes, for calling corruption by its name—sin. The cross, of course, does not merely provide a philosophical framework for moral absolutes. It also *delivers* us from sin.

3. *The cross and power*

The cross makes service the true source of power, turning democracy into meritocracy. Corruption enables a person to attain advantages, opportunities, contracts, offices, and promotions on the basis of family connections, influence, bribes, conspiracies, crime, and force. Without the cross, we can have the form of democracy but not its soul. The cross is a symbol of the sublimation of power.

Imagine this scenario: Christ is arrested, falsely accused, and unjustly condemned. The Roman soldiers are dragging him outside Jerusalem to crucify him. After mocking him as the "king of the Jews," they begin to mock the impotence of the Jewish race itself. The mobs that had gathered in Jerusalem for the festival are following him, wailing loudly. Some women cry out, condemning their menfolk for their cowardice in the face of the audacity of the Roman authorities to humiliate their most prominent public figure. People are seething with rage. They have not forgotten Herod's cowardly act of secretly beheading John the Baptist, their other prophet. John's disciples have been waiting for an opportune moment to take revenge. Some of them have forged an alliance with the zealots who are recruiting and arming comrades during the festival. The Roman centurion in charge of the crucifixion is the same officer whose servant Jesus had earlier healed. He is double-minded, unsure whether to hang Jesus or save him. Highly respected Jews, such as Nicodemus and Joseph, are publicly condemning their colleagues for conspiring with the Romans to murder their own prophet.

Then, just when his enemies thought that they had won, Jesus, sensing the groundswell of public opinion in his favor, springs a

dramatic surprise. On a narrow bend he makes a daring escape.
The crowds go ecstatic. The soldiers attempt to chase Jesus but
are met with a volley of stones. As they attack the crowd, including unarmed women, the Jewish temple guards switch sides. The
zealots turn the mutiny into a battle for liberation. Within minutes the palaces of Pilate, Herod, and Caiaphas go up in flames.
The three of them are hung upon the three crosses on Golgotha.
The revolution is a spectacular success. The Jews are free. Jesus,
son of Joseph, age thirty-three, becomes the first Jewish king for
the whole of Israel after almost a thousand years. He proves to be
greater than his illustrious forefathers, David and Solomon. His
disciples control the new regime.

  This script matches our world's expectations. (After all, it was
the disciples who expected the story to end this way.)

  What happened instead is mind-boggling. While the disciples were debating who would be the greatest in the new kingdom, Jesus stood up from the table, took off his robe, took a towel
and a basin of water, and started washing the feet of his disciples.
As they were trying to understand what was going on, Jesus said
that the problem with the kingdoms of this world is that their
rulers make their followers drink the water in which they have
washed their feet. He had come to establish a kingdom in which
he who serves would be the greatest. Before the message had fully
penetrated the disciples' minds, Jesus dropped another bombshell.
He was not headed, he said, for a throne with a golden crown on
his head. That very night he was going to be arrested, mocked
with a crown of thorns on his head, and crucified, for he had come
to serve to the extent of giving his own life for the salvation of the
world. His disciples, if they wanted his kingdom, had to walk in
his footsteps. The power he wanted them to have was not power
to lord over others, nor power to exploit and oppress, but power
to sacrifice themselves for others.

  St. Paul gave this classic summary of the nature of the kingdom of God:

Your attitude should be the same as that of Christ Jesus:
    Who, being in very nature God,
        did not consider equality with God something to be
            grasped,
    but made himself nothing,
        taking the very nature of a servant,
        being made in human likeness.
    And being found in appearance as a man,
        he humbled himself
        and became obedient to death—
            even death on a cross! (Phil. 2:5–8)

Is this exposition of the cross a repetition of some ancient idealistic religious discourse, or is it a discussion of a kingdom that is present now? Is it an aspect of Christianity that is "Western," or can it transform global culture?

As a thirteen-year-old boy, I once cycled many miles to hear Pandit Jawaharlal Nehru, our first prime minister. Panditji's opening statement was moving: "My countrymen," he said, "I have come to address you as your 'First Servant,' for that is what the term 'Prime Minister' literally means." I don't remember Panditji talking about Jesus on that occasion. For that reason, many in the audience may not have understood what exactly he was talking about, or from where he got that definition of democratic leadership. However, even as a young boy I could see that the ancient cross had not lost its power to transform our world.

Pandit Nehru was "made in England." Within two decades after his speech, the "world's largest democracy" became a vast jungle of authoritarian leaders surrounded by sycophants or conspiratorial followers. We have over nine hundred registered democratic parties, but not one of them has internal democracy. Why? The gospel of the cross came to us, but we have preferred the script where the hero hatches a conspiracy to escape the cross and overcome with the sword.

The cross is power. But it is the power of faith, the power of knowing the sovereign God enough to trust him and, therefore, to surrender to him and wait for his vindication. The cross is the power to put principle above power.

4. The cross and civility

Civility is not a matter of the organizational form of society but of its heart. It is a matter of recognizing each person's worth and rights, and giving to them what is their due as individual persons. Corruption denies to some what is due to them and gives to others what they do not deserve. A corrupt society is the opposite of a civil society.

It is common to denounce "Western individualism" and extol "Asian values" of family and community. But compare the scene at the domestic terminal of Indira Gandhi International Airport in New Delhi on any given morning with the scene at a bus stop in London. You expect to see the most educated and sophisticated Indians at the airport, and the working-class people at the bus stop in London. The Europeans are individualists; we Indians are supposed to be respectful toward others in the community. Surprisingly, however, it is the Western individualists who would spontaneously form a queue (even if it is after a hard day's work, when they are anxious to get home), while we Indians push, shove, and try to jump the queue. The folks in the West would even allow someone with special needs to go ahead of them. What makes the difference?

The cross of Jesus Christ symbolizes radical individualism, for it implies both Christ's rejection *of* and Christ's rejection *by* the world, that is, by his own culture. To take up one's cross means to have the strength to stand alone, to reject and to accept rejection. St. Paul, who faced persistent persecution by the world and finally changed the world, said that he would boast of the cross through which he is dead to the world and the world is dead to him (Gal. 6:14). Paul's fiercest enemies were the Jews—his own people—who saw him as the greatest threat to their culture.

The individualism that the cross symbolizes is not only radical but also radically different from what the term now means to the secular mind. Secular individualism is self-centeredness; the

cross is the opposite, for it means denial of self in favor of surrender to God.

Neither Jesus' family nor his disciples wanted him to go to
the cross. Before his arrest, in the Garden of Gethsemane, Jesus
himself prayed, "My Father, if it be possible, let this cup [the
cross] pass from me." But then he added, "Not as I will, but as you
will." (Matt. 26:39 ESV). A person cannot reform his community
unless he is willing to transcend his community by surrendering
to God alone. Thus, the cross does symbolize individualism—
a rejection of one's family and community. But the cross is not
self-centeredness, for it is surrender to God. Moreover, the cross
is not only an individual's self-giving to God; it is his self-giving
to God for others.

During the Last Supper, a few hours before his arrest, Jesus
explained to his disciples that in choosing the cross he was giving his body to be broken for them. He took the Passover bread,
gave thanks, and broke it, and gave it to his disciples, saying
that it symbolized his body. As bread gives life when it is broken
and eaten, so would his body. Likewise, he took the cup, gave
thanks, and gave it to them to drink, saying that this was his
blood, which was about to be shed for the forgiveness of their sins.
The cross, thus, is simultaneously a rejection of the world and a
giving of oneself to God for the world, to serve the world's real
interest. This makes the cross the source of civility—of affirming
every individual's worth, preferring others before oneself, winning with sacrificial love rather than with the sword.

5. The cross and suffering

By themselves, moral absolutes are not enough. Islam has a
divine law, but the Islamic civilizations have not been able to
get out of the closed circle of power-driven politics. Why? Islam
does not have the cross. That is not to say that no Muslim ruler
has ever been just, but to affirm that no Muslim ruler has ever
been able to establish a durable political system in which the
highest political power is under the rule of righteous law. Force

remains supreme in Islamic societies. It is up to the individual ruler whether he uses his power more frequently for good or for evil. Power stays above principles. Historically, the record of Hindu, Chinese, and Japanese rulers was generally worse than Muslim rulers because they did not even have an objective law against which their rule could be judged.

The cross breaks through closed circle. It puts a commitment to principles above the love or fear of power. A "commitment to principles" could, of course, mean a heartless legalism. But the cross escapes that because the supreme "principle" that it represents is love for God and for one's neighbors.

Corruption, that is, the kingdom of Satan, survives by fear: the fear of being shamed, the fear of persecution or physical harm, and most supremely the fear of martyrdom or death. The cross takes the weapon of the kingdom of Satan and turns it against Satan. The New Testament explains: "Since the children have flesh and blood, he too shared in their humanity so that by his death he might destroy him who holds the power of death—that is, the devil—and free those who all their lives were held in slavery by their fear of death" (Heb. 2:14–15).

It is helpful to look at how each of these forms of suffering— shame, persecution, and martyrdom—contributes to corruption and is dealt with by the cross.

Shame. Many social scientists have pointed out a basic difference between Western civilizations that were shaped by the preaching of the cross and non-Western civilizations. Traditionally, the consciousness of *guilt* has been a driving factor in the West. The non-Western world, by and large, has been more concerned with *shame.* In his *Apology for Promoting Christianity in India* (1814) Claudius Buchanan told a heartrending story that illustrates the power of shame in Indian culture. A widow of Vaucha-ramu, a Brahmin, had to commit sati with her dead husband at Mujilupur, south of Calcutta. The cremation got delayed until sunset. The smoke and the heat made the widow change her mind. She managed to wriggle out of the funeral pyre and hide in the bushes. When the smoke had cleared, the mourners saw that there was only one body on the pyre. A manhunt began. The son found his mother and began to drag her to the fire. She cried and begged to live. The son replied that if she lived, he would be shamed in his caste and that would be worse than death.

Sati, of course, was banned in 1829, but the culture of shame continues. A typical Indian family would pay a huge dowry to marry their daughter to a government officer because he has the power and plenty of opportunity to abuse his position to extract bribes. To take a bribe and pervert justice does not bother us, but for the son-in-law to get caught would be a matter of shame. Purity is more a matter of external rituals and appearance than a matter of heart. Given a choice, the family would reject an equally good young man who did not have the power to extract bribes. The family would be ashamed of marrying their daughter into a relatively poor, although principled, home. We do not have many young heroes who have the spiritual resources to prefer the shame of relative poverty to the sinfulness of corruption. A culture cannot fight corruption without first dealing with this shame-driven social milieu. We condemn Western individualism and boast of our family and community orientation. In reality, it is our individualistic pursuit of wealth at the cost of the community's need for social ethics that makes us a corrupt and poor nation. When Jesus said, "Seek first the kingdom of God and his righteousness, and all these things will be added to you" (Matt. 6:33 ESV), he taught an important paradox: prosperity comes to a culture that has strong individuals who can choose the shame of poverty by putting righteousness above wealth.

Western Bible teachers do not teach how the cross liberated Christendom from the oppressive culture of shame. They focus on the verses that teach that Jesus took our guilt upon him. The gospel story, however, says more. Luke explains how the cross was as much about shame as about sin:

The men who were guarding Jesus began *mocking* and beating him. They blindfolded him and demanded, "Prophesy!

Who hit you?" And they said many other *insulting* things to him. . . .

Then Herod and his soldiers *ridiculed* and *mocked* him. Dressing him in an elegant robe, they sent him back to Pilate. . . .

The people stood watching [Jesus on the cross], and the rulers even *sneered* at him. They said, "He saved others; let him save himself if he is the Christ of God, the Chosen One." The soldiers also came up and *mocked* him. . . . There was a written notice above him, which read: THIS IS THE KING OF THE JEWS.

One of the criminals who hung there hurled *insults* at him: "Aren't you the Christ? Save yourself and us!"
(Luke 22:63–65; 23:11, 35, 36, 38–39)

The cross is a typical expression of an Asian culture using shame to coerce its members to fall in line, to conform to its code. The New Testament says that in enduring the cross Jesus turned his culture's weapon of shame against his culture: he "scorned" or "despised" its shame (Heb. 12:2). He refused to be ashamed of what they wanted him to be ashamed of. Instead, he made *them* ashamed of what they ought to have been ashamed of. We are to follow Jesus, who "suffered outside the city gate to make the people holy through his own blood. Let us, then, go to him outside the camp, bearing the *disgrace* he bore" (Heb. 13:12–13).

Persecution. The power to inflict physical pain is a second form of suffering that sustains corruption. In the 1990s Mr. Ram Jethmalani, an eminent lawyer who became a Union Minister, said in a public lecture in New Delhi that every police officer in Punjab had become a multimillionaire since the law gave special powers to the Punjab police to detain suspected terrorists without trial. A police officer needs to kill only one young man in a fake "encounter" to extort ransom from a thousand families. A culture of corruption obliterates the distinction between criminals, police, politicians, and religious leaders! Europe's religious history is full of popes and bishops who were criminals and murderers.

Today the Western church reduces the Holy Spirit to a matter of personal ecstasy or, at best, of emotional catharsis and physical healing. In the New Testament, one of the transformations that the Holy Spirit brought about in the disciples was to strengthen them to take up their cross in a confrontation with the kingdom of Satan. In the Garden of Gethsemane they had fled from persecution, but the Holy Spirit turned them into martyrs—those who live unto God.

The contemporary Western exposition of the cross fails to notice that the cross does more than deliver us from our sin and its consequences. Jesus died and rose again so that "by his death he might destroy him who holds the power of death—that is, the devil—and free those who all their lives were held in slavery by their fear of death." Past Hindu leaders, such as Swami Vivekananda, found the Western gospel to be obnoxiously cheap: its beginning and end appeared to be that Jesus died so that Christians can get a free ride to heaven. Did Jesus ask us to pray that we might go to heaven, or that the kingdom of heaven might come on this earth?

Martyrdom. The cross is the way into the kingdom of heaven because it makes death—the ultimate weapon of the kingdom of Satan—impotent. The Jews could not have arrested Jesus, let alone killed him, during the Passover festival. The crowds that followed him enthusiastically were his buffer during the day. The soldiers that were sent to arrest him returned saying it was impossible to arrest him without causing riots. At night Jesus did not sleep in a building that could be raided. A group of soldiers marching with torches cannot find a small group in a garden on a mountain. The soldiers would be visible; the darkness would be a cover for Jesus and his disciples. Jesus said no one could take his life from him; he was laying it down voluntarily (John 10:14–18).

The message of the cross, the invitation to die, *is* foolishness. But, as Paul says, the foolishness of God is wiser than the wisdom of man (1 Cor. 1:25). The point about the cross is that Jesus waived the advantages that he had to save his life in favor of doing his Father's will for him to go to the cross. Choosing the cross, thus, is a matter of knowing God enough to trust him. Eternal life is to know God, not just to go to heaven (John 17:3). A faith that is willing to choose the cross is the power that "overcomes the world" (1 John 5:4).

Without the resurrection, it would be a hopeless task to inspire people to choose the cross. If death is the unpredictable but final reality, then the present moment is all that we have; to deny ourselves is foolishness. Yet to deny ourselves, to save, to invest in the future, whether we live to enjoy it or not, are among the basic ingredients of the traditional economic wisdom of the West. Christ's disciples, such as St. Thomas, could deny themselves, come to India, and choose martyrdom because, having met with the risen Christ, they knew firsthand that death was not the end. Jesus had overcome it.

Jesus' death and resurrection freed his disciples from the fear of death, making Satan's ultimate weapon redundant. The cross is not a commitment to abstract moral absolutes. It means to trust and obey the living God, our Father and the Giver of life. No individual is more powerful than one who has ceased to fear death. He walks with his coffin over his head, that is, with his cross on his shoulders. The trapeze artists are able to perform their wonderful feats at fearsome heights because they know that if they fall the net below them will save them. The resurrection gives us a robust spirituality because it plays a similar role in Christian life. Eternal life is not a selfish enjoyment of heaven; it is a life of conflict and triumph here on this earth, a spirituality that turns the world upside down.

6. *The cross and community*

The foregoing exposition of the cross could give an impression that the cross is a matter of individual heroism: the daring individual, unafraid of death, commits himself or herself to moral principles and takes on a corrupt system. That would clearly be inadequate. The cross has triumphed because it succeeded in creating a voluntary community of disciples—the church. That is why true spirituality involves substantial healing in the area of human relationships. The cross is the antithesis of the Hindu ideal of a spiritual person who renounces community in pursuit of *self*-realization. The most "holy" saints are often those who are so immersed in themselves that they do not even talk to those who visit them in their caves.

Some Christians do seem to think that the only purpose of Jesus' death was to take their souls into the bliss of heaven. But is Jesus seeking individual souls or a bride—the church? Jesus' body was broken to make his disciples into one body, his church; his washing of the disciples' feet was meant to teach them to serve one another; Jesus' last prayer for his disciples was that they may be one (John 17:21). Corruption is a social issue, and community problems usually do not have individualistic solutions.

Suppose our village is infected with malaria. We learn that the mosquitoes that breed in stagnant waters spread malaria. Can you be safe from malaria if you clean up your backyard and do not allow mosquitoes to breed there? Obviously not! Your safety is dependent on an organized, united effort by the whole community. So it is with corruption. An individual's determination to make fifty trips to the telephone department rather than pay a bribe for a minor repair would achieve little unless a community is created that shares his values and is stirred up by his voluntary suffering. His suffering can become a blessing to everyone if it moves us out of our apathy.

We do have to come to the cross as individuals. It does call us to assume moral responsibility for our own choices. Just as Jesus died when he became sin for us, so shall we suffer unless we repent. Repentance means to take individual responsibility for our sins and to accept God's grace for our salvation. It is right to be concerned with the flaws in our society, but the cross calls us, first of all, to come to terms with our own flaws and transgressions. We (human beings) are more important to God than our social structures. Although God made us in his triune image for family and community (Gen. 1:27), Jesus said that ultimately each of us would have to stand before God as individuals (Matt. 25:31–46).

To repent is to ask for forgiveness for the sins that we have committed. We must go on to receive God's Holy Spirit so that we may live by his law, not by our private values. God's law is summed up in the command to love God with all our being and to love our neighbor as ourselves. Repentance toward God, therefore, involves getting right with our neighbors. We find forgiveness for our sins because of Christ's righteousness, not ours. However, the proof of forgiveness is that we forgive others who sin against us. Jesus went to the extent of saying that we will not be forgiven, our worship and sacrifices will not be accepted, unless we first forgive others and get reconciled with our brothers and sisters (Matt. 5:23–24; 6:14–15).

Becoming a community implies going beyond forgiving one another. John explains the community-creating power of the cross:

> This is how we know who the children of God are and who the children of the devil are: Anyone who does not do what is right is not a child of God; nor is anyone who does not love his brother. . . . This is how we know what love is: Jesus Christ laid down his life for us. And we ought to lay down our lives for our brothers. If anyone has material possessions and sees his brother in need but has no pity on him, how can the love of God be in him? Dear children, let us not love with words or tongue but with actions and in truth." (1 John 3:10, 16–18)

The battle against corruption calls us to carry our cross, to become a community by a willingness to "carry each other's burdens, [which fulfills] the law of Christ" (Gal. 6:2).

7. *The cross and conflict*

Why is the power of darkness growing in our world? One reason, as we saw earlier, is that far too many people confuse spirituality with ecstatic experiences, meditation, "going within," or with spiritism, astrology, numerology, palmistry, and fatalistic resignation to Karma, fate, or destiny. In contrast, Jesus asked us to pray that God's kingdom may come and his will may be done on earth as it is done in heaven. Often our prayers do not seem to go beyond a desire to go to heaven and have a comfortable life here on earth.

The cross is a radical refusal to compromise with the evils of the social status quo. It is a costly confrontation with corruption. Jesus said that the world hates him because he testifies that what it does is evil (John 7:7). Although he is the "prince of peace," Jesus is a peacemaker, not a peace lover. A peace lover stays away from conflicts. The peacemaker gets involved in unjust, oppressive situations. A peacemaker is necessarily a troublemaker. He disturbs an oppressive social system in order to make "all things new" (Rev. 21:5 RSV). Jesus said, "I have come to bring fire on the earth, and how I wish it were already kindled! But I have a baptism [cross] to undergo, and how distressed I am until it is completed! Do you think I came to bring peace on earth? No, I tell you, but division" (Luke 12:49–51).

To compromise with corruption is to enslave ourselves. It is to build a society where we are not even free to be honest. The cross is not a passive acceptance of evil, but a fearless opposition to evil—and of taking the consequences of that opposition.

Why is an acceptance of the evil status quo a violation of our humanity?

I often ask my audience: "Suppose you have returned home late. Your home is dark. What is the first thing you would do?"

"We'd turn on the light," is the usual reply.

"But you're in Mussoorie, and there's no power."

"We'd light a candle."

"But you've forgotten to buy matches."

"Well, we'd just go to sleep."

"What if the lights don't come on the whole next day and you face the prospect of spending another night in darkness? Suppose there has been a riot, and the city is in curfew. The markets are closed."

"We'd try to borrow matches, or else get two stones or sticks to get a spark to start a fire."

"Good! Now imagine that it is your dog which goes ahead of you into your dark house. What would it do?"

"Nothing. It would just find its place and lie down."

My final question is: "Why is it that you do something or the other to create light, but your dog does not?"

Normally I find that very few people give a satisfactory answer to the last question. The correct answer is that we make light because, while we are made in the image of the Creator who made light, our dog is not. Animals are not creative in the sense that they do not create culture and history.

The first chapter of the Old Testament tells us what it means for God and us to be creative. God is not limited by what is. The existing realities do not determine his boundaries. He is the Creator. That means that he transcends what is. He imagines what ought to be and creates it. He saw darkness but was not limited by it. He proceeded to create light (Gen. 1:2–3). What is true in the physical sphere is equally true in the social sphere. The New Testament begins a description of Christ's ministry with the declaration that "the people living in great darkness have seen a great light; on those living in the shadow of death a light has dawned" (Matt. 4:16). Jesus' audience had their lamps, but Jesus declared, "I am the light of the world. Whoever follows me will never walk in darkness, but will have the light of life" (John 8:12). Jesus went on to promise his disciples that if they followed him, their lives too would become lights of the world (Matt. 5:14).

Because we are creative, neither our homes nor our society need to remain in darkness. Neither the physical darkness nor the socio-spiritual darkness is invincible. God does not accept our moral/spiritual darkness as final, nor should we. Jesus came as the light to transform our lives into lights of this world. True spirituality is to become light. It is by burning himself out on the cross that Jesus became the light of the world. To accept the darkness of the social status quo is to deny our humanness as creative creatures. It is to disobey God's call to us to be light, to expose the works of darkness (Eph. 5:11), to "live as children of light" (Eph. 5:8).

A clash of darkness and light is unavoidable. The cross, like every other war, is a bloody and costly affair. The only thing worse than a war is to be in a war and not know that you are in a war, for then your doom is assured. A church that chooses not to fight corruption will be destroyed by it.

From Worldview Programs to Kingdom Movement

Forging Alliances to Restore the Gospel of the Kingdom

T. M. MOORE

A Kingdom Initiative: Restoring the Gospel of the Kingdom

A *modern Babylonian captivity*

In 1520 Martin Luther argued passionately that the church in his day had been taken captive by an inadequate, and in many ways false, gospel. His was not the only voice auguring for reform within the Catholic Church. Luther's pamphlet *The Pagan Servitude of the Church* likened the church's situation in sixteenth-century Europe to Israel in Babylon. The people of God were prisoners of a false gospel, a false worldview, and the extent to which they were able to realize the full promise of Christ's rule was strictly curtailed by their captive status.

T. M. Moore is dean of The Centurions Program of the Wilberforce Forum and principal of The Fellowship of Ailbe, a spiritual fellowship in the Celtic Christian tradition.

Jesus and the apostles proclaimed the gospel of the kingdom, the bold and exuberant declaration that a new order had broken into human experience, bringing power to cleanse, forgive, renew, and reconcile all of life back to God in a kingdom of righteousness, peace, and joy in the Spirit. The first Christians boldly proclaimed and embodied this gospel, turning their upside-down world right side up for Jesus Christ.

This theme of liberating the church from an inadequate or false gospel has been repeated in nearly every age. It was the rallying cry of the orthodox against the followers of Arius, culminating in the Council of Nicea in AD 325. It has been part of the burden of every spiritual order that has come into being since the days of Anthony, Paul the Hermit, and Benedict. It was the burden of the scholastic theologians, the founders of the medieval universities, and the leaders of the Catholic Reformation of the sixteenth century. It motivated the courage of the separatists against the liberalizing efforts of latitudinarians in seventeenth-century England. The concern to recover the gospel and revive the church impassioned Whitefield, Edwards, Wesley, and revivalists and reformers in every age. It was the great burden animating much of the work of Abraham Kuyper; it fueled Newman's argument for recovering the idea of a university; it inspired the movement to recover the Fundamentals at the turn of the twentieth century; it laces the great classic *Christianity and Liberalism* by J. Gresham Machen; it was the motive force behind the Second Vatican Council; it fueled the Jesus Movement of the '60s and '70s; and it was the guiding force behind the papacy of John Paul II. Each of these efforts was, in its own way, remarkably effective in setting the church free to express the faith of Christ beyond the mere perpetuation of a kind of status quo Christianity into arenas of personal, social, and cultural transformation as well.

An inadequate gospel

In our day again the gospel of the kingdom has been replaced by an inadequate and false gospel, a gospel of personal peace and well-being. This false gospel loads believers with false assurances about their eternal state, even as it distracts them from the pursuit of holiness, minimizes the life of discipline and obedience, fosters an idolatry of material success, redefines the "go/tell" mission of the church, and leaves the larger issues of culture and society in the hands of the children of the kingdom of darkness.

The gospel of the kingdom has become captive to mere personal interest, felt needs, aspirations of prosperity, postmodern relativism, and social and political ambitions. Certainly there are aspects of most of these in the gospel of the kingdom; however, the gospel of the kingdom is much broader, much deeper, much more integrated, and much more sweeping in its implications and power than any or all of its present-day substitutes. What we need today is a movement to restore the gospel of the kingdom—Christianity as a worldview—to the churches and the public square. This will not happen without the deliberate, coordinated effort of those who share a burden for such a broad and deep renewal.

Questions for Reflection or Discussion

1. Do you see any evidence that the gospel embraced by many contemporary Christians is not having the kind of "right-side-up" effect on our society we might expect?
2. How would the believers you know define the Christian's hope? Why not ask a few of them? Is this hope sufficiently broad, powerful, and all-encompassing to be able to turn the world right side up for Christ? Why or why not?
3. What do we mean by the phrase "Christianity as a worldview"? What is a worldview? Why should we consider Christianity to be a worldview?

Worldview Ministries

Over the past twenty years or so, a number of ministries have emerged, all focusing on a common theme: understanding and applying a biblical worldview. Ministries like Summit, L'Abri, *World* magazine, *First Things*, the Wilberforce Forum and the Wilberforce Forum Centurions, the Acton Institute, the C. S. Lewis Institute, *Touchstone*, the Truth Project, American Vision, Reflections Ministries, and others—together with such colleges as Calvin, Belhaven, Cedarville, Union University, Steubenville, and Westmont, as well as certain publishing houses—have, independently of one another, sensed the present state of the captivity of the church and have argued for a broader interpretation and more consistent and far-reaching applications of the Good News. All these ministries acknowledge the generally biblical and evangelical character of contemporary American evangelicalism and evangelical Catholicism, yet all have sensed a need for some broader proclamation and ministry.

Each of these ministries has provided its own program for renewal, focused on one segment of the larger Christian community. Each of these ministries could provide a summary of the success of their programs similar to what follows for that of the Wilberforce Forum Centurions.

Wilberforce Forum Centurions: A Summary to Date

The Wilberforce Forum Centurions Program of Prison Fellowship Ministries (PFM) has been a success to this point in at least three areas:

1. It has confirmed and enlarged the widespread and growing interest in biblical worldview currently taking hold in many sectors of the church.
2. It has attracted and trained an impressive cohort of over five hundred men and women from all walks of life and a wide range of Christian communions, and has deployed them to live and teach biblical worldview within the context of their own personal mission fields.

3. It has provided impetus, direction, content, resources, feedback, and networking for a growing array of impressive transformational ministries, which are bringing the gospel of the kingdom to bear on the lives of hundreds and thousands of men and women, in and outside the church.

For this we must give thanks and praise to God, who brought this ministry (and others committed to the same kingdom objectives) into being, raised up its leaders and participants, carried the burden of instruction, and is bringing forth the fruit of these programs in ways similar to those summarized above.

On the glorious splendor of your majesty
    and on your wondrous works, I will meditate.
They shall speak of the might of your awesome deeds,
    and I will declare your greatness.
They shall pour forth the fame of your abundant goodness
    and shall sing aloud of your righteousness.
(Ps. 145:5–7 ESV)

Undoubtedly, should the Centurions Program do nothing more than continue in its present mode as a training program and resource center, it is reasonable to expect that such results as outlined above might continue to be increasingly in evidence.

But for the Centurions Program and for all other programs and ministries focusing on biblical worldview to realize their full potential and make their maximum contribution to the progress of Christ's kingdom, they must develop beyond being merely worldview programs; they must begin orienting toward becoming a unified *kingdom movement* committed to restoring the gospel of the kingdom, restoring the true hope of the gospel, and recovering the church from its captivity to what theologian David Wells has called a "shrunken" version of the faith of Christ.

Some Observations Concerning Social Movements

A social movement is a widespread and far-reaching network of men and women united by a common vision and devoted to the task of changing their society and their times and, hence, the course of history itself. Over the years, social movements have gathered impressive power and achieved lasting results in the ways people live and societies develop. Think of the abolitionist movement of the nineteenth century, the movement to enfranchise women in the early twentieth century, the civil rights movement, the labor movement, the anti-war movement of the 1960s and 1970s, the women's rights movement, and the gay rights movement of our own time. Social movements do not simply happen; they are the product of earnest thought, careful planning, deliberate action, powerful communications, compelling purpose and vision, and a wide array of devoted labors.

We may make three observations concerning effective social movements:

1. They form in order to redress some clearly identified and boldly defined social evil.
2. They form around six essential features, which scholars and historians describe by different terms, but with essentially the same aspects.
3. They are temporary phenomena. Social movements do not form in order to create a permanent movement but to overturn existing evils, create new ways of social thinking and acting, and establish movement members in permanent social and cultural institutions.

Where these three features are in place and consciously pursued, social movements can exert enormous power. Let's look a little more closely at each of these.

Social Evils: The Other

Social movements form to redress some clearly identified and boldly defined social evil. The leaders of a social movement must be crystal clear as to what they are trying to overthrow. They must identify their enemy—the "Other"—in clear and uncompromising terms, and labor diligently to explicate and demonstrate why it is an evil, where it lurks, what are its harmful effects, and how it may be eradicated. They must declaim against their identified Other and seek to persuade the public and relevant powers concerning the utter necessity of its overthrow and eradication. We have no problem recognizing enemies such as slavery, segregation, or the oppression of workers or women as social evils; however, in their day, such recognition was not obvious and had to be developed by movement intellectuals and others.

What social evil—what Other—have the Wilberforce Forum Centurions and other worldview ministries sought to address? I would suggest that the evil we are seeking to overturn can be summarized by the words *the Lie*.

What is the Lie? Paul explains it in Romans 1:21–25. Whereas the biblical worldview insists that God is Truth, the Lie asserts that God is a construct and man is the arbiter of truth:

Biblical Worldview	The Lie
God is Truth	God is a construct; man is the arbiter of truth

The Lie develops into a worldview according to certain corollary lies and half-truths:

- Truth is relative and pragmatic.
- Ethics are utilitarian.
- The cosmos is an accident.
- Life is a fleeting and meaningless journey to oblivion.

- Man is a product of evolution.
- The principal concern of man is man.
- Spiritual concerns are private, merely.
- Christianity is a pliable, changeable thing.
- Christ is one option among many as a way to eternal life.

And so forth. The Lie has implications for every area of life, as is patently clear. And what is equally clear, in a day when over half of confessing Christians believe that there are many ways to God, the Lie easily leaches into the body of Christ, diverting her focus, undermining her mission, and sapping her strength. Asked for a reason for the loss of reality that many Christians experience concerning their faith, Francis Schaeffer answered, "Surely the greatest reason for this loss of reality is that, while we say we believe one thing, we allow the spirit of the naturalism of the age to creep into our thinking, unrecognized."

The naturalism of our secular age—the Lie—has inundated the unbelieving world and swept into the church, and as yet has not been fully exposed and forcefully evicted. The various worldview ministries mentioned above came into being to address this situation, especially since it seemed to them that the large majority of Christian voices were remaining silent concerning the Lie and its effects on the gospel and the church, and were content merely to seek a kind of pietistic accommodation with what has seemed an intractable status quo. These worldview ministries have consistently worked, independently of one another but often with overlapping formats and foci, for over twenty years. As a result, awareness of their efforts is now growing and, in many ways, beginning to coalesce.

We do not insist that those who embrace and promulgate the Lie are themselves consciously and purposefully liars; rather, they are deceived, living in the darkness of unbelief, and unable or unwilling to embrace the Truth that God is everywhere revealing to them about himself (Eph. 4:17–19; 2 Cor. 4:1–6). They have been blinded by the father of lies, so that they cannot see the Truth about God that is everywhere on display (John 8:44). Yet they are willing conspirators in their own ignorance; they prefer gods of their own devising, which they can manipulate or change at will, to the unchanging God of heaven and earth and his eternal law and gospel. Against those who promote the Lie, embrace the Lie, or remain silent before the Lie, the prophets of old consistently proclaimed, "Thus saith the Lord!"

Further, we should note that the Lie does not, nor ever can, satisfy the deep needs and concerns of the human soul. Even those who embrace and promulgate the Lie show by various critical inconsistencies and incongruities, as well as an unquenchable longing for transcendence, that they cannot live with the Lie. They are constantly "borrowing against" biblical truth to prop up their patently flimsy worldviews, although they do so generally unchallenged. Moreover, captive to the Lie, men everywhere live as prisoners to the fear of death, to which they are reluctantly resigned as the end state of all life and the cosmos (Heb. 2:15). This explains why we hear so much talk about "quality of life" and about extending and enriching human life, as well as so many euphemisms for death. Thus the Lie has made prisoners—of fear, uncertainty, disappointment, despair, deception, and death—everyone who continues under its sway. Within the church the Lie has subverted the power of the gospel of the kingdom by creating false hopes, inadequate aspirations, missional complacency, ethical confusion, and cultural indifference among a great many members of the body of Christ. The Lie is an unmitigated evil and must be attacked directly and earnestly if it is to be overthrown.

For these various worldview ministries to become a kingdom movement, we will have to agree on an Other, or an enemy, against which we are organizing to assert our most cherished claim that God is Truth. If our burden is Truth, then our ultimate enemy can only ever be the Lie. In an age where there is no truth, there must also perforce be no lies. And so the modern world has convinced itself that every man is free to do what is right in his own eyes, and many church leaders have subscribed to this agenda, careful, however, to give it a scriptural gilding, but without scriptural basis or substance. If we are to unite against the Lie, we will need to be willing to name names, point the finger at specific offenders, engage the Lie wherever it has established a base of operations, challenge and expose the Lie in all its forms, demonstrate the many and variegated forms of evil for which the Lie alone is responsible, and patiently and lovingly point the way beyond the Lie to the basic premise of the biblical worldview, that God is Truth. All this we must learn to do with reverence and respect, with gentleness and compassion, with patience and love, and in a context of winsome reasoning, unbreakable unity, and uncompromised obedience to God (2 Tim. 2:24, 25; 1 Pet. 3:15).

Questions for Reflection or Discussion

4. Get a concordance and look up the listings under the headings "lie," "lies," and "liars." Why do you think this theme is so pervasive in the Scriptures?

5. Do you agree with the biblical teaching that people who have not come to the truth of God in Jesus Christ are deceived and living under the influence of the Lie? What evidence would you point to in order to support your answer?

6. Do you see evidence that you and your Christian friends are in some ways influenced by the Lie? How does this happen?

Social Movements: Six Essential Features

Social movements form around six essential features. While these are variously described by scholars and historians, I will examine them under the following headings:

- Vision
- Values
- Vernacular

- Volunteers
- Vehicles
- Validation

We might think of a social movement as a wheel, consisting of an inner hub, six spokes, and an outer rim.

1. Vision

Every social movement must articulate a vision of what it hopes to achieve. The vision determines the direction and speed with which the movement rolls along. It is the agreed-upon end result or destination to which all the members of the movement subscribe and all its energies are bent. For the kingdom movement we envision, this vision can be nothing more or less than what Christ taught us to pray: that his kingdom would come and his will would be done, increasingly, on earth as it is in heaven. We are called to seek first the kingdom of God and his righteousness for every area of human life and interest and all the cosmos.

This vision must be spelled out in imaginative language through a wide range of media, including speech, writing, the arts, and the formation of new institutions. Here we can look at one example within the Christian worldview community. The Centurions vision is already spelled out for us in the statements of mission and vision of PFM, the parent ministry of the Wilberforce Forum and the Centurions.

Our mission is: "To seek the transformation of believers as they apply biblical thinking to all of life, enabling them to transform their communities through the grace and truth of Jesus Christ."

Our vision is: "That Jesus Christ's transforming grace and truth be manifested in the lives of believers, enabling the Church to influence every arena of life, advancing truth, justice, mercy, love, goodness, and beauty."

For the purpose of movement formation, this kingdom vision and mission must be further developed and explained at the levels of personal spiritual formation, personal mission field, disciple-making, church renewal and reformation, social and cultural transformation, and historical transmission and transformation of the vision and mission. In addition, for the Wilberforce Forum to unite with other worldview ministries in a kingdom movement, the essential components of its vision and mission must be matched with the statements of vision and mission from the other ministries joining the movement to restore the gospel of the kingdom and the hope of that gospel.

It is not enough to articulate a vision. That vision must be worked into the movement at every level, and continuously. It must be reiterated and evaluated over and over to discover and celebrate progress over time and in specific areas.

Questions for Reflection or Discussion

7. How would you describe the vision and mission of your own local church? Would you describe this as a "kingdom" vision? Why or why not?
8. How about your own vision of the Christian life? What hope gives direction to your daily walk with the Lord?
9. What do you understand by the term *kingdom of God*? Use a concordance to look up some instances of this term, then meditate on or discuss what you see there.

2. Values

A movement's values are those core convictions its members cherish above all else, indeed, even enough to die for, if necessary. The values of a movement constitute the hub of the wheel. They integrate all the parts, focus the energy, and coordinate all the efforts of the movement. Again, the values of PFM suggest a starting point for thinking about a movement to restore the gospel of the kingdom:

• Centered in Jesus Christ—in our obedience to the Risen Lord

- Grounded in the Bible—in our life and ministry
- Dependent on prayer—as the foundation for ministry
- Partnered with the church—as the biblical means for ministry
- Committed to unity—with all believers in Jesus Christ as our Lord Jesus commands
- Compelled to evangelize and disciple—to bring Jesus Christ to the lost and to help people grow in Him
- Loving others—by treating all people with grace, trust, and respect
- Seeking excellence—by demonstrating integrity and wise stewardship

These values must be elaborated as to how they relate to a kingdom movement such as we are envisioning and as to what they imply as we seek to live them out in our biblical worldview. As with the statement of vision and mission, these values must be refined and clarified against the organizational and program values of other likeminded agencies and individuals. More specifically, these core values must be elaborated in terms of the gospel of the kingdom, the restoration of which provides the motive force for the movement.

Questions for Reflection or Discussion

10. What ultimate values organize and give direction to the ministries of your church?
11. What would you say are the organizing values and priorities of your own life? What would others who know you say?
12. Where do we get our values? Do you think the values of our churches and fellow believers, as well as our own values, are at all affected by the Lie? Explain.

3. Vernacular

Any social movement has its own vernacular, a vocabulary of terms, ideas, mottoes, and catchphrases that are broadly understood and embraced and used consistently throughout the movement to provide integrity, direction, and unity. This vernacular represents the grease, the screws and bolts, and the bands and braces of the wheel. In the Centurions Program we have a start on a common vernacular, which includes such terms and ideas as:

- Truth—both the story of truth (*How Now Shall We Live?*) and its structure (*The Faith*)
- Culture—the artifacts, institutions, and conventions by which people define, sustain, and enrich themselves
- Biblical worldview—including the key questions by which this is developed

To a lesser extent, other terms have begun to find their way into the training, but not with the kind of focus that indicates they are becoming the lingua franca of a movement. These include:

- Kingdom of God—what we have entered and what we embody and proclaim
- Spiritual formation—the shape and means of personal transformation
- Personal mission field—each believer's personal calling to culture and disciple-making
- Teaching and learning—what we seek and how we seek it
- Making disciples—what this process involves and what it seeks to achieve
- Cohorts—including co-laborers, cadres, and communities
- Transformation—mind, character, relationships, ministry, influence
- Revival, renewal, and reformation

Questions for Reflection or Discussion

13. Are you aware of any mottoes, slogans, catchphrases, recurrent terms, or other forms of "vernacular" that guide your church's life and ministry?
14. Why is it important to agree on a common vernacular if we expect to become a kingdom movement?
15. Review the terms listed above. How many of these are part of your own speech and communication? Which are not?

4. Volunteers

In a social movement, everyone is a volunteer in the sense that he or she is committed to the project by conviction of mind, heart, and conscience, as well as devotion of life. This is not to say that there are no paid staff members in a social movement; rather, it only insists that everyone, paid staff or field volunteer, is committed to the effort to the depths of his or her being, no matter what sacrifice and self-denial may be required.

Social movements require six kinds of volunteers; while these are separate and distinct functions, in a very real sense every member of the movement carries out some aspect of each of these functions whatever may be his or her calling or place in the movement:

- Visionaries—define and articulate the vision in clear and compelling terms
- Vocalizers—communicate the vision to volunteers, public, and the Other
- Vanguard—leaders in the field who translate the vision into action
- Voles—men and women "on the ground" who carry the work through to realizing the vision
- Vestry—organizers, tabulators, evaluators, and accountants
- Versifiers—those who celebrate the achievements of the volunteers and the progress of the movement

These different functionaries are the spokes of the wheel, the inner hub of which contains the core values and vision of the movement, and the outer rim of which consists of the various programs and activities that encounter the "ground" and keep the movement going forward as it makes progress in realizing its vision. While there are separate and distinct spokes, each spoke partakes of the strengths of all the others, and every spoke must be kept fit and strong to bear the weight of the movement as it progresses. The spokes collaborate in their common endeavor by drawing on the vernacular of the movement in all their planning, evaluating, working, communicating, teaching, and ministry development.

Questions for Reflection or Discussion

16. Which of the above "spokes of the wheel" do you see active in your church? Which are conspicuously missing or underrepresented?
17. In a social movement, everyone fulfills all the requirements of every spoke in some way. However, each spoke represents a different group of movement participants. With which of these spokes do you most readily identify?
18. In a sentence or two, relate everything we've said thus far about social movements, expressing your summary in terms of the wheel, its various parts, and its direction.

5. Vehicles

The vehicles of a social movement—the rim of the wheel—are those organized entities by which the movement expresses its convictions, mobilizes and resources its volunteers, sustains and guides its energy, advances its progress, communicates its vision, and engages the world on the ground. In the Centurions Program these include:

- The training program
- The Centurions Web site

- The BreakPoint Web site
- Various communication vehicles: *BreakPoint WorldView* magazine, Worldview Church eReport, weekly Centurions Newsletter, etc.
- Regional Cohorts—subdivided and supplemented by Colleagues-in-Ministry, Cadres, and Communities of Transformation
- BreakPoint staff—structure and protocols
- Additional training programs of the Centurions: Bible studies, Sunday school classes
- BreakPoint resources: Wide Angle, etc.
- The Wilberforce Project
- Ongoing Centurions Training: Tuesdays with T. M., Second Year, Cohort Leaders Training

For these vehicles to succeed, they must have certain common components, including (1) goals and outcomes, (2) movement resources, (3) means of evaluation, (4) feedback and celebration. In a kingdom movement involving several agencies, some agreement will have to be reached concerning the structure, formats, and proper functioning of these various vehicles and the way the vehicles of various ministries can be related to one another in coordinated and complementary ways.

Questions for Reflection or Discussion

19. What are the primary vehicles for ministry of your church? Does your church depend on outside ministries for part of its own work? Which?
20. Review the four common components such vehicles of ministry require. Which are employed in your church? In what ways?
21. How might better coordination and collaboration of various worldview ministries make all their ministry vehicles more effective for restoring the gospel of the kingdom?

6. *Validation*

A social movement, to succeed, must be able to demonstrate progress. It should leave marks on the ground wherever it has rolled through society and culture. It must be able to show that it is gaining ground against the Other across a broad spectrum of visible and undeniable results. These results must be intentionally sought, assiduously assessed, and faithfully celebrated at every level of the movement and to the public at large.

Validation must be so much a part of the movement that every participant has some basic orientation in the hows and whys of assessment and is continuously seeking evidence that the movement is gaining ground against the Other.

Questions for Reflection or Discussion

22. How do you evaluate your own progress in the Lord?
23. How does your church evaluate its progress in ministry?
24. Reflect on or discuss for a few minutes the mounting impact of secular, unbelieving thought on our culture and society. Does this suggest anything about the "validity" of what our churches have been doing to advance the cause of Christ and his kingdom?

Social Movements: Temporary Phenomena

Effective social movements exist not to perpetuate themselves but to achieve their vision. Thus, for as long as a social movement continues its momentum, it must focus on four overarching objectives:

1. Achieving specific, immediate victories and measurable outcomes against the Other
2. Growing and expanding the movement
3. Placing members in permanent social and cultural institutions for the long-term
4. Defining the legacy it hopes to leave once it has ceased to

> function as a movement (e.g., revived churches, changed
> laws, reformed values and ethics, new institutions,
> changed lives, transformed communities)

A movement to restore the gospel of the kingdom such as we
are herein envisioning will itself be, like the revivals of the past,
a temporary phenomenon. At the same time, it could last for a
generation or more. The Celtic revival, we recall, continued for
nearly four centuries. However, this kingdom movement must
not take as its focus the perpetuation of the movement as such.
Instead, it must continue to focus all its energies on overcoming
the Lie and restoring the gospel of the kingdom and the hope of
that gospel to the churches and the public square.

Questions for Reflection or Discussion

25. What is the relationship between a movement, which may
    involve various parachurch organizations, and the church
    itself? What is the church's function and mission, and how
    can a movement support the church?
26. What overarching objectives guide your church's life and
    ministry? Are you making progress in achieving these?
27. Are you aware of any effort on the part of your church's
    leadership to coordinate the activities of your church with
    other congregations in your community? Do you think this
    would be a good idea?

From Programs to Movement

The various worldview ministries are even now beginning to
converge and congeal, as is evidenced by the wide representa-
tion of individuals who are lending their vision and skills to
the Centurions Program. The faculty of this burgeoning ministry includes representatives from each of the following worldview ministries: the Acton Institute, the C. S. Lewis Institute,
World magazine, Joni and Friends, Summit, The Truth Project,
and Reflections Ministries. The Centurions Program also has on

its faculty instructors from such diverse institutions and locations as Central Connecticut State University, Calvin Theological Seminary, Fuller Theological Seminary, Reformed Theological Seminary of Istanbul, and Westminster Theological Seminary. In addition, writers associated with the Centurions are published by a wide range of evangelical and Catholic houses, which seem ready to receive further work from them and their associates and disciples. The Wilberforce Forum is thus strategically positioned to assume a critical role in calling these and other ministries together for more focused, cooperative, and intensive effort to recover the gospel and liberate the church. Indeed, initial efforts have indicated that representatives of these and other ministries are willing and eager to discover ways of making this kingdom movement a reality.

What might we hope to realize from such a united effort? That is, what legacy for the future might we unite to pursue?

The Mission: Personal Transformation

We might believe that this kingdom movement could provide a significant impetus for change in personal and social values and practices. Let this be a movement for outreach and equipping, and let us take as our common mission to promote and nurture Christian transformation in the minds, lives, relationships, ministries, and spheres of influence of those we will be serving. By sharing resources; collaborating on projects and in specific geographies and fields; training and deploying platoons of volunteer evangelists, apologists, activists, and reformers; reaching out more aggressively and helpfully to pastors and church leaders; maintaining mutually edifying communications and accountability; and, above all, covenanting to pursue the Lord in united, extraordinary prayer for revival, worldview ministries united in a kingdom movement might reasonably expect to see the enhancement and improvement of their efforts to effect change in the lives of the people they serve. Thus, by pursuing the gospel of the kingdom together, we might hope to unite the missions of disciple-making and cultural transformation into one restored and fully embraced Great Commission (Matt. 28:18–20).

The Objective: Social and Cultural Transformation

Let these united ministries take as their common objectives (1) to raise up a generation of men and women equipped for transformed kingdom living, according to the mission outlined above; (2) to provide them with the finest resources for outreach and disciple-making; and (3) to aid them in linking up with one another in ministry teams and action platoons, so that they are able to raise up others for the work of prayer, study, and kingdom living and action. Thus, those we serve will be able to equip and encourage others in the transformed life, working together for social and cultural change at the local level, and thereby contributing to a growing movement of transformed individuals who are seeking to restore health and wholeness to our culture and society through the recovery of the gospel and the revitalization of the church (2 Tim. 2:2).

The Vision: Transformed Times

Let us take as our common vision to serve as a catalyst for achieving a watershed moment in history. Let us aim to impact the times in which we live so that future generations will look back and agree that in our generation a turn was accomplished; a new direction was proclaimed; and a vanguard of men and women, organized in working teams and national networks, was equipped and resourced to lead our churches in revival and reformation, our culture in renewal, our society into a new Great Awakening, and our world into a spiritually and ethically more wholesome and prosperous future. Let us, in other words, articulate a clear, compelling, and comprehensive vision of the kingdom of Christ developing in our twenty-first-century world, transforming lives, homes, churches, communities, societies, and cultures. Let it be our earnest longing that those who persist in the Lie might be compelled to admit that we have, indeed, turned their world upside down for Jesus Christ.

No one of these worldview ministries can hope to accomplish such a grand vision by itself; nor will they likely do so by continuing to work independently of one another, without any conscientious and coordinated effort to intensify, through a kind of spiritual and organizational fusion, the energy for transformation that each of these ministries represents.

But if it pleases God and he responds to our earnest pleadings and united steps of faith, these ministries could well accomplish, by the power of God at work in them together, exceedingly more than all that any of them has ever dared to ask or think (Eph. 3:20). They will do this by working together, praying together, communicating often, sharing vision and values, planning and sharing resources with one another, and, above all, embodying in their loving service to one another and to the church the vision of renewal they seek.

Where To From Here?

What will it take for the various worldview programs and ministries to unite in bringing about a kingdom movement to restore the gospel and free the church from her captivity to a shrunken faith? Many things, but I would like to suggest the following:

1. Immediate and sustained discussion of the implications and ways and means of forging these disparate ministries and programs into a spiritual movement with lasting, transformational effects. This conversation must be broached and pursued up and down the ranks of these ministries, with sufficient and effective incorporation of new ideas and feedback to all participants.
2. A move by representatives of these ministries to adopt a

form or framework for identifying the players, program, and progress of the movement (such as the six elements outlined above). They must seek to understand how each facet of their ministries fits into the overall movement— what its contribution should be and how it must be strengthened and resourced to make that contribution.

3. Deliberate, intentional effort to integrate the language and form of a social movement into the various ministries, and the various ministries into the framework of a social movement. This may involve such things as summit meetings, joint planning sessions, the creation of a manifesto, discovering means of mutual accountability, joint communiqués, creation of a board of oversight, and developing new communications media.

4. Agreement on the Other against which the movement is to be organized, and further development of the rationale for and means of moving to overthrow and eradicate the Other to the fullest extent of the movement's ability.

5. Identification and adoption of movement vernacular, together with exploration of ways of integrating that vernacular into existing ministries and new endeavors.

6. Establishment of criteria for the development of movement vehicles and the validation of movement endeavors.

7. Development of ways and means for placing movement members in the permanent structures of society and culture.

Conclusion

The time is ripe for such a movement to restore the gospel of the kingdom—a movement of biblical worldview forged out of the common vision and convictions of existing ministry leaders and united in a conscious effort to overthrow the Lie and seek the Lord for revival and renewal in every area of life. The failures of the modernist worldview, the flimsiness of postmodernism, the looming danger of militant Islam, the renewal of evangelical Catholicism and its growing dialog with the rest of the church, and the implosion of evangelicalism and its manifest longing for a renewed identity—all make this an ideal time for worldview ministries to unite to reclaim the high ground for the gospel of the kingdom; to lead the church into the fuller liberty of the sons and daughters of God; and to lead the world into the light of truth in new, more powerful, and more lasting ways.

Let your work be shown to your servants, and your glorious power to their children. Let the favor of the Lord our God be upon us, and establish the work of our hands upon us; yes, establish the work of our hands! (Ps. 90:16–17 ESV)

Questions for Reflection or Discussion

28. How do your respond to this call for an initiative to restore the gospel of the kingdom? Do you think this is needed? Why or why not?
29. Is this a movement you would like to join? In what ways? What might you contribute?
30. Are you willing to begin praying for such a movement and seeking to discover ways you might become involved?

What You Can Do

If you answered the last question in an affirmative way, here are some things you can do to become part of this movement to restore the gospel of the kingdom and the hope of that gospel to the churches:

1. Pass this paper, "From Worldview Programs to Kingdom Movement," on to as many of your friends as you can. Urge them to read it and begin praying about its challenge. Meet to discuss the paper, using the questions provided.

2. Meet with leaders from your church, and invite them to read and study this paper with you or in their own groups.

3. Write to receive our weekly e-mail prayer letter, "Restoring Hope: A Kingdom Movement." Each issue shares insights, updates, prayer requests, and items for action to help you become informed and involved in this growing effort. Write by e-mail to Steve_Bradford@pfm.org and request to be on the mailing list for this prayer letter.

4. Each time you receive the prayer letter, forward it to several friends and encourage them to subscribe and to request their own copy of this paper.

5. Pray daily that God will honor the efforts of those who are involved in this movement, and that together we might seek the renewal of the church and the transformation of culture and society in our day.

T. M. MOORE
Fall 2008

APPENDIX 3

Transform America

Retake Education

"I feel as if I'm sending my teenage boy to live, not in a college, but in a red-light district," complained Anne.

"But why do you have to send him to *that* college?" I was curious.

"Well," answered Anne's husband, Ted, "my grandfather was one of the founders. He built a steel factory here to supply the railways. He made a small fortune and built our church and *that* college. He believed that in order to build our nation it was more important to build churches and colleges than to build railways, which would be replaced by another mode of transportation anyway."

"Ted's father," added Anne, "was the chairman of the college board when *we* studied there. He became a pioneer in making our city the Mecca of medical equipments. He wasn't trained for it, but stumbled into that line after the railways went out of business and steel had no market."

"Anne's father also served on the college board," Ted added. "He was a pastor, and the college belonged to our denomination."

"My parents," Anne continued the story, "had no problem sending their daughters to the college. All my siblings graduated from there. That's why we want John to continue our family tradition. The college still has a good reputation, especially in sports . . . but things have also changed."

"Sexual permissiveness is not *my* primary concern," Ted said, distancing himself from his wife's thinking. "We've made our mistakes, and the children will make theirs. Hopefully they'll learn, as did we. I have done stupid things. Anne and I have had our struggles like every other couple, and our failings have hurt our children. They know our weaknesses, but John doesn't seem to appreciate God's grace that made it possible for us to repent, forgive, and grow together as a family."

"Then why are you reluctant to send John there?" Anne asked.

"My problem," Ted explained, "is that the college no longer turns the hearts of the children to their fathers. It undermines the important values of marriage and family. In our day, the college promoted missions. Now, legalizing same-sex marriage seems to be the most important mission on campus. I'm not homophobic. My complaint is that the college no longer builds character, virtues, and skills that are necessary for succeeding as a family, a business, or a nation."

"John is a born manager—" Anne tried to turn the conversation in a positive direction, but Ted interrupted.

"Management is in his genes, but my father always said that managerial leadership is not merely talent and skills. It's also character. Your team, your clients, your church, and your family have to be able to trust that you'll always act in the interest of your common vision and mission; that you'll put people above profits; that you'll act justly and love mercy. Your team will follow you if they know that you're for them. When you have to act against one of them, the rest of the team doesn't need to know all the reasons; they have to have the confidence that you discipline your subordinates only because you walk the path of righteousness and expect your team to do the same. That's lovin' your neighbor as yourself. That's what it means to be a disciple of Jesus Christ. Your team and your community tend to trust you when they know that you are following the Lord with a clean conscience. That's what made American management so successful and attractive, but these days education discourages children from trusting and following the Lord. No wonder the world is losing its confidence in our banks, institutions, and economy! Our managers are more educated than ever, but colleges no longer care about character. The church does, but the university drives students away from the church."

"That's the issue," Anne said, putting the finger on the problem. "It will cost us $100,000 to see John through college. This money will come from a family trust that Ted's mother created when John was born. But we're afraid this money will be spent only to help John lose his faith and the values that have been important to our family and its success. In Africa, $100,000 might see a hundred kids through college. Are we being wise stewards? John's grandmother was very strict. She never would have given her money to send her children or grandchildren to the red-light district."

"Surely the professors know," I said to the couple, "that character is crucial for America's economic success. So why doesn't the college care about character?"

"I've thought about that a lot," Ted said, "because the college is more than my alma mater; it's a part of my family heritage, and I'm attached to it emotionally. I think the college does care about character. But the problem is that it has discarded its moral compass. Character requires having a stable North Star and following it scrupulously, no matter the temptations from within or the pressures from outside. God's Word was the moral compass for our culture—our education, business, and politics. Both the church and the college taught the Bible. But now the college turns young people away from the Bible and the church. It leaves them to follow their pop stars or their own foolish minds and sinful hearts. Without a compass, they no longer know which of their ideas are noble and which are merely trendy or harmful. Without a compass, they've become vulnerable to all sorts of Pied Pipers. That's why we're seeing lives shipwrecked all around us."

"I understand your dilemma," I said to Ted and Anne. "Your forefathers built the churches that built colleges and universities for the glory of God. They knew that wholesome education should help students discover truth, cultivate character, and grow in social skills, as well as acquire vocational skills and physical fitness. But now Satan has taken over the institutions your fathers built. First he gave them over to secularism and now, increasingly, to paganism. You can either lament this loss or seek the pioneering spirit of your parents to reclaim education."

"But what can a family do?" Anne sounded skeptical.

"A family may not be able to do much," I said, "but a church can certainly do more. It was through your church that your grandfather helped build that college. In fact, the church played a pivotal role in the Revolution that liberated America. Now it needs to liberate education from far more destructive tyranny of the secular lie that each child should become the compass of his own truth and morality."

"But how?" Ted and Anne asked together.

"And why," Anne continued, "would our church want to get involved in education?"

"You just told me that your church started that college and that Anne's father served on the college board because he was a pastor. The Christian church is the mother of Western education. The church started all the universities in Europe and most of the early universities and colleges in America. The church is losing America because it has given over to the world the responsibility to educate her youth."

"That's true," Ted agreed. "The separation of church and state has now come to mean the separation of truth and education, morality and education. Education is in a mess because it is no longer under the moral and theological influence of the church.

But how can an average church teach subjects that require specialization?"

"Education has several aspects: worldview formation, character formation, life-skills formation, and teaching of vocational skills. John can still go to *that* college to learn management, but the church has to take back from *that* college the responsibility of helping him develop his worldview, character, and life skills. This could happen if John went back to your church for the first two years of college education, formed his primary friendships and community there, got established in his faith, received an Associate of Arts degree, and then went to *that* college for the final two years of his degree."

Anne, still unconvinced, commented, "One church here runs a high school, and it is frustrated with how parents and church leaders keep interfering with the school."

"That was an important reason why universities separated from churches," I explained to her. "But don't forget, secular schools face similar interference from all sorts of lobbies. That is what it means to be a democratic society. However, just as a wise pastor does not interfere with how you run your family, the church and the parents will have to learn to respect the carefully defined autonomy and intellectual liberty of the college. Not everyone in the congregation agrees with everything a pastor or a Bible teacher says. Nor would everyone in the church agree with how a college is run or what it teaches. A church chooses its pastor carefully and then gives him the liberty to teach what he believes is biblical. If the pastor is wrong, there are usually wise people in the church who will study the issue with him respectfully. So should college professors be open to intellectual or methodological challenges from others who may not be professionals but may be right on a specific matter. In subjects such as science, history, arts, literature, or economics, where the Bible gives us greater freedom to study and explore, there ought to be greater room for sincere differences of opinion. If a church is mature enough to respect teachers' authority in the sphere of education, then a church and a college can benefit from each other and reinforce each other."

Anne began to think positively. "I still don't know how our church can do that . . . but come to think of it, the church does have empty classrooms from Monday through Friday. Plus there's an immense amount of unused talent within the congregation— gifted teachers, managers, executive assistants—not to mention financial resources. If all of John's friends were there the whole week, studying, playing, practicing music, and making films, they might want to keep coming on weekends, even when they go that *that* college. But tell me, how can the church double as a college?"

"I'm not thinking of duplicating the kind of colleges that are already failing," I assured her. "Academically, spiritually, morally, socially, financially, the education system in America is falling apart. The church doesn't need to imitate a system that is boring students to death. It can create a new pattern."

"American education has certainly failed to inspire our younger son Tim," Anne added. "He doesn't even want to go to college. I'll be grateful if he completes high school."

"Students that appear to be underachievers are only the first victims of this failing system," I said. "In fact, the system is destroying your entire civilization. At best it prepares young people to earn a living. It doesn't teach them how to live or to make sense of life. Pastor Rick Warren's book *Purpose Driven Life* has had such a phenomenal reception because secular education has systematically deprived life and universe of all meaning and purpose.

"Obviously, I don't know what makes Tim uninterested in education, but I do know that many students become underachievers because their teachers never become their friends and mentors as Jesus did with his disciples. How many students have a teacher who takes personal and self-sacrificing interest in their education? President Obama says that he was inspired to study because his mother woke him up at 4:30 AM to make him complete his homework. When he complained, she would say, 'Get up and do it—this is no picnic for me either.' Parents can do that when you are young. Once you are as old as Tim, you may need an adult mentor who believes in you—even though you appear to be a failure—and takes an interest in your education at personal cost. A close relationship with a teacher could inspire young people to put in the extra effort in learning. Most college professors cannot relate with students in depth because they see students for an hour or so, two or three times a week. Jesus was able to inspire his students to change the world because he became their friend. The problem may not be with Tim. The problem may be that the schools and colleges are not following Jesus' model of inspiring and teaching students."

"But," Ted interjected, "realistically, how can a church succeed where experts are failing?"

"Studies are showing," I contended, "that on average, parents who homeschool their kids are doing a better job than credentialed teachers in public schools. At college level, a church would need to replace parents with intelligent and motivated mentors who help a small group of students educate themselves with the help of a curriculum that some of us are developing.

"In our scheme, Monday to Friday, John and Tim will go to your church for 'college.' For two years they will be a part of a small class with two qualified and trained mentors. They will stay with the same teachers, just as the disciples stayed with Jesus the whole time—they didn't change professors every few hours. Together their small group of friends and their mentors will devote an hour or so to studying the Bible, not just devotionally, but also "worldviewishly." They will work through intellectual and moral questions raised by the text. The rest of the time will be spent on a carefully crafted curriculum. They'll follow a modular system. They may spend a whole month studying politics—biblical and secular—with the help of Great Books, CDs, DVDs, Internet, satellite and live seminars. Another month may be spent studying literature or philosophy or science.

"As a requirement for their AA degrees, John and Tim will need to invest one evening a week in community service as a part of your church's outreach to the community. John may tutor an inner-city kid from a single-parent family; Tim might drive an elderly person to the store. They may work with a small group in dreaming up and developing income-generating projects for single moms in community housing. John and Tim will be helped to think what it might mean for them to love their neighbors. They will study the problems and possibilities of the community they are serving, and conceptualize practical projects that could improve the community. This will include understanding actual beliefs and practices of the community and responding to them biblically. As part of their two-year degree program, they may come with me to India or go to Israel with your Bible teacher."

"This sounds interesting," Ted exclaimed. "I know our senior pastor would be open to these ideas. He is very busy, but he is a visionary. He is concerned because his daughter lost her faith when she went to college. If he invited you, would you come and speak to our church on how this might work?"

"I would love to come to your church with my friend Davis Norment and his father, Bobby, to speak in a weekend conference called 'Retake Education.' Bobby is a successful businessman, and Davis an experienced teacher. Together we are developing Rivendell Sanctuary, which is blazing a new kind of college, creating sanctuaries of higher education based on Jesus' model of apprenticeship. Rivendell Sanctuary will be launched in September 2010, but we can come to your church before that to speak in the 'Retake Education' conference. We would discuss the history and philosophy of education and apply Jesus' apprenticeship model to our contemporary needs. We would also consider what is wrong with secular and 'Christian' education today and what your church can actually do take back from the world those aspects of education that are destroying your nation."

"We have a dedicated group of families in our church who could take this on," Ted said. "And if they really do, I'll suggest to our church that we train ten mature couples and help them buy or rent large houses so that students can stay with them for two years before going to live in secular dorms. These Christian house-parents should become life mentors to young people, teaching them life skills, from personal devotions to dinner menu planning to budgeting, shopping, cooking, cleaning, serving, hospitality, dating, dancing, gardening, and just getting along with difficult people."

By now Anne was excited. "Man! If this happens, I wouldn't think twice about sending my little Leah to live in a coed house when she goes to college."[1]

---

1. For more information, please visit www.RivendellSanctuary.com.

Study Guide

The author and the publisher wish to thank the Disciple Nations Alliance and the following individuals who helped create this study guide: Scott Allen, John Bottimore, Kim Bottimore, Tim Williams, Heather Hicks, Dwight Vogt, Darrow Miller, Tyler Johnson, and Bob Moffitt.

Chapter 1
Morality: *The Floundering Secret of the West's Success*

1. Using the illustration of a dairy, Vishal lists several negative economic and social consequences for the dairy, its customers, and the larger society when a culture of dishonesty and distrust takes root. Describe these consequences.

2. "Moral integrity is a huge factor behind the unique socioeconomic/sociopolitical success of the West." Do you agree with this statement? Why or why not?

3. According to Vishal, not all societies are equally trustworthy. How did the gospel message that John Wesley (1703–1791) preached contribute to creating a culture of trustworthiness in England?

4. What, specifically, did Dutch churches do in the years following the sixteenth-century Reformation to form a culture of trustworthiness in the Netherlands? Compare this to your local church. Is it doing the same?

5. Read Deuteronomy 5:19–21 and Ephesians 4:28. How do these passages provide a foundation for a culture of trustworthiness?

6. How does postmodern relativism understand morality? How are pantheism and polytheism in India similar to Western postmodern relativism in regard to morality?

7. "Economists have lost the secret of the West's [social and economic] success." Do you agree with this statement? What will happen to the West if it cannot be recovered? What can Christians and churches do to help the West recover this lost secret?

8. A moral society begins with the moral integrity of its people, particularly in the seemingly small decisions they make

when no one is watching (for example, riding a bus without paying for a ticket, as the two American girls in Amsterdam did in Vishal's illustration). Take some time to think through any ways that you may be stealing. Write these down, confess them to God (and others if necessary), and make a commitment to change.

Chapter 2
Rationality: *The Forgotten Force Behind Western Technology*

1. Historically, how have Christian cultures differed from other cultures in the creation and use of technology?

2. For what purposes did Christian monasteries develop technologies? What biblical truths or principles motivated this?

3. What worldview differences prevented Eastern monks, e.g., Hindu and Chinese, from making technological progress despite living in civilizations much older than the West? What were the consequences of this?

4. What happened to the pursuit of truth and reason during the latter half of the twentieth century? Why did this occur? How are the effects of this visible in your culture today?

5. In what ways has the church given up the pursuit of rationality and learning? Would you say that your church or Christian community supports the development of education and learning? Discuss.

6. What can you do within your circles of influence to educate and assist others to understand and communicate the powerful linkage between biblical revelation, reason, and societal development? How can this be communicated and applied in everyday life?

Chapter 3
Family: *The Failing School of Western Character*

1. How has monogamy liberated women by giving them "unique power over their husbands" in ways that cohabitation and polygamy do not?

2. Why did Martin Luther believe that marriage is a better "school" for the development of character than a celibate, monastic life?

3. Reflect on the following passages and the biblical understanding of marriage and family that they form:

   • Genesis 2:18, 24: Who created sexuality and marriage? Did this happen before or after the Fall?
   • Genesis 1:26–27: Why did God create marriage?
   • Malachi 2:15: Why else did God create marriage?
   • Ephesians 5:21–33: How are husbands and wives to treat each other?
   • Ephesians 6:1–4: How are parents and children to treat each other?

4. "Monogamy is tough because it cannot be sustained without a spirituality that mandates love above lust, submission as the secret of greatness, meekness as the source of glory, and service as the path to power." Given this, what is the relationship between the valued principles of contemporary Western culture and the decline of monogamy?

5. Noah Webster's 1828 *American Dictionary of the English Language* defines marriage as:

   "The act of uniting a man and woman for life; wedlock; the legal union of man and woman for life. Marriage is a contract both civil and religious by which parties engage to live together in mutual affection and fidelity, till death shall separate them. Marriage was instituted by

God himself for the purpose of preventing the promiscuous intercourse of the sexes, for promoting domestic
felicity, and for securing the maintenance and education
of children."

A widely used contemporary dictionary defines marriage this
way:

"A legally recognized relationship, established by a civil
or religious ceremony, between two people who intend to
live together as sexual and domestic partners."

In what ways do these two definitions differ? What might be
some of the consequences of this redefinition of marriage in
the West?

6. Vishal makes the bold claim that "Islam [will] take over
   Europe through reproduction alone, without firing a gun or
   winning a debate." What evidence does he cite to support
   this claim?

7. "For Luther sex was for pleasure, procreation, and bonding a
   family into permanent unity." How did the sexual revolution
   of the 1960s change this understanding of sexuality? What
   are the consequences of this change for men? For women?

8. How has this chapter challenged your understanding of marriage and its role in society?

Chapter 4
Humanity: *The Forsaken Soul of Western Civilization*

1. In the powerful and tragic story of Sheela, Vishal concludes
   with this statement: "What we experienced . . . was a clash of
   two worldviews, both of which cannot be true. We saw this
   child very differently than the parents saw their own daughter." Our worldviews, or our deeply held religious beliefs,
   determine our values, which in turn determine our actions
   and behaviors. Based on this, fill in the table below:

	Ruth & Vishal	Sheela's parents
Religious beliefs that informed their view of Sheela (be specific)		
The value that each had for Sheela based on these beliefs		
Specific behaviors or actions taken based on these beliefs and values		

2. Along with accepting polygamy, the Netherlands has legalized infanticide under certain circumstances. Other Western
   countries are following this example. What beliefs underlie
   these countries' actions? How would you argue against these
   beliefs?

3. More and more people have decided that a human being is nothing more than an animal. What consequences of this belief do you see in your own country?

4. "The belief in the unique dignity of human beings was the force that created the Western civilization, where citizens don't exist for the state but the state exists for individuals." Explain what this means in your own words.

5. What could change the opinions of people who believe that human life is not important and should not be protected? How can you help with this?

6. Consider and write down what God is calling you to do in response to what you have read.

Chapter 5
His Wounds: *For the Healing of the Nations*

1. Vishal discusses ways in which Americans are losing their freedom. In what ways have you or people you know experienced a loss of freedom? What has been the cause of this?

2. Christians are often seen by secular society as intolerant people. Vishal points out ways in which secular society is intolerant. Are both of these views correct?

3. Read Genesis 12:2–3. What does this passage reveal about God's purposes for history? What, in light of this, were the purposes of Jesus' death? How did his death accomplish these things?

4. In what ways has Christianity become "privately engaging but publicly irrelevant"? How has this affected you personally?

5. Think of people you know who model biblical boldness for truth in society. How do they do this well, and how can you imitate them?

6. What will it cost you to stand boldly for truth in your sphere of influence? Are you willing to pay the price to protect your freedoms? Pray and then write down what God is calling you to do in response to what you have read.

Chapter 6
His Compassion: *Jesus the Troublemaker*

1. In John 5, what reason does the lame man give for why no one has helped him into the pool? What are some examples in your culture that illustrate a lack of compassion for those who are needy?

2. Healing the blind man in John 9 was not the only objective of Jesus' service. What was his other objective? How did he accomplish it?

3. "Because an 'unknown' blind beggar is special to God, we must have compassion for him individually. This compassion must be visible in specific acts of mercy, but our compassion for him must go deep enough to create a society that can see that a blind man is a special person." Write three ideas you (or your family or church) could do to help society respond to the value of the marginalized and vulnerable.

4. Vishal argues that Jesus intentionally cultivated a mass following. What are the differences between how and why Jesus built up his following and the motives and methods of other religious and national leaders throughout history? What can you learn from the way Jesus stirred social change?

5. Why didn't the disciples understand Jesus' responses to the Canaanite woman in Matthew 15?

6. Jesus confronted the sin that separates people into groups. If he were alive today, what do you think he would confront in your nation, your church, or your life?

7. What reasons does Vishal give for why our service lacks the power that Jesus demonstrated in his service?

8. What is one way you could "take up your cross" to fight a corrupt establishment with moral weapons this year?

Chapter 7
His Kingdom: *The Natural and the Supernatural*

1. What evidence is given for the existence of a supernatural realm (from Jesus' experience, from Daniel's, and from the author's)? What evidence could you add from your life?

2. How did John know that "the whole world is under the control of the evil one" (1 John 5:19)? Why is it important to understand the true nature and power of evil?

3. "Daniel had acquired all the political power that a Jew could expect in the Babylonian and Medo-Persian empires. But he spent weeks in fasting and prayer for the rebuilding of Jerusalem." Why did he do this? What does this reveal about prayer and the way the kingdom of God works?

4. What system of power, in particular, makes war against Christ and wants to govern in place of God? What does this mean for how we should pray for our leaders? Take some time right now to pray for leaders.

5. How, according to Vishal, does the kingdom of Satan begin? What can we do to stop the kingdom of Satan from taking root and ruling around us?

6. Why is the principle of human equality not self-evident? Describe a situation you have seen when a particular group of people were not treated with the same value, worth, and dignity as others. How was the group impacted?

7. What is the source of the idea that the future can be better than the past or present, and that individuals and groups can make a difference? What is lost when a person has "hope" but does not know or acknowledge its source?

8. What are some false or damaging beliefs that people you know hold? What can you do to help them discover the source of these "truths" which they hold so dear?

Chapter 8
His Truth: *The Key to Transformation*

1. The Protestant Reformers, following the biblical pattern, saw no conflict between *reason* and *revelation*. Because of this, they taught that all Christians should pursue wisdom and knowledge. What, in turn, did the Reformers promote and establish?

2. On the graph below, identify in which of the four quadrants each of the following would belong:

   - Biblical Christians
   - Atheists (secular humanists)
   - Animists, neopagans, Eastern philosophies
   - Jihadists
   - Modern "liberal" Christians
   - Many modern evangelical and charismatic Christians
   - YOU

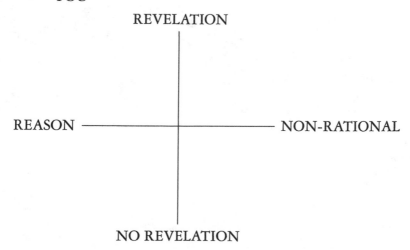

What are some of the implications of your understanding?

3. Vishal quotes a number of Old and New Testament texts about *knowing* and *understanding*. What point is he trying

to make? How does this broaden your view of the Christian life?

4. What are the consequences of a person or nation believing lies? What are the consequences of a person or nation believing Truth?

5. What has led to the spread of anti-intellectualism in the evangelical church? What has been the result of this anti-intellectualism in the church? In our nations?

6. Vishal says, "Deception has to rely on force." Where do you see deception and force at work in your own community or nation?

7. Where did you place yourself in the question #2 quadrant? Why are you there? What one thing will you do in this coming week to move from where you are to being closer to the center of the revelation–reason quadrant?

Chapter 9
His Law: *Sin and Its Consequences*

1. Vishal tells a story from his time working with "untouchables" in 1977. Describe in your own words the lesson of the story.

2. Vishal warns the West of what will happen as we move from worshiping God the Creator to worshiping his creation (man and nature). List some of the consequences of modern nature worship (neopaganism).

3. "Societies that worship make-believe gods or refuse to worship the living God cannot have moral order and discipline that come from within." What does this mean? Why is this so? What happens in a nation whose citizens do not internally self-govern themselves based on God's moral law?

4. On the following scale, where would you place yourself?

Strong need for external authority[1]	———————————	Strong internal self-government

    What does this tell you about yourself?

5. What is the purpose of God's moral law?

6. How does obedience to God's laws lead to the health and prosperity of a society? In contrast, how does disobedience of God's laws lead to the breakdown and impoverishment of a society?

7. Which of Vishal's discussions of the Ten Commandments most captured your imagination? Why?

8. How can you strengthen your internal self-government? Pick an area where you need better moral discipline. What will you do this week to grow in this area?

1. External authority includes parents, laws, police, and more rules and regulations in society.

Chapter 10
Evangelism: *Heralding Truth*

1. "Ultimately it is ideas, not armies, that rule the world."
    What ideas are ruling the society you are living in? Take a
    few moments and write down the implications of those ideas.
    Are they leading to freedom or oppression? In what ways?

2. In your own words, describe the biblical role of the evangelist.
    In what ways does Vishal's description of the evangelist in
    this chapter differ from how you previously understood it?

3. This chapter makes a clear argument that "slavery is a mat-
    ter of belief." In what ways can believing the wrong things
    lead to enslavement? How have you seen yourself enslaved
    because of wrong beliefs?

4. Why did Luther's preaching of justification by faith alone stir
    up the masses?

5. Review Vishal's ideas on the centrality of Paul's doctrine of
    salvation. How was Paul's message of salvation a message of
    social reform?

6. Vishal discusses three options for reforming a society. What
    are the three options? List the strengths and weaknesses of
    each. Which option does Vishal propose as the best? Do you
    agree? Why or why not?

7. In what ways does the message that "Jesus is Lord" conflict
    with the ideas of your society? Would it be dangerous to pro-
    claim that message? Why?

8. After reading this chapter, what conclusions have you come
    to about how God wants to use you as an evangelist? Be
    specific.

Chapter 11
The Holy Spirit: *The Spirit of Truth and Power*

1. In chapter 8 Vishal made clear that societies are destroyed by a lack of knowledge. In this chapter he makes the same statement but says, "Knowledge alone is not enough." Why is knowledge not enough in making us witnesses?

2. In your own words, define and describe *prophetic evangelism*.

3. "Salvation and judgment are the inseparable sides of the same coin: God's holiness and hatred of evil." With this in mind, what is the church's role as Christ's body in the world in bringing about holiness and justice?

4. By your evaluation, has the church been a solid voice for justice? Why or why not?

5. "The tragedy of the contemporary church is that those Christians who rightly stress the necessity of the work of the Holy Spirit in our lives are often mistaken about the purpose of God's gift of the Holy Spirit to the church." In what ways are they mistaken? What is the purpose of God's gift of the Spirit?

6. What was the transformation that the baptism of the Holy Spirit brought about in the disciples?

7. What is the connection between *prophetic evangelism* and *cross-bearing*?

8. Be honest and journal what the reactions are in your heart when you contemplate our call as Christians to prophetic evangelism. Reflect upon the need for the Holy Spirit to fulfill this call.

Chapter 12
The Church: *The Pillar of Truth*

1. Do you agree with the statement that the church should be "a threat to those who have vested interests in false and oppressive ideas"? Why or why not?

2. How is self-sacrificing love an antidote to poverty?

3. On a scale of 1 to 10, where would you place your local church's view of people? Do they view them primarily as souls to be saved from hell (1) or as individuals to support physically, socially, or economically (10)? If you are not part of a local church, rate yourself. What are your reasons for this placement?

4. Pick a vested interest in your community that you believe is responsible for oppression (e.g., employers that intentionally take advantage of workers, abortion clinics, strip bars). On a scale of 1 to 10, how might these groups see the churches in your community—as harmless (1) or as a threat (10)? Why?

5. What are the social implications of Jesus' statement in Matthew 16:18, "I will build my church, and the gates of hell will not prevail against it"?

6. In *Twilight of the Idols* Nietzsche said, "Christianity . . . is the *anti-Aryan* religion *par excellence*." What did he mean?

7. Make a plan to do one thing this week that expresses self-sacrificing love for someone in your sphere of relationships outside your family or church (something you would not have done without this assignment). What will you do? For whom? Where? When in the next week?

Chapter 13
Hope: *He's Making All Things New*

1. With a multitude of forces arrayed against optimism for the future, how would you summarize the basis of Christian hope and communicate it to both Christian and non-Christian audiences?

2. What thoughts underlie the pessimism toward the future often found among today's Christians? How is this a hindrance in effectively engaging the world for Christ? Give specific examples of how Jesus responded to similar challenges.

3. What happens when believers focus too much on the strength of the powers of darkness? What biblical truths ought to override the ensuing pessimism?

4. Can you detect evidence in your own life of the prevalent pessimistic outlook sapping your hope or even disabling your efforts for God? What do you plan to do about it?

5. Have you, consciously or unconsciously, sought return for your efforts? Do we have any right to lay claim to the fruits of our efforts? By what standard does God measure our success or failure?

6. Knowing that death is inevitable, why are our labors and trials on this earth worthwhile? In what ways is 2 Peter 3:7, 10, and 13 appropriately read as a source of hope for believers in this world?

7. What will the renewed earth and glorified man be like when finally redeemed by God? What is the eternal destiny of the Christian? How should this tremendous hope shape your behavior today?

For bulk orders of *Truth and Transformation*
call **YWAM** Publishing at (800) 922-2143
or e-mail books@ywampublishing.com.

www.ywampublishing.com

VISHAL MANGALWADI, described by *Christianity Today* as "India's foremost Christian intellectual," is an international lecturer, social reformer, political columnist, and author of fourteen books.

Born (1949) and raised in India, Dr. Mangalwadi studied philosophy at secular universities, at L'Abri Fellowship in Switzerland, and in Hindu ashrams. In 1976 he turned down several job offers in the West to return to India, where he and his wife, Ruth, founded a community to serve the rural poor. Their efforts to transform rural India resulted in violent opposition, several arrests, and the burning down of their home and community. Vishal continued to work for the empowerment and liberation of peasants and the lower castes at the national headquarters of two political parties. His firsthand experience of social evils motivated him to study how the West became a relatively just, free, and prosperous civilization. *Truth and Transformation* is one of several results of that study.

In 2003 William Carey International University honored Vishal's life, service, and books with a Doctor of Laws (LLD) degree. Vishal and Ruth have two daughters and four grandchildren. They are looking forward to their fifth grandchild in June 2009.

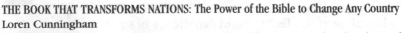

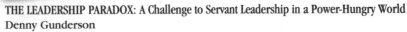